ON THE
FRONTIERS
OF HISTORY

RETHINKING EAST ASIAN BORDERS

ON THE FRONTIERS OF HISTORY

RETHINKING EAST ASIAN BORDERS

TESSA MORRIS-SUZUKI

PRESS

GLOBAL THINKERS SERIES

Published by ANU Press
The Australian National University
Acton ACT 2601, Australia
Email: anupress@anu.edu.au

Available to download for free at press.anu.edu.au

ISBN (print): 9781760463694
ISBN (online): 9781760463700

WorldCat (print): 1182556687
WorldCat (online): 1182556433

DOI: 10.22459/OFH.2020

Cover design and layout by ANU Press.
Cover image from Mamiya Rinzo's 'Tōdatsu Kikō'.

CONTENTS

LIST OF ILLUSTRATIONS

INTRODUCTION

The date is 1 August 1996, and I am aboard a ferry as it sets off from the northern Japanese port of Wakkanai on the sea crossing to Korsakov, on the Russian island of Sakhalin. It is a quiet, calm day and the sea is a silver-lead colour, with few waves in the bay, although my cabin companions warn me that it will get rough out in the straits. They remember the crossing 50 years ago, when the cups rolled around on the table, and people went down below decks to escape the storm, only to find that the heaving of the waves was even worse down there. On the quay, the scene is much as I had expected. A number of elderly couples, some with adult children, returning to visit their long-lost birthplaces; a few stray younger travellers, and one small party of Russian teenagers on a school exchange. But look more closely, and matters become more complicated. The young couple in front of me in the boarding queue – a skinny man in a loose black jacket and a girl in a pink trouser suit, whom I had automatically registered as Japanese – were speaking Russian as they said farewell to a very Japanese-looking elderly lady on the docks, and showed their Russian passports as they went through emigration.

My Japanese cabin companions are going back on a nostalgia visit. They have been friends since childhood and meet every year to recall memories of Karafuto (the Japanese colony that occupied the southern half of Sakhalin Island from 1905 to 1945). Their other friends in Japan have no interest in sharing these memories. Until the end of the war, they lived in the 'old city' of Toyohara (now the Russian city of Yuzhno-Sakhalinsk). Their neighbours included a Russian, a Polish family and a German family who ran the local bakery. The children all went to school together, and they say that they had no sense of any of them being 'foreigners'. Later, sitting on the upper deck, I find myself next to a woman with sadder memories. She went to Karafuto when she was five, and was nine when the war ended. Her family lived in Maoka (now Kholmsk), until the Russians came and burned everything. She remembers playing with her sister among the burnt ruins, picking up broken cups and plates. They took shelter for a while in her grandmother's house, which was still standing, but then the Russians came with rifles and took her father away.

Sakhalin appears on the port side before I expect it: beautiful and mountainous, with fold upon fold of hills in different shades of blue-grey, and sometimes sharper peaks appearing behind. When I go to the stern of the ferry, I find, sheltering from the wind, three women: one small and elderly, one middle-aged and the third younger and dressed in a smart grey suit. I start talking to them in hesitant Russian. The woman in grey turns out to be Nivkh, and the other two are Uilta (members of the indigenous Sakhalin communities discussed later in this book). They have been on a visit to their relatives in Abashiri, in northern Hokkaido. Only the elderly lady speaks Japanese – though she explains that she can also speak Uilta and Russian, as well as some Nanai and Korean – so we make do with Russian. The Nivkh lady speaks no Nivkh, but mentions that there is a nursery school in their area that teaches the language. They say that few people have any interest in their culture, and the middle-aged Uilta lady laments that it is now too late for her people. Later, they are joined by her son, who is about 20 and works in a fish-processing factory in central Sakhalin. He is dressed in trendy denim and sports dark glasses. He is friendly and polite, and says that he has enjoyed his first visit to his relatives in Japan. He speaks some English and expresses and interest in coming to Australia.

***

This book brings together thoughts and writings that span a period of 25 years, from the mid-1990s to the end of the 2010s. All journeys, of course, have multiple starting points, and the ideas that I explore here have grown out of hundreds, maybe thousands, of encounters with remarkable people in Japan, other parts of East Asia and beyond. But one crucial starting point for the journey of exploration undertaken in this book was the crossing from Hokkaido to Sakhalin, which I have described in the paragraphs above, using notes that I jotted down in my diary at the time. The people I met on that crossing gave me new insights into the complexities of history.

Like many people who originate from the British Isles, I come from a family of border-crossers, though few of them have crossed frontiers in such traumatic circumstances as the people I met on the ferry to Korsakov. I had Irish relatives who served in the British army in India, a half-Irish and half-Scottish mother who grew up in Istanbul, and today I have sisters who live in France, Italy and Greece and a son who lives in the United States, while I am an Australian. We are children of empire, and children of the globalisation that followed in the wake of empire, so it was perhaps inevitable that my interest in the history of Japan would turn to an interest in history of the borderlines surrounding Japan. But once I started looking at history from the vantage point of frontiers, I found myself confronting profound questions about the nature of history itself. Why is it that we so readily accept the boundary lines drawn around nations – or around regions like East Asia – as though they were natural, self-evident and eternal, when in fact they are so mutable and often so very arbitrary? What happens to people not only when the borders they seek to cross become heavily guarded, but also when new borders are drawn straight through the middle of their lives? In trying to answer those questions, it soon becomes clear that time and space are woven together in complex ways. Questioning spatial frontiers therefore also forces us to question the frontiers that we draw through time.

All of the essays that I have brought together in this book try to address aspects of these problems. In some of them, I take the stories of small places, and of events that seem minor in 'global' terms, and endeavour to look outwards from the small towards the large, asking what these 'minor pasts' tell us about the grand narratives of history. The borderline between Japan and Russia on the shores of the Okhotsk Sea is, for me, one small place that offers such a vantage point, and is the geographical focus of several of the chapters that follow. The history of this area is itself fascinating and insufficiently known; but, more importantly, it creates a space for posing broader questions that apply to the problem of frontiers in many times and places.

A number of the chapters published here are based on articles I have published in the past quarter of a century, though some have never been published, and some have never appeared in English before. In revising and updating essays that I had published earlier, I have been surprised and somewhat alarmed to discover how little has altered in those 25 years. Of course, the details of political regimes and current events have changed, and a wealth of new research has offered fresh material and concepts with which to address the questions that lie at the core of this book. But the underlying issues of frontiers and their impact on human lives have changed only in the sense that they have become ever more visible and more urgent. In the mid-1990s, debates and predictions about the force known as 'globalisation' were gathering momentum, but it was already starting to become clear that the popular visions of globalisation as sweeping away national borders and weakening the power of nations and nationalism were wide of the mark. In the decades since, nationalist passions and concerns about border controls have become ever more intense. The more economics and technology unite us (it seems) the more political borders divide.

Making sense of these forces, I think, requires a look at the deep history of boundary-drawing that has shaped our modern world. In this book, I begin by looking back at the history of area studies, and at the hopes expressed by some pioneers of the field that area-focused research would promote global understanding and weaken the divisive forces of narrow nationalism and ethnocentrism. As a researcher working in Japanese and East Asian studies in the late twentieth and early twenty-first centuries, I found myself asking why those hopes had not been fulfilled, and feeling that part of the answer lay in the nature of the spatial boundaries devised and used by area scholars themselves. These reflections take us, in Chapters 2 and 3, into the history of frontier-drawing – an exploration of the conceptual ways in which the lines between nations, continents and civilisations have been defined, and of the influence that this process of definition has had on understandings of the human past and present. In Chapter 3, I use the wide area surrounding the Russo–Japanese border and extending into Eastern Siberia as a focus for sketching how boundary-drawing was used by Western thinkers to make sense of the bewildering diversity of places and peoples they encountered in the travellers' tales sent back by merchants, explorers, freebooters and others. Chapters 4 and 5 go on to use the same area as a site for exploring possible alternative ways of writing history from the vantage point of the societies of the frontier, rather than from the vantage point of nation-states or 'civilisations'.

In Chapter 6, we trace the history of border encounters between Russians and Japanese, and the processes that created a sharply defined but repeatedly shifting frontier line between the two nations, and in Chapter 7 we look at the effects that the drawing and redrawing of this frontier had on the people who lived in the heart of the border zone: in one small village that stood at the point where Japanese-controlled Karafuto confronted Russian-controlled northern Sakhalin. While most of the book moves inwards from the global and general towards a single specific point on the face of the globe, Chapter 8 moves outwards again. There I make use of ideas explored in earlier chapters to re-examine the changing mental boundaries that have shaped the study of Japanese history as a whole. In all of these chapters, I am interested particularly in linking the political dimensions of border-drawing to their social and cultural dimensions: how do political borderlines affect daily life, and how are they translated into lines within the human mind and imagination?

The questions posed and discussed in this book have no simple answer. The aim is not to offer decisive resolutions to the debates that swirl around these issues, but rather to encourage the processes of debate and imagination themselves. This book therefore is a sometimes offbeat voyage through many times and places, but one that I hope you will enjoy sharing.

Acknowledgements

Putting this volume together has reminded me once again of the enormous debt of respect and gratitude that I owe to all the many travelling companions who made it possible.

They are far too numerous for me to be able to name them all, but my particular thanks go to Tonohira Yoshihiko, Buddhist priest and founding member of the Sorachi People's History Group; Tsurumaki Hiroshi, Satō Takumi and other members of the Okhotsk People's History Group; the late Tanaka Ryō of the Okhotsk People's History Group and Uilta Association; Ainu Elders Ogawa Ryūkichi, Shimizu Yūji and Kuzuno Tsugio; the late Kitagawa Aiko, co-founder and head of Jakka Dukhuni; Tazawa Mamoru and Naraki Kimiko of the Karafuto Ainu (Enchiw) Association; Dr Tatyana Roon, former Director of the Sakhalin Regional Museum and eminent scholar of Sakhalin indigenous cultures; filmmaker Fujino Tomoaki; Oda Hiroshi, Professor of Cultural Anthropology at Hokkaido University; Hyun Mooam, Professor in the Faculty of Media and Communication at Hokkaido University; and Professor Jeffry Gayman and Dr Svetlana Paichadze of Hokkaido University. I have learnt so much from all of them. Any errors that remain are, of course, mine alone.

I would also like to express my warm thanks to Professor Bruce Batten, Resident Director of the Inter-University Centre for Japanese Language Studies in Yokohama, for his very helpful comments on an earlier version of this manuscript; to Associate Professor Andrew Kennedy of The Australian National University for initiating and guiding the process that led to the completion of this book; and to the ANU Publication Subsidy Fund for supporting this publication.

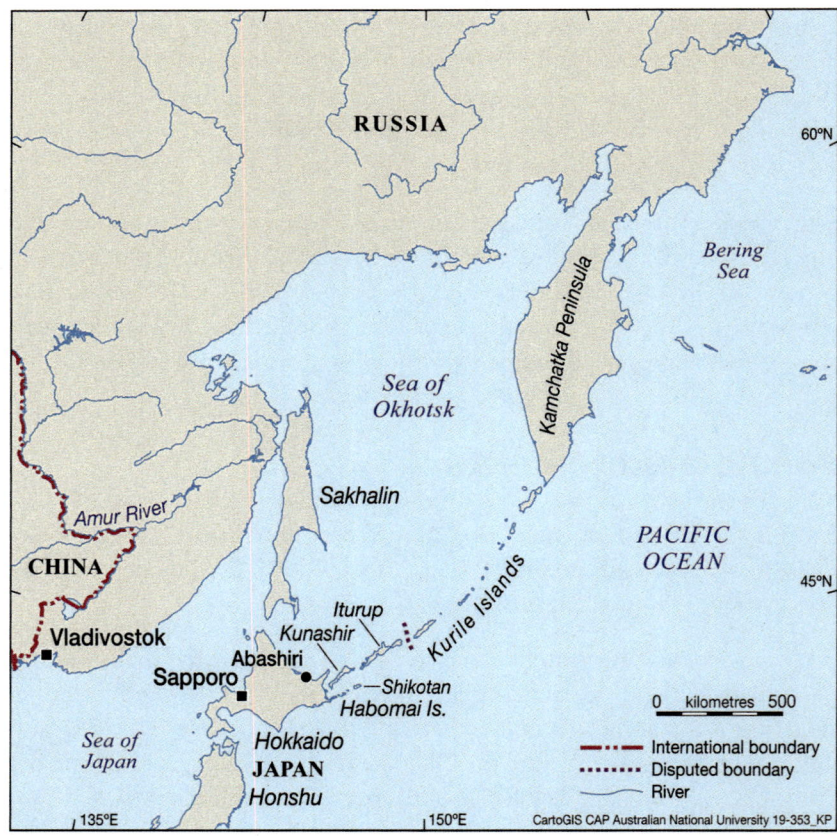

Map 1.1. The Okhotsk region.

Source: CartoGIS, The Australian National University.

1

ANTI-AREA STUDIES REVISITED

Writing in the middle of the twentieth century, as area studies came into its own in the US, anthropologist Julian Steward proclaimed that there was 'general agreement' about four key objectives of this new field of research. The four objectives, wrote Steward, were to 'provide knowledge of practical value about important world areas'; to 'give students and scholars an awareness of cultural relativity'; to 'provide an understanding of social and cultural wholes as they exist in areas'; and to 'further the development of a universal social science'.[1] Elaborating his theme, Steward pointed out that 'anyone who becomes familiar with a new and different culture experiences what has been called a "cultural shock" – an awareness that everything in the new culture is somehow unfamiliar but is also part of a self-consistent and intelligible whole'. By understanding that each unfamiliar culture had such a 'self-consistent and distinctive pattern', the student would come to appreciate that 'none is absolute or inherently superior to the others'. This understanding, Steward continued, 'gives the layman greater tolerance of the peoples of the other areas, and it gives the scholar an objectivity which will help him avoid the methodological fallacy of ethnocentrism'.[2]

Rereading those words many decades on, several thoughts spring to mind. One is that 'cultural shock' no longer seems to be the exclusive preserve of area scholars who journey to distant regions. Rather, it has become

---

1   Julian H Steward, *Area Research: Theory and Practice* (New York: Social Science Research Council, 1950), p. 2.
2   Steward, *Area Research*, p. 4.

a regular part of daily life. In a world of global flows, unfamiliarity presses in from every side, but, far from being part of a 'self-consistent and intelligible whole', this unfamiliarity is overwhelmingly experienced as *unintelligible* in terms of conventional notions of region, area and space. International frontiers become at once more porous and more ferociously guarded, while new internal frontiers, often patrolled by the invisible but all-seeing eye of the surveillance camera, divide islands of glittering wealth from seas of urban decay. Transport and communication technologies increasingly detach temporal from spatial proximity, making the centres of the great world cities closer to one another in terms of travel-time, consciousness and culture than they are to their own rural hinterlands. It has become commonplace to speak not of the end of history but of the end of geography.

A related thought is that the contemporary encounter with the unfamiliar has ambivalent implications for the promotion of 'tolerance' or the conquest of ethnocentrism. On the one hand, old certainties about national, ethnic or cultural belonging are constantly exposed to challenges. But on the other, a rather common response to the unintelligibility of the world is precisely an attempt to *re-establish* these certainties by reasserting the power of national boundaries and patriotic symbols. The current influence of globally resurgent nationalisms can be seen not only in the appearance of certain new forms of right-wing politics, but also (more alarmingly, perhaps) in the popularity of mass-consumption chauvinism. As an Australian scholar working mostly on Japan, I am repeatedly intrigued but alarmed both by striking similarities in the rhetoric of popular nationalism in Australia and Japan, and by the way in which nationalist fears and stereotypes in different countries seem to feed off each other, creating a continuing spiral of incomprehension.

Area Studies and Ethnocentrism

Having been involved in Asian studies – and more specifically in Japanese studies – in Australia since the early 1980s, I find myself increasingly impelled to reflect on the effect that education about 'Asia' has had within Australian society. To what extent has the enormous expansion of the study of 'Asia' fulfilled Julian Steward's mid-century vision of area studies as a cure for ethnocentrism? Has the effort to understand 'unfamiliar cultures' as self-consistent and intelligible wholes served the cause of giving laypeople greater tolerance? In attempting to answer those questions, I have to begin by admitting to a deep discomfort with the word 'tolerance'. (Who, after all, wants to be tolerated?) At the same time, though, it would seem unreasonable not to sympathise with Steward's obvious longing for a field of study that would promote human understanding and mutual appreciation rather than fear and loathing. It would also be a mistake to underestimate the profound contribution the great growth of Asian studies in Australia over the past four decades or so has made to that understanding.

I feel, though, that there are good reasons for some self-critical reflection, not simply about the amount of 'Asian' content in the curriculum and in our media, but about the whole framework within which knowledge of the world beyond Australia's boundaries is taught, researched and debated. One issue that prompts that reflection is the enduring influence of simplistic and reductionist generalisations about 'Asia' and 'Asians' in the Australian media and in public discourse. More widely than this, though, there is also the problem that I referred to earlier as the unintelligibility of the world. The global resurgence of nationalisms and ethnocentrisms in the past decade seems to reflect a very real and widespread feeling of powerlessness – almost, one might say, of disenfranchisement – among the citizens of many countries. This feeling of powerlessness appears to derive from a sense of being at the mercy of forces and institutions – many of them crossing the boundaries of nations and regions – whose workings are not just beyond the control of ordinary people but are also almost totally inscrutable.

Very few people now, I think, would subscribe to Julian Steward's vision of the development of a universal social science that would render these forces and institutions totally transparent. But it is worth asking how well education and research serve the cause of helping to make a complex and rapidly changing world at least a little more comprehensible to the population at large. The argument I want to make here is that the spatial framework of understanding – the image of areas – that has emerged from area studies is in some respects an obstacle that makes the nature of the contemporary world system *less* rather than *more* visible and comprehensible. A rethinking of the spatial frameworks of teaching and research is therefore an important element in working through ways in which education confronts the problem of an unintelligible world. And the first step in that rethinking has to be a re-examination of the origins of the existing framework of area studies.

The Origins of Area Studies

Area studies can be understood as having emerged from a reimagining of space that took place in the middle decades of the twentieth century. A particularly important feature of this reimagining was that it created a *common* spatial framework that could be used by a variety of different humanities and social sciences, and that therefore marked out a space for the interdisciplinary study of societies as totalities. In the late nineteenth and early twentieth centuries, the various disciplines had tended to operate on different spatial planes. For geographers, the major large-scale divisions of the world were continents, whose boundaries were defined by the physical geography of oceans, mountain ranges and so on. For political scientists, on the other hand, nations and colonial empires were more significant divisions of space. Historians, meanwhile, also tended to operate mostly at the national level, but if they thought in larger terms were more likely to use concepts such as Occident and Orient (as employed by writers like Oswald Spengler and Karl Wittvogel). The contemporary image of 'areas' such as the Middle East, and East and Southeast Asia, crystallised in the early twentieth century against the background of the rising international tensions that culminated in the Second World War. The expression 'Middle East' has been used since the nineteenth century, but the current sense of the word was firmly established by the British and US military only in the 1930s–40s, while the label 'Southeast Asia' 'entered popular consciousness in the Second World War, when military strategists used it to "designate the theatre of war commanded by Lord Louis Mountbatten"'.[3] During the war, the work of the US Ethnogeographic Board helped to lay the foundations for the postwar boom in area studies by defining the new classificatory system of 'world regions'.[4]

The war and its aftermath drew attention to the strategic value of cultural knowledge: information about the languages, histories and traditions of geographically distant allies and enemies was vital to the conduct of war, and to the international power struggles of the Cold War world. During the 1950s US policymakers explicitly recognised that the development of

---

3   MW Lewis and KE Wigen, *The Myth of Continents: A Critique of Metageography* (Berkeley: University of California Press, 1997), pp. 65–66 and 172.
4   Lewis and Wigen, *The Myth of Continents*, pp. 162–66.

area studies programs could contribute to the successful exercise of US world power, and substantial funding for this development was provided under the terms of the 1958 National Defense Education Act.[5]

In Australia, too, the Pacific War drew attention to the need for expertise in the languages, societies and political systems of neighbouring regions (particularly Asia), and 'Oriental Affairs' (as it was then called) was seen as an area of study deserving special national attention.[6] This led, among other things, to the establishment of a School of Pacific Studies with a strong focus on East Asia at the newly created Australian National University (ANU) in 1946, and to the creation of a School of Oriental Languages at Canberra University College (later incorporated into ANU) in 1952.[7] During the course of the 1950s, funding for Indonesian and Malayan studies was also provided to both Sydney and Melbourne universities. In the postwar development in Asian studies, therefore, most courses tended to be offered in interdisciplinary, regionally focused departments.[8]

Fundamental to postwar visions of area studies, at least in the English-speaking world, were the notions of 'culture' and 'civilisation', which became key unifying concepts connecting varied disciplinary approaches to the study of a given region. As we have seen, an emphasis on the relationship between society and culture, and on cooperation between the disciplines, was central to the work of Julian Steward, who played a leading role in the US Social Science Research Council's Committee on World Area Research. Meanwhile, other scholars such as Robert Redfield, who in 1951 helped to establish the Ford Foundation's Cultural Studies Project, were focusing attention on the comparative study of civilisations: 'civilisation' being defined by Redfield as a culture that possessed not only a 'little tradition of the largely unreflective many' but also a 'great tradition of the reflective few'.[9] Redfield, like Steward,

5   GB Nash, C Crabtree and RE Dunn, *History on Trial: Culture Wars and the Teaching of the Past* (New York: Alfred A Knopf, 1997), p. 91.

6   Daniel Botsman, 'Deconstructing the Past to Redefine the Future: A History of Japanese Studies at the Australian National University', in *Japan and the World: Proceedings of the Seventh Biennial Conference of the Japanese Studies Association of Australia*, vol. 3 (Canberra: Australia Japan Research Centre, 1991), pp. 240–48.

7   Botsman, 'Deconstructing the Past'; William Sima, *China & ANU: Diplomats, Adventurers, Scholars* (Canberra: ANU Press, 2015), doi.org/10.22459/ca.12.2015.

8   John Ingleson and ME Nairn, *Asia in Australian Higher Education*, vol. 1 (Report Submitted to the Asian Studies Council, 1989), p. 34.

9   A Sartori, 'Robert Redfield's Comparative Civilizations Project and the Political Imagination of postwar America', *Positions: East Asia Cultures Critique* 6, no. 1 (1998): pp. 33–66, doi.org/10.1215/10679847-6-1-33; Robert Redfield, *Peasant Society and Culture: An Anthropological Approach to Civilizations* (Chicago: University of Chicago Press, 1956).

saw great potential for bringing together humanities and social science disciplines in collaborative efforts to comprehend the past and present of particular societies. Knowledge of the dominant civilisational patterns of each major world region would, it was felt, provide a historical basis for interpreting the contemporary and future destiny of each region in an interconnected modern world. Such US approaches had a substantial impact on the development of area studies in other countries including Australia, where studies by US area specialists (like John Fairbank, Edwin Reischauer and Albert Craig in Asian studies) came to be widely used as texts for an expanding range of area-focused courses.

The development of area studies in the US and Australia also resonated with emerging European approaches to the study of the world. Redfield's concept of comparative civilisations, for example, drew on the ideas of British scholar Arnold Toynbee, whose massive study of civilisational history was published in 12 volumes between 1934 and 1961. Toynbee's classification of civilisations was idiosyncratic – based above all on the foundational role of the great religions – but his research was driven by many of the impulses that inspired other varieties of mid-century area studies.[10]

Meanwhile, in France a somewhat different version of civilisational history was emerging from the postwar work of the Annales school. From its founding in the late 1920s, the Annales group had envisioned large-scale collaborations between scholars trained in demography, psychology, social statistics and other disciplines, working together to produce a 'total history' of the everyday life of particular societies.[11] During the 1950s and 1960s, Fernand Braudel built on this approach to present a vision of global history centred upon major civilisational areas, each of which 'has its own geography with its own opportunities and constraints, some virtually permanent and quite different from one civilisation to another'.[12] Braudel's famous textbook for French high school students, *Grammaire des civilisations*, divided the world into six major areas: America, the Muslim World, Africa, the Far East, Europe and that 'Other Europe' constituted by the Soviet Union. Each area, he argued, possessed

10   AJ Toynbee, *A Study of History* (Oxford: Oxford University Press, 1961). Original published in three parts: 1934, 1939 and 1954.
11   See, for example, Lucien Febvre, *A New Kind of History: From the Writings of Lucien Febvre*, ed. P Burke (London: Routledge and Kegan Paul, 1973); François Dosse, *New History in France: The Triumph of the Annales*, trans. PV Conroy Jr (Urbana: University of Illinois Press, 1994).
12   Fernand Braudel, *A History of Civilizations*, trans. R Mayne (London: Allen Lane, 1994), p. 11.

its own deep underlying structures – 'religious beliefs, for instance, or a timeless peasantry, or attitudes to death, work, pleasure and family life': structures that persisted with only the most gradual of changes beneath the ever-shifting surface of transient historical events.[13]

Mapping Cultures

Braudel's study indeed offers a vivid illustration of some of the key strengths and weaknesses of the postwar area approach. On the one hand, it represented a genuine and deeply felt desire for a more universal understanding of social phenomena – an approach that would transcend the bounds of narrow nationalism or ethnocentrism. On the other, however, its temporal and spatial frameworks almost inescapably imposed particular limitations on the image of the world it presented. In order to deal with the study of very large areas such as 'the Far East', Braudel's account begins by singling out certain features seen as fundamental cultural characteristics of the entire area. In the case of the 'Far East', for example, these included rice cultivation, the tenacious influence of old-established creeds such as Buddhism and Confucianism, and the eternal antagonism between settled civilisations and the 'barbarian hordes' who constantly threatened their borders.[14] Such deep structures provided the foundations on which the distinctive, and more rapidly changing, political, economic and social formations of individual nations within the area were built. Nations in turn embraced local regions, which – with their particular productive systems and cultural traditions – formed the locus of everyday life. This structure closely parallels that of many of the major area studies texts of the postwar decades – works like Reischauer and Fairbank's *East Asia: The Great Tradition*, in which an overview of the underlying civilisational patterns of the region provided the starting point for more detailed analysis of the individual destinies of particular nations.[15]

The difficulty with this approach is that, since a region like 'the Far East' or 'East Asia' is a vast and diverse one with few overarching commonalities, those few characteristics that *are* shared by much of the region tend

---

13   Braudel, *A History of Civilizations*, p. 11.
14   Braudel, *A History of Civilizations*, pp. 155–70.
15   Edwin O Reischauer and John K Fairbank, *East Asia: The Great Tradition* (Boston: Houghton Mifflin, 1958); Edwin O Reischauer, John K Fairbank and Albert M Craig, *East Asia: Tradition and Transformation* (London: Houghton Mifflin, 1973).

to be singled out as 'fundamental' and (it could be argued) given disproportionate weight. A good example of this is the almost obsessive attention paid to that shifting complex of ideas and practices commonly labelled 'Confucianism'. It seems clear that the influence of Confucianism has varied enormously across the region according to place, time and social class, and that for many people in many times it had little or no influence at all. But the visions of Chinese, Japanese and Korean histories as contained within the framework of East Asian history makes it almost inevitable that plausible common denominators like 'Confucianism' will come to be seen as the underlying motive forces of the region's past.

The overall outcome tends to be an image of the individual as standing at the centre of a series of ever-expanding circles of shared history, culture and memory. The richest and most varied array of common experiences, traditions and beliefs is shared with the immediately proximate communities of family, local community, village or town. As one moves outward in space, the sharing of more transient memories and experiences diminishes, leaving only the deeper strata of enduring culture that (it is suggested) are shared, first with other members of the national community and, at the profoundest level, with fellow inhabitants of the entire civilisational area.

US area studies scholars like Steward and Redfield, rather similarly, saw area studies as operating at a number of spatial levels, ranging from 'communities through regions, states and nations to large cultural areas'.[16] Area studies required both detailed, usually ethnographic, studies of small local communities and larger interdisciplinary studies of nations and world regions. Steward thus likened multilevel area research on human societies to multilevel biological research on living organisms, in which 'the cell is incompletely understood if it is not studied as part of an organ; and an organ is intelligible only as part of a total organism'.[17]

But mapping the world in this way obscures human commonalities not based on geographical proximity, not containable within the frontiers of nation, area or 'civilisation'. Of course, the area scholars of the 1950s recognised that civilisations interacted, and above all that 'modern Western civilisation' affected the lives of people throughout the world. The very nature of area studies, however, made it difficult to pursue

---

16   Steward, *Area Research*, p. 20; see also Redfield, *Peasant Society and Culture*, Chapter 3.
17   Steward, *Area Research*, p. 109.

investigation of the cultural commonalities that might link people in widely dispersed geographical locations on the basis of occupation, age or interest (for example, the commonalities between Catholics in Ireland and Zimbabwe, or between soccer fans in The Netherlands and Brazil).

Rather than opening the way to exploration of shared – or differing – experiences of the 'modern', area studies encouraged a comparative approach to the understanding of a process called 'modernisation'. To what extent, in other words, did 'modernity' represent the triumph of the Western model of civilisation? To what extent could the fundamental patterns of other civilisations survive within, and adapt to, the modern order? Which areas possessed the patterns of culture and tradition that would best equip them for participation in the competitive struggle for social and economic development?

Area studies also involved a distinctive relation of scholars to their subject matter. The classical Orientalists of the nineteenth century had found it necessary to rely substantially on the interpretation of the written archive. Their work, until the mid-twentieth century, was supplemented by the writings of colonial officials, whose social experiences were shaped by the hierarchical structures of life in the colonies, yet who had often been required to immerse themselves in the details of administering a particular confined territory. The postwar area scholar lived in a different world: a world of air travel, an age of fieldwork – a concept extended from anthropology to a wide range of other disciplines in the middle decades of the century. From their base in the campuses of the developed world, area specialists were able to venture forth, armed with a training in disciplinary techniques and theories as well as language, for regular stints of research in 'the field'. Implicitly, this research was envisaged as using the latest (supposedly universal) social theories, generated within the academic realms of Western Europe and North America, to interpret the diverse complexities of the particular region on which the area specialist focused. The scholar would thus return from the field with empirical data and case studies to enrich the development of universal social theory. No one can doubt that postwar area scholars in the still-dominant nations of Western Europe and North America contributed greatly to a deeper understanding of Asian, African and other societies and histories. Yet the very frameworks within which their work was conducted meant that this understanding did not necessarily lead to any fundamental rethinking of the vision of 'Western civilisation' as interpreter of the world, and as crucible of the modern.

Critiques of Area Studies

In more recent decades, of course, area studies have been criticised from several directions. A frequent focus of criticism has been the intimate connection between this field of research and US Cold War strategy.[18] While many US scholars resolutely resisted efforts by the state to mobilise their research for strategic purposes, there are numerous well-documented examples of government manipulation of area research in the Cold War period. One case, cited by George Kahin, was the ostensibly academic journal *Vietnam Perspectives*, which was launched in 1967 with substantial support and funding from the US military's Historical Evaluation and Research Organization.[19] As late as the start of the twenty-first century, United States–based historian of Japan Harry Harootunian could write:

> Fifty years after the war, we are still organizing knowledge as if – in the case of Japan, China and the former Soviet Union – we are confronted by an implacable enemy and thus driven by the desire to know it in order to destroy it or learn how to sleep with it. While nobody would deny that this has produced mountains of empirical data on the peoples of these societies, this accomplishment has kept these areas from being assimilated into new theories of knowledge and categorizations that promise to end their isolation.[20]

As Harootunian's critique suggests, challenges to the link between area studies and strategic concerns are part of a wider questioning of the methodological underpinnings of the area approach. At one level, area specialists have been accused of exaggerating the autonomy of individual cultures and for paying insufficient attention to connections between one region and another. The civilisation theory of scholars like Toynbee has also been taken to task on the grounds that, by identifying 'civilisation' with powerful urbanised communities, it neglected large swathes of

---

18 For example, Immanuel Wallerstein, 'The Unintended Consequences of Cold War Area Studies', in *The Cold War and the University*, ed. N Chomsky, L Nadar, I Wallerstein, RC Lewontin, I Katznelson and H Zinn (New York: New Press, 1997), pp. 195–232; Bruce Cumings, 'Boundary Displacement: Area Studies and International Studies during and after the Cold War', *Bulletin of Concerned Asian Scholars* 29, no. 1 (1997): pp. 6–29, doi.org/10.1080/14672715.1997.10409695.
19 George M Kahin, 'The Making of Southeast Asian Studies: Cornell's Experience', *Bulletin of Concerned Asian Scholars* 29, no. 1 (1997): pp. 38–42, doi.org/10.1080/14672715.1997.10409699.
20 Harry Harootunian, *History's Disquiet: Modernity, Cultural Practice and the Question of Everyday Life* (New York: Columbia University Press, 2002), p. 28.

human society.[21] Yet this critique has not necessarily led to a rejection of the organising framework of large contiguous regions defined in terms of an underlying common culture. Instead, it has tended to produce modifications of that image, in which boundaries are redrawn in the effort to create a more coherent and inclusive picture.[22]

One important modification to the postwar image of area studies was the emergence of the concept of the 'Asia-Pacific' or 'Pacific Rim', which enjoyed a vogue particularly in the 1970s and 1980s. This vision of geography transcended traditionally defined visions of 'civilisations', and sought to bring together the study of Asian, American and Australasian regions, which were in fact increasingly being linked by economic and cultural flows. As Arif Dirlik points out, though, the new concept itself was deeply embedded in the emerging economic and political power structures of the late twentieth century. The concept of the Asia-Pacific area served to:

> set up a domain of economic activity and power for those who play a hegemonic role in the area (at present, the United States and Japan), to contain within it the relationships that in and of themselves are not confined to it, and thereby to assert a regional identity (and power bloc) against other similar regions in the world system, of which the European Economic Community is the immediate instance.[23]

Meanwhile, however, a different criticism of area studies was increasingly making itself heard. Area studies schools and departments, it was argued, were not giving their students a sufficiently rigorous disciplinary grounding. In Australia, for example, at the end of the 1980s, the *Report of the Inquiry into the Teaching of Asian Studies and Languages in Higher Education* observed that the 'Asian studies model' had:

> tended to marginalize the study of Asia, by cutting it off from the major disciplines and producing graduates who had a great deal of knowledge of one or more Asian country, often proficiency in a language as well, but who were inadequately trained in one of

---

21   See Lewis and Wigen, *The Myth of Continents*, pp. 130–31; Nash, Crabtree and Dunn, *History on Trial*, pp. 164–71.

22   See, for example, Lewis and Wigen, *The Myth of Continents*, p. 157.

23   Arif Dirlik, 'The Asia-Pacific Idea: Reality and Representation in the Invention of a Regional Structure', *Journal of World History* 3, no. 1 (1992): pp. 55–79.

the social sciences disciplines, such as history, politics, sociology or economics. It also acted as an excuse for discipline departments ignoring the study of Asia.[24]

The report went on to propose greater integration of Asian content into 'mainstream' humanities and social science departments, recommending that by the year 2000 at least 20 per cent of student enrolments in those departments should be in 'Asia related' subjects.[25]

In practice, though, this proposal proved remarkably difficult to put into effect. The 1998 Australian Research Council review of the humanities in Australia revealed that initial efforts at greater integration had wilted in the face of the harsh economic climate of the 1990s.[26] Although some of the newer cross-disciplinary areas like postcolonial studies paid substantial attention to various Asian societies, many of the older disciplines remained overwhelmingly focused on Europe and North America. In philosophy, which (according to one observer) 'is usually thought of as a distinctively Western discipline', developments in the teaching of Asian philosophy could still be dealt with in a couple of sentences.[27] The situation in relation to areas like early modern studies was even more interesting. Here, Asia rated a mention only because Asian history was seen as a potential competitor with early modern studies for student enrolments. This begged the question: did places like Japan have an 'early modern' (as most Japanese historians clearly seem to believe it did), and, if so, how might this relate to the early modern studied by 'early modern studies'?

The ongoing tension between area studies and disciplines reflected, I think, something more than institutional rigidities and budgetary constraints. It reflected the fact that *both* the traditional disciplines *and* area studies often incorporate similar underlying assumptions about the nature of social space. Both, in other words, tend to take for granted the reality and integrity of entities like 'Latin America' or 'Southeast Asia'.

---

24 Ingleson and Nairn, *Asia in Australian Higher Education*, p. 260.
25 Ingleson and Nairn, *Asia in Australian Higher Education*, p. 265.
26 Beverley Hooper, 'Chinese Studies', in *Knowing Ourselves and Others: The Humanities in Australia into the 21st Century*, ed. Reference Group for the Academy of the Humanities (Canberra: Australian Government Publishing Service, 1998), pp. 57–66, reference from p. 58; William Coaldrake and Kenneth Wells, 'Japanese and Korean Studies', in Reference Group for the Academy of the Humanities, *Knowing Ourselves and Others*, pp. 151–63, reference from p. 155; Ingleson, 'Southeast Asian Studies', in Reference Group for the Academy of the Humanities, *Knowing Ourselves and Others*, pp. 251–60.
27 Stephen Gaukroger, 'Philosophy and Intellectual History', in Reference Group for the Academy of the Humanities, *Knowing Ourselves and Others*, pp. 215–24, reference from p. 223.

They also incorporate similar ideas about the relationship between scholar and subject of study. That is to say, disciplines as well as area studies often embody an implicit image of 'the West' as the fountainhead of theories with which to interpret the rest of the world. So, commendable efforts to encourage the inclusion of material from Asian societies in various disciplinary courses in Australia went hand in hand with a worrying tendency to insist that the object of the exercise was to promote 'Asia literacy' – as though 'Asia' were a sort of hieroglyphic document that would become legible if only one could crack the code.[28] The Western scholar was still assumed to stand within a legible, transparent space that is the source of theories with which to interpret the enigmatic areas outside. From this perspective, Australia could all too readily come to be presented as an outpost of Western universalism fortunately located close to the perplexing realms of Asia, and so offering a convenient salient from which to 'interpret' Asia to the (English-speaking) world.

The Possibility of Anti-Area Studies

In this context, it is crucially important to resist one particular variant of the critique of area studies: the view that area studies should be subordinated to a new brand of universalism based on the dominance of disciplinary knowledge. This view proposes that societies are to be understood in terms of scientific models, centred around notions such as 'rational choice'. Detailed knowledge of language and history of specific societies thus becomes irrelevant, or at least of secondary importance, in interpreting contemporary trends, for once one has mastered the rules contained in the latest texts from Chicago or MIT, the behaviour of everyone from Javanese rice farmers to Taiwanese pop stars will be readily understandable and predictable. A version of this critique, for example, was controversially put forward in the mid-1990s by political scientist Robert Bates, who saw 'area programs as a problem for political science' because of their 'resistance to the search for theory and to the use of rigorous methods for evaluating arguments'. He did not seek the abolition of area studies, but argued for something that he called a 'mutual infusion' of area and discipline approaches. By this, though, he meant that mathematics-based Western sociology and political science possessed the

---

28   For example, Commonwealth of Australia, *Australia in the Asian Century White Paper* (Canberra: Commonwealth of Australia, 2012), p. 167.

tools necessary to 'handle area knowledge in rigorous ways'. For example, forms of game theory developed for the study of politics in the United States could (he argued) be universally applied to explain the impact of culture and history on politics in any context.[29]

But, as Vincent Houben has suggested, this urge for universality needs to be complemented by a sensitivity to diversity and specificity: 'Whereas disciplines look for the universal within variety, Area Studies want to highlight variation within global universality'.[30] What is needed, then, is a different approach to the rethinking of area studies – one that retains that sensitivity, and therefore continues to emphasise the importance of detailed knowledge of human lives in particular places. At the same time, this approach would seek to reverse the process of spatial integration, through which area studies sought to create a single framework for the interdisciplinary study of social wholes. Rather, in trying to make sense of the contemporary system it seems important to be able to make simultaneous use of a range of *different* spatial maps to analyse *different* social processes and interactions.[31]

The point is not that the concept of areas like East or Southeast Asia is an anachronism to be thrown onto the intellectual scrap heap. The area studies vision of world regions as a basis for understanding has obvious uses. For a historian who wants to study the spread and evolution of the character-based writing system that originated in China, for example, the geographical category 'East Asia' makes sense (though it would make even better sense if it were expanded to encompass most of Vietnam, now usually classified under the heading 'Southeast Asia'). But using 'East Asia' as the primary space for understanding the whole past and present of the area now encompassed by the nations of China, Mongolia, Japan, Korea and Taiwan is much more problematic. Difficulties arise when concentric circles of contiguous space come to be seen as the framework for a total understanding of the past and present, for this model of space obscures a host of experiences vital to interpreting the contemporary global system.

---

29   Robert H Bates, 'Letter from the President: Area Studies and the Discipline', *APSA-CP: Newsletter of the APSA Organized Section in Comparative Politics* 7, no. 1 (1996): pp. 1–2.
30   Vincent Houben, 'New Area Studies, Translation and Mid-Range Concepts', in *Area Studies at the Crossroads: Knowledge Production after the Mobility Turn*, ed. Katja Mielke and Anna-Katharina Hornidge (London: Palgrave-Macmillan, 2017), pp. 195–211, quotation from p. 202.
31   B Mazlish, 'Crossing Boundaries: Ecumenical, World and Global History', in *World History: Ideologies, Structures and Identities*, ed. P Pomper, RH Elphick and RT Vann (Oxford: Blackwell, 1998), pp. 41–52.

What I would like to suggest, then, is not a bland erasure of differences, but rather an attempt to rethink the way in which to map difference. One important element in this new mapping might be the development of an 'anti-area studies', whose aim is not to plot the communal trajectory of a civilisational area within the march of global progress, but to observe major global forces from a variety of positions that are far apart. Let us consider some examples of possible themes of this type of 'anti-area studies'.

One theme could be a topic I am particularly interested in: the past and present of indigenous communities in various parts of the world. Despite their great diversity, indigenous societies worldwide face certain sorts of common challenges and problems that arise not from innate cultural similarities, but from shared experiences of the encounter between small, relatively decentralised communities and modern empires and nation-states. Forms of study and teaching that link the experiences of indigenous societies in (say) Australia, the Philippines, Japan, Russia and Brazil can bring to light important issues, differences and commonalities, which remain invisible when the history of indigenous societies is studied in a national or even a conventional area studies framework.

Another type of anti-area studies concerns the way in which a particular set of ideas or ideologies is understood, applied and developed in quite different situations. Examples of this are research projects on the varied experiences around the world of the late 1960s student movement. Here it becomes possible to consider how people from a broadly similar social stratum – mostly young, middle-class and university-educated – related to a broadly common set of ideologies in radically different circumstances. What is important, though, is that the 'map' of 1968 should include not only places like Paris, Berkeley and London but also Tokyo, Mexico City, Melbourne and Calcutta. In a similar vein, one might consider the way in which various new (and not so new) forms of religious thought – Scientology or the Unification Church – are received and evolve in distinct locations.

A third possible variant of anti-area studies would be research on the social formation of global systems or organisations: organisations like the World Bank or UNICEF. Such studies would explore both the evolution of these organisations and their interaction with local society in many parts of the world. This research might help to illuminate the ways in which international bodies, with their worldwide networks of employees and offices, develop their own set of cultural resources and behavioural patterns: shared 'traditions' that transcend the boundaries of conventionally defined 'areas'. The map appropriate for this sort of study cannot be predicted in advance but would need to be carefully tailored to the research task. It might, however, focus on selected points in Asia, Africa and the Americas, and include urban as well as village communities. Research and teaching on these themes seems particularly important as a means of confronting the sense of incomprehension and powerlessness induced by the increasing complexity of international rules, systems and cultural flows in the contemporary world.

Many other variants of anti-area studies might be imagined, but here I will sketch just one more that is particularly central to the theme of this book. Anti-area studies might also be advanced by placing oneself not within the boundaries of traditionally defined world regions such as 'Latin America' or 'Asia', but precisely *on* the boundaries: in the frontier zones where these regions interact and intersect. The focus of research then becomes the shifting and fluid nature of these boundaries themselves. By observing the ways in which conceptual and political boundaries have been redrawn over time, we become aware of the sometimes arbitrary forces that determine how frontier lines are defined, and can observe the way in which each redrawing of frontiers makes certain social or political features more visible while rendering others more obscure. This in turn, I would argue, can destabilise some of the certainties of conventional area studies approaches to history, culture and society, and open up new ways of looking not merely at the border zones themselves, but at the world and the mental constructs through which we perceive it. It allows us, in other words, to (as it were) reverse the angle of vision. Instead of using modern Western academic theories to elucidate the peculiarities of places in Asia or elsewhere, we can use a viewpoint from the borderlands to look back at those modern Western theories with questioning eyes, and probe the processes by which they came into being.

Over the past couple of decades, the rapid expansion of various forms of 'border studies/frontier studies' has provided a rich source of inspiration for such a frontier-based approach. On the one hand, scholars such as Malcolm Anderson and Stefan Wolf have explored the history of frontier-drawing and its role in the generation or resolution of conflicts.[32] On the

---

32 Malcolm Anderson, *Frontiers: Territory and State Formation in the Modern World* (Cambridge: Polity Press, 1996); Stefan Wolff, *Disputed Territories: The Transnational Dynamics of Ethnic Conflict Settlement* (New York and Oxford: Berghahn Books, 2003).

other, Donna Guy, Thomas Sheridan, Janet Carsten, Martin Stokes and many others have focused on the experiences of interaction between the groups who inhabit those borderlands that Guy and Sheridan term 'contested ground'.[33] Frontier studies open up an alternative vantage point for viewing social space. And, as we shall see in the chapters that follow, focusing on and questioning the nature of spatial borderlines also leads us inevitably to cast a questioning eye on the borderlines that historians draw through time; for, as Imogen Seger Coulborn has argued, temporal boundaries are created not by the facts themselves, but rather by 'what one wants to know or compare'.[34]

Anti-area studies in this sense would require many of the skills traditionally demanded of area studies specialists. It would need people with a real knowledge of different languages and societies, and with a strong theoretical understanding of the issues to be researched or taught. It would also often involve collaboration between several scholars studying, and based in, different places. But it would differ from conventional area studies in the sense that it neither pulls together a range of disciplines into the study of a single social whole, nor combines a variety of area specialisms into a single discipline. Instead, it uses knowledge of a variety of places and a variety of disciplinary approaches in order to elucidate problems that cross boundaries. In doing this, it accepts the need to draw its own maps.

This book aims to contribute to anti-area studies in several ways: by highlighting the contingent and shifting nature of the boundary lines we draw between nations and regions; by viewing history from the perspective of a zone that has been repeatedly subdivided by ever-moving political and conceptual frontiers; and by focusing on the 'imbricated history'

33   Donna J Guy and Thomas E Sheridan, 'On Frontiers: The Northern and Southern Edges of the Spanish Empire in the Americas' in *Contested Ground: Comparative Frontiers on the Northern and Southern Edges of the Spanish Empire*, ed. Donna J Guy and Thomas E Sheridan (Tucson: University of Arizona Press, 1998), pp. 3–15; Janet Carsten, 'Borders, Boundaries, Tradition and State on the Malaysian Periphery', in *Border Identities: Nation and State at International Frontiers*, ed. Thomas M Wilson and Hastings Donnen (Cambridge: Cambridge University Press, 1998), pp. 215–36, doi.org/10.1017/cbo9780511607813.009; Martin Stokes, 'Imagining "the South": Hybridity, Heterotopias and Arabesk on the Turkish-Syrian Border', in Wilson and Donnen, *Border Identities*, pp. 263–88, doi.org/10.1017/cbo9780511607813.011.
34   Imogen Seger Coulborn, 'A Question of Utility?', in *The Boundaries of Civilizations in Space and Time*, ed. Matthew Melko and Leighton R Scott (Lanham and New York: University Press of America, 1987), pp. 268–69, quotation from p. 268; on the relationship between temporal and spatial boundaries, see also Johannes Fabian, *Time and the Other: How Anthropology Makes its Object* (New York: Columbia University Press, 2002). Original published in 1983.

that emerged as diverse social formations came into contact within this zone (an approach that will be developed particularly in Chapter 4). The geographical focus here will be a relatively narrow one, mostly confined to the area around the Okhotsk Sea, though sometimes extending a little further to Japan and the broader East Asian region. The hope, though, is that this may offer ideas and approaches that can also contribute to the wider rethinking of spatial and temporal boundaries occurring in the study of many realms of our world's complex and interwoven history.

An earlier version of this paper was published in the journal *Communal/Plural* 8, no. 1 (2000): pp. 9–23.

2
MAPPING TIME AND SPACE

It is not drawn on any map; true places never are.[1]

From the end of the sixteenth century, in response to contact with European missionaries and merchants, a new fashion appeared in Japan: a fashion for lavishly decorated screens depicting maps of the world. The maps were often accompanied by pictures illustrating the landscapes of distant cities or (in sometimes fanciful style) the dress and customs of foreign peoples. A remarkable feature of these world maps is their colour. They usually depict the world as being divided into a patchwork of countries, each surrounded by a boundary line and each coloured so as to distinguish it from its neighbours. The seventeenth-century Japanese decorative painting of the lands and peoples of the world shown below (with its world map oriented towards the east) follows the same convention: Japan, coloured cream, is distinguished from the Korean Peninsula, which is green. The British Isles are coloured brown, Iberia is golden-yellow and so on. The result is a feast for the eye.[2]

---

1   Herman Melville, *Moby Dick, or The Whale* (New York: Harper and Brothers, 1851), p. 61.
2   Muroga Nobuo, 'Atarashii Sekai no Ninshiki: Nanban Sekaizu Byōbu', in *Daikōkai Jidai no Nihon 5: Nihon kara Mita Ikoku* (Tokyo: Shōgakukan, 1978), pp. 93–102; for further discussion of the development of Japanese map-making traditions, see Kazutaka Unno, 'Cartography in Japan', in *The History of Cartography*, ed. JB Harley and David Woodward, vol. 2, book 2 (Chicago: University of Chicago Press, 1994), pp. 346–477; Kären Wigen, Sugimoto Fumiko and Cary Karakas, *Cartographic Japan: A History in Maps* (Chicago: University of Chicago Press, 2016); Oda Takeo, *Chizu no Rekishi: Sekai Hen, Nihon Hen* (Tokyo: Kōdansha, 2018).

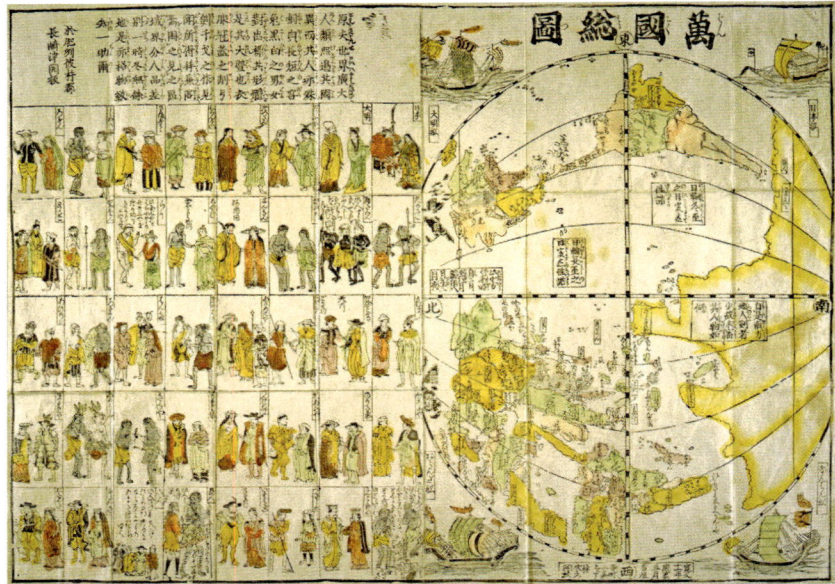

Figure 2.1. Japanese map and accompanying image of peoples of the world, 1671.

Source: University of British Columbia Library Open Collections, Creative Commons (CC BY-SA) licence.

For the contemporary viewer, looking at these images it is easy to underestimate the revolutionary nature of their representation of space. This is, after all, the way we are accustomed to seeing the world today. Contemporary atlases still follow the same convention. But at the time when these works were produced, this was a novel image of the world, which had only recently begun to appear in Europe itself. During the sixteenth century, the work particularly of famous map-makers like Abraham Ortelius and Petrus Plancius had popularised the use of coloured 'political' maps of the world. But as Jeremy Black points out, at least until early modern times, national boundaries were hazy, and ruling dynasties claimed control over territories that were often physically scattered. All of this made it extremely difficult to depict space in terms of clearly bounded blocks of 'national territory'. 'A more spatially territorial approach to frontiers', Black notes, 'developed in the seventeenth and eighteenth centuries, although this process remained incomplete at the time of the French Revolution'.[3]

---

3   Jeremy Black, *Maps and History: Constructing Images of the Past* (New Haven and London: Yale University Press, 1997), p. 17.

Japanese artists' early adoption of an image of the world as a patchwork of bounded political territories seems to owe more to their sense of visual aesthetics than to a premature awareness of the emerging importance of the nation-state. The multicoloured design of these political world maps made them attractive subjects for the two-dimensional decorative surfaces of the lacquered screen, and this aesthetic appeal was probably more important to the designers than the precise location of political frontiers. The national boundaries they imposed on Europe often followed the lines drawn by European map-makers, but other parts of the world left greater scope for the visual imagination. In the map shown in Figure 2.1, China is divided into several parts and the political boundaries of Africa are quite fanciful. Most interesting, perhaps, was the treatment of the Japanese nation in screens and maps that focused on Japan itself. Japanese screen painters generally used local knowledge to improve on the sketchy depictions of Japan provided in European world maps. They also, however, quite often chose to depict Japan, not as a single block of colour, but rather as attractively divided into a multicoloured diversity of territories, their boundary lines often following those of the ancient Japanese *kuni* (which in fact had no political or administrative significance at the time the maps were drawn, but which remained deeply ingrained in popular identity and imagination).[4]

Reinventing the Frontier

By contrasting sixteenth- and seventeenth-century political maps of the world with the maps produced in earlier centuries, we can begin to grasp the profound impact that European nation-state formation had upon the human sense of space and time. The most immediately visible revolution is the invention of the frontier as a single, clear, definable line separating one nation-state from another. The idea of such borderlines was not entirely new. For example, the Emperor Charlemagne, dividing his territories between his sons in the ninth century, provided detailed verbal descriptions of the lines separating one heir's territory from another. However, such lines were seldom inscribed on maps, and throughout much of Europe the relationship between political control and territory was much more complex.

---

4   On the persistence of the notion of *kuni* in Japanese mapping, see Kären Wigen, *A Malleable Map: Geographies of Restoration in Central Japan 1600–1912* (Berkeley and Los Angeles: University of California Press, 2010).

Figure 2.2. Fifteenth-century map of the Iberian Peninsula.
Source: British Library Harley MS 3686, public domain.

Medieval dynastic rulers often exercised control over widely dispersed, non-contiguous collections of territories. In the middle of the twelfth century, for example, the area that we now know as 'Spain' was divided into several political units, including the (sometimes united and sometimes separate) Kingdoms of Castile and Leon, Navarre, Aragon (which also incorporated the territory of Catalonia), the Muslim kingdom of Valencia and the Islamic Almohad Dominions in the south of the Iberian Peninsula. After a dynastic alliance in the early twelfth century, both Aragon and Catalonia were ruled by the same monarch, but his status in the two realms was different: in Aragon he was a feudal king; in Catalonia a count with distinct and more circumscribed powers. The kings of Aragon also exercised various types of feudal authority in Occitania (the area that now forms the south-western region of France): Jaume I of Aragon (1208–76), for example, was also count of the city of Montpellier. In 1238 Jaume conquered the kingdom of Valencia and began to encourage the colonisation of this region by Christian settlers from elsewhere in Spain, yet the Christian population remained a minority, living alongside, but largely separate from, the remaining Muslim inhabitants.[5] Thus political control in no sense implied cultural integration, and diverse and widely dispersed collections of territory were often under the control of the same ruler. Even in the sixteenth century, Philip II of Spain continued to control the Netherlands, parts of Italy and Franche-Compté (in what is now France), as well as the vast Spanish empire in the Americas.

Elsewhere in medieval Europe the nature of frontiers was equally multilayered and complex. In Wales and Ireland, for example, waves of invasion from England had created small pockets of territory which were more or less under the control of an Anglo-Norman aristocracy, but were surrounded by large areas controlled by assorted native rulers. So, to travel just a few kilometres out of towns like Radnor in Wales or Dublin in Ireland 'was to enter a different world and to cross a frontier, or rather frontiers, all the more profound for not being delineated on a map'.[6] As Rees Davies points out, in such regions there existed multiple superimposed borders 'of conquest, settlement, peoples, culture and units of power', and none of these borders precisely coincided with the others.[7]

The modern concept of the national frontier owed much to the processes of European overseas expansion and colonisation. It was Spanish and Portuguese expansion into the New World that prompted the first (and perhaps most famous) artificial creation of a linear territorial boundary, the 1494 Treaty of Tordesillas, which drew a straight north–south line 370 leagues east of the Cape Verde Islands, separating the colonies of the kingdom of Castile from Portuguese colonies in the Americas. This division of the world between Castile and Portugal treated

---

5   Robert I Burns, 'The Significance of the Frontier in the Middle Ages', in *Mediaeval Frontier Societies*, ed. Robert Bartlett and Angus MacKay (Oxford: Clarendon Press, 1989), pp. 307–30, doi.org/10.1093/acprof:oso/9780198203612.003.0013, see particularly pp. 319–29.

6   Rees Davies, 'Frontier Arrangements in Fragmented Societies: Ireland and Wales', in Bartlett and MacKay *Mediaeval Frontier Societies*, pp. 77–100, doi.org/10.1093/acprof:oso/9780198203612.003.0004, reference from p. 78.

7   Davies, 'Frontier Arrangements', p. 80.

'the world' as a flat plain: a map rather than a globe. However, the early sixteenth-century voyages of Magellan and others made European rulers aware of the potentially rich resources of Southeast Asia, and encouraged them to envisage the world as a globe. This in turn prompted the Castilian and Portuguese kings to reimagine the Tordesillas border not as a flat line on a flat map, but as a line encircling a spherical world, dividing the globe in two as one might split an apple. This extension of the Tordesillas line into the eastern hemisphere was enshrined in the 1529 Treaty of Saragossa, which was remarkable for the fact that it specifically required the drawing up of a map showing the location of the frontier between 'Castilian' and 'Portuguese' spheres of influence.[8]

The drawing of such linear boundaries both encouraged and was made possible by the development of new surveying techniques, and these in turn were then applied by European administrators and map-makers to their home territories: producing, for example, sixteenth-century maps of the Iberian Peninsula that redefined the frontier between Castile and Portugal, no longer as a rather hazy 'border zone', but as a precisely plotted line – a line that sometimes ran right through the middle of villages, and even through the middle of family homes.[9] These technical developments in the surveying of frontiers of course coincided with the sixteenth-century emergence of the notions of 'national sovereignty' and of the contractual treaty between nation and nation. While overseas expansion stimulated the emergence of new images of the world as a whole, the consolidation of state power within Europe encouraged the production of highly detailed and mathematically accurate maps of frontier regions liable to invasion by neighbouring powers.

For example, sixteenth-century conflicts between England and France over control of the area around Calais (part of which remained under the control of the English crown until 1558) led to the production of whole series of precisely plotted charts of the north-western French coastline. Among them is one that (in the words of historian Peter Barber) 'must

8   Jerry Brotton, *Trading Territories: Mapping the Early Modern World* (Ithaca: Cornell University Press, 1998), pp. 119–50.
9   Geoffrey Parker, 'Maps and Ministers: The Spanish Hapsburgs', in *Monarchs, Ministers and Maps: The Emergence of Cartography as a Tool of Government in Early Modern Europe*, ed. David Buisseret (Chicago: Chicago University Press, 1992), pp. 124–52; William Kavanagh, 'Symbolic Boundaries and "Real" Borders on the Portuguese-Spanish Frontier', in *Border Approaches: Anthropological Perspectives on Frontiers*, ed. Hastings Donnan and Thomas M Wilson (Lanham: University Press of America, 1994), pp. 75–87.

rate as among the earliest of the detailed "frontier" maps', depicting an English interpretation of the border between English and French territory as a line of red dots close to the town of Boulogne.[10] In France, too, early modern mapping of the national territory was stimulated, first by military and defensive needs, but during the seventeenth century also by the demands of an increasingly centralised state for the geographical knowledge necessary to supervise local administration, collect taxes and carry out public works projects.[11]

The political theorists of the emerging modern state, such as Baldassare Castiglione (1478–1529) and Thomas Elyot (c. 1490–1546), stressed the importance of accurate maps for administration of the nation. Elyot's advice to rulers, *The Boke Named the Governour* (1531), described accurate maps of the nation as being essential to the monarch 'as well for the safeguard of his country, as for the commodity and honour thereof' – in other words, both for defensive and political purposes.[12] The gradual appearance of an order in which European nations were seen as clearly bounded territories under the control of a single sovereign state thus had profound implications for the depiction of geographical space. From the time of the 1648 Treaty of Westphalia onwards, a whole series of treaties among the emerging world powers put these ideas into effect, ultimately producing the familiar modern vision of the world as a patchwork of nations each with its own clear boundary lines.

During the seventeenth and eighteenth centuries, with the processes of European expansion and the emergence of the modern global order, such notions of linear frontiers gradually spread to other parts of the world, including East Asia. In Japan during the Edo period (1603–1868), for example, the most familiar frontiers, for the majority of people, were the boundaries between domains, or the checkpoints (*sekisho*) created by the shogunate along major highways to control the movement of people in and out of key centres of power. By contrast, the boundaries surrounding the nation as a whole were, at least in the early Edo period, rather vague

10   Peter Barber, 'England I: Pageantry, Defense and Government: Maps at Court to 1550', in Buisseret, *Monarchs, Ministers, and Maps*, pp. 26–56, quotation from p. 37.
11   See David Buisseret, 'Monarchs, Ministers and Maps in France Before the Accession of Louis XIV' in *Monarchs, Ministers, and Maps: The Emergence of Cartography as a Tool of Government in Early Modern Europe*, ed. David Buisseret (Chicago: University of Chicago Press, 1992), pp. 99–123.
12   Barber, 'England I', p. 32.

and porous.[13] As Bruce Batten notes, the overriding ideological image at this time was the 'Japan-style middle kingdom order' (*Nihon-gata kai chitsujo*) – a Japanised variant of China's middle kingdom system, with Japan proper posited as a centre surrounded by outlying 'barbarians'.[14] Efforts were made to control the contact points between 'Japan' and the 'barbarians', and in Ezo (Hokkaido) a firm borderline was drawn between the territory directly controlled by the Japanese Matsumae family and the Ainu realms beyond (see Chapter 4). But even:

> the border in Hokkaido … was not conceived as an absolute limit to Japanese authority, for the notion of territorial sovereignty remained unknown. The border merely represented the outside limits of the sphere of directly administered territory within the larger world order defined by the 'middle kingdom ideology'.[15]

It was growing awareness of European expansion (and particularly of Russian expansion into Siberia, Kamchatka, Sakhalin and the Chishima Archipelago) that prompted the first Japanese efforts to define clear national frontiers. By the 1780s, mathematician and political thinker Honda Toshiaki was speaking of the need to 'establish a mutual frontier between Japan and other countries in order to create a fortress to withstand northern enemies'.[16] And two decades later, in 1808, growing friction with Russia to the north of Japan prompted a famous expedition by officials Mamiya Rinzō and Matsuda Denjirō to establish the northern 'limits of the territory of Great Japan' (discussed further in Chapter 6).[17]

---

13   On early concepts of boundaries and borders in Japan, see Iida Momo, *'Nihon' no Genkei: Kikaigashima kara Sotogahama made* (Tokyo: Heibonsha, 1994); Bruce Batten, *To the Ends of Japan: Premodern Boundaries, Frontiers and Interactions* (Honolulu: University of Hawai'i Press, 2003); Marcia Yonemoto, *Mapping Early Modern Japan: Space, Place and Culture in the Tokugawa Period (1603–1868)* (Berkeley and Los Angeles: University of California Press, 2003).

14   Batten, *To the Ends of Japan*, p. 44.

15   Batten, *To the Ends of Japan*, p. 47.

16   Kaiho Mineo, *Kinsei no Hokkaidō* (Tokyo: Kyōikusha, 1979), p. 129.

17   On Mamiya Rinzō and mapping, see Brett L Walker, 'Mamiya Rinzō and the Cartography of Empire', in Wigen, Sugimoto and Karakas, *Cartographic Japan*, pp. 140–43, doi.org/10.7208/chicago/9780226073194.003.0032.

Figure 2.3. Hayashi Shihei's *Illustrated Outline of the Three Countries* [*Sankoku Tsūran Zusetsu*], 1785.

Source: Wikimedia commons, public domain.

The astronomer and geographer Hayashi Shihei's 1785 *Illustrated Outline of the Three Countries [Sankoku Tsūran Zusetsu]* represented an early attempt to define Japan's borders with its neighbours: Korea to the west; the Ryukyu Kingdom (now known as Okinawa) to the south; and Ezo (now known as Hokkaido) to the north. Hayashi's map of East Asia differs in several important ways from the sixteenth- and early seventeenth-century depictions of the world in Japanese screen paintings. In the screen paintings, the outer limits of Japan remain obscure. Much of the island of Ezo was still unmapped, and the region is normally either entirely omitted altogether or depicted as a small and variably shaped blob. Other islands like Hachijojima may or may not appear on the map, and are often painted in different colours from the neighbouring regions of Japan. On Hayashi's map, by contrast, Hokkaido is depicted in far more detail (though in a curiously elongated shape) and colour is now used to represent an emergent concept of national territory. The whole of 'Japan', from Matsumae Domain in the southern part of Hokkaido to Satsuma in the south of Kyushu, is uniformly coloured to distinguish it from neighbouring countries, though this colour coding also identifies both 'Ezo' and the Ryukyu Kingdom as territories distinct from 'Japan'.[18]

Separating Space and Time

But post-Renaissance political maps of the world do not only reveal the emerging notion of the clearly bounded nation-state. They also represent another and perhaps even more profound revolution in notions of time and space, though one that is not so readily obvious to the viewer. To grasp the nature of this revolution, we might begin by looking at one of the most remarkable pre-sixteenth-century maps, the 1402 *Map of the Integrated Territory of Historical Countries and their Capitals [Honil gangni yeokdae gukto jido]*, usually referred to as the *Kangnido*. Produced in Korea in the early Chosŏn Dynasty, the *Kangnido* has been described as having been, in its day, 'the most complete map of the world that any East Asian country had to offer'.[19] Indeed, it was probably one of the most complete maps on offer anywhere. The map combined information drawn from earlier Chinese sources (most notably a now lost map by the monk

---

18   See Terasawa Hajime et al., eds, *Hoppō Mikōkai Komonjo Shūsei 10: Ezo Kochizu* (Tokyo: Sōbunsha, 1975).
19   Gari Ledyard, 'The Kangnido: A Korean World Map, 1402', in *Circa 1492: Art in the Age of Exploration* (New Haven: Yale University Press, 1991), pp. 329–32, quotation from p. 329.

Qingjun) with local knowledge of Korean geography and information apparently obtained from Arab traders. The result is an image of the world that extends from a fairly detailed image of Japan in the east, through a very large Korea and through China and India (depicted as consolidated into the western side of the Chinese landmass), to Arabia, the Nile and the Mediterranean in the west.

The accompanying text tells us that 'in the 4th year of the Jianwen era (1402), Left Minister Kim [Sahyeong] of Sangju and Right Minister Yi [Mu] of Tanyang, during moments of rest from their governing duties, made a comparative study of [earlier] maps and ordered Yi Hoe, an orderly, to collate them carefully and then combine them into a single map … One can indeed know the world without going out of his door! By looking at maps one can know terrestrial distances and get help in the work of government'.[20]

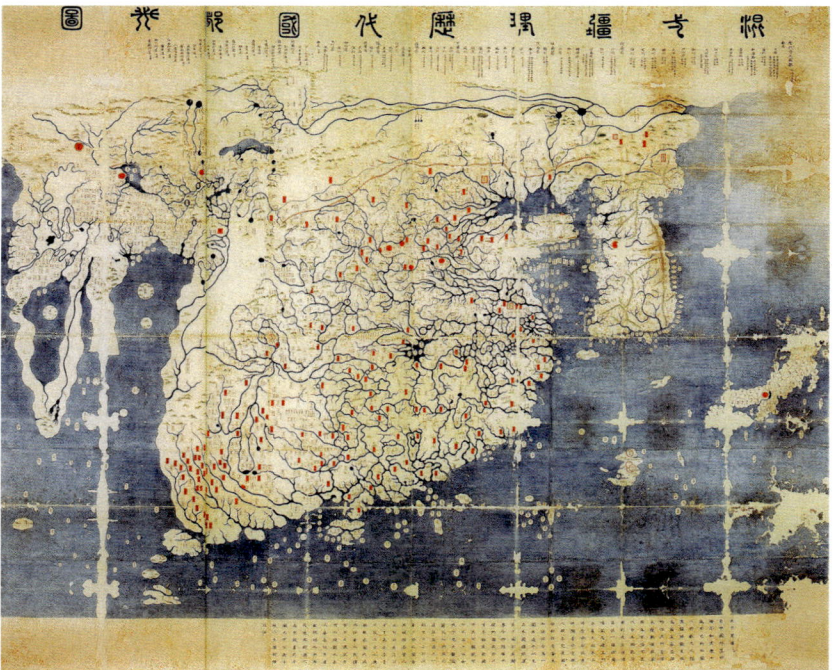

Figure 2.4. *Map of the Integrated Territory of Historical Countries and their Capitals [Honil gangni yeokdae gukto jido]* **(The *Kangnido*), 1402.**
Source: Wikimedia commons, public domain.

20   Ledyard, 'The *Kangnido*', pp. 329–30.

The origins and significance of the *Kangnido* (which is now known only from three copies) have been widely debated. The date of its production, and the fact that it was drawn up just seven years after the completion of a famous and officially commissioned map of the heavens, suggests that its purpose was partly ideological – it was a visual statement affirming the legitimacy of the Chosŏn Dynasty, and asserting the Dynasty's place in space and history. One of the most interesting and obvious features of the map, however, is that it is (as the words 'historical countries' in its title suggests) a map of time as well as space. It represents not only the geography of the world but also its history. Like earlier Chinese maps (which often combined image and words to show changes in place names and administrative structures) it used both cartographic symbols and accompanying text to illustrate the changing territories and capitals of successive dynasties.

The use of maps to represent time as well as space was not confined to East Asia. Many pre-Renaissance European maps also combined text with imagery to convey ideas about the passage of historical time as well as the shape of geographical space. Evelyn Edson observes that '"reading a map" in the Middle Ages could mean scanning great blocks of written matter, describing geographical, anthropological and historical features'.[21] A striking example of the fusion of space and time in medieval European mapping comes from the great thirteenth-century wall map preserved at Hereford Cathedral in England. Like most medieval world maps, this is oriented towards the east, with a depiction of the Garden of Eden at the top, detailed scenes from Biblical events and classical mythology below, and the outlines of contemporary Britain and its neighbours at the bottom. As Edson explains, 'historical time flowed down the map, from the expulsion from Paradise in the east, through the parade of empires, to the newest cities in the west'.[22]

---

21 Evelyn Edson, *Mapping Time and Space: How Medieval Mapmakers Viewed their World* (London: The British Library, 1997), p. 134.
22 Edson, *Mapping Time and Space*, p. 140; see also PDA Harvey, *Mappa Mundi: The Hereford World Map* (London: British Library, 1996).

Figure 2.5. The Hereford wall map.

Source: Wikimedia commons, public domain.

If pre-Renaissance maps often represented time as well as space, pre-Renaissance histories often incorporated a spatial as well as a temporal dimension. About 150 years before an unknown artist composed the Hereford wall map, Otto, Bishop of Freisling, wrote one of the most famous of all medieval European histories of the world: *The Two Cities*. The 'two cities' of the title are the eternal city of God and the transient city of human life. Freisling begins his story with the Biblical origins of humanity in the Garden of Eden before moving on through tales of the classical world to recent times: Viking expansion, the rule of Charlemagne, the crusades, etc. The structure of his image of the world, in this sense, parallels the structure presented in the Hereford wall map. Here too, time and space are inseparable. Movement through historical time is also movement through geographical space, from east to west. As Otto of Freisling wrote, 'it is observed that all human power or learning had its origin in the East, but is coming to an end in the West, that thereby the transitoriness and decay of all things human may be displayed'.[23]

Against this background, the revolutionary nature of the vision of the world represented by sixteenth- and seventeenth-century mapping practices becomes obvious. Here, time has been separated from space. It is true that some of the great map-makers of early modern Europe (including Abraham Ortelius) were deeply interested in history, and Ortelius indeed included historical maps of the classical world in his famous 1570 atlas, the *Theatrum Orbis Terrarum*. But the key transformation was that the maps of Ortelius and his successors were not diachronic but synchronic: each map represented only one moment in time, whether present or past. The map had become a pure representation of space – a miniature representation of the physical shape of the world itself. As one of Ortelius' admirers wrote to him, 'you have compressed the immense structure of land and sea into a narrow space, and have made the world portable, which a great many people assert to be immovable'.[24]

Just as the early modern revolution in mapping produced a notion of 'homogenous, empty space', so a concurrent revolution in social thinking produced the discipline of history with its concept of 'homogeneous, empty time'.[25] Writing in the Western European context, John Lukacs notes that:

> the modern concept of *history* (like the political concept of *Europe* and the social concept of the *bourgeois*) grew with the Renaissance. But the origins of the real development of our awareness of this kind of thinking … [was] a relatively recent development, beginning in the seventeenth century.[26]

---

23   Otto, Bishop of Freisling, *The Two Cities: A Chronicle of Universal History to the Year 1146 AD*, trans. CC Mierow (New York: Octagon Books, 1996), p. 95.

24   Quoted in Brotton, *Trading Territories*, p. 175.

25   Walter Benjamin, 'Theses on the Philosophy of History', in *Illuminations*, ed. Hannah Arendt, trans. Harry Zohn (New York: Schocken Books, 1969), pp. 253–64, quotation from p. 261. Original published in 1950.

26   John Lukacs, *Historical Consciousness or the Remembered Past* (New York: Harper and Row, 1968), p. 12.

Figure 2.6. Abraham Ortelius's world map, *Theatrum Orbis Terrarum,* 1570.

Source: Wikimedia commons, public domain.

The word 'historian', for example, seems to have appeared in English around the beginning of the sixteenth century, and the distinction between the terms 'ancient' and 'modern' around the beginning of the seventeenth. Until the seventeenth century, the word 'progress' referred to movement through space: it was probably the political administrator and scientific thinker Francis Bacon (1561–1626) who first gave it the new meaning of 'advance through time'. During the seventeenth century, too, alongside the appearance of a new English vocabulary of scientific terms (such as 'fluid', 'gas', 'temperature' and 'pressure') came the emergence of a new vocabulary of historical time: 'century', 'decade', 'epoch', 'contemporary', 'historic' and 'primeval' are all seventeenth-century words.[27] Anthony Giddens links this separation of space from time to the rise of mechanical methods of measurement – particularly the use of the mechanical clock, which was associated with growing 'uniformity in the social organization of time'.[28] But, as David Gross suggests, the institutions of nation-states made use of these tools of modernity to challenge older religious visions of time and advance their own 'political conceptions of duration'.[29]

Space, Race and Progress

This revolutionary separation of time from space, which coincided with the emergence of the modern nation-state, was to have profound consequences for social thought – consequences that continue to influence our vision of the world in the present day. On the one hand, the re-envisioning of the surface of the globe as 'homogenous, empty space' encouraged a gradual but profound reordering of geographic concepts. Classical and medieval European world-views envisioned the lands of the earth as a single contiguous block of territory, the *Orbis Terrarum*. But growing knowledge of the Americas forced a rethinking of this conceptual framework. The seventeenth and eighteenth centuries saw the gradual emergence of the notion of 'continents' as large masses of land containing the many nations. The precise classification and division of continents, however, remained a matter of controversy. Increasing awareness of the geography of central Russia, for example, raised questions about the dividing line between 'Europe' and 'Asia'. It was not until the eighteenth

---

27   Lukacs, *Historical Consciousness*, pp. 12–13.
28   Anthony Giddens, *The Consequences of Modernity* (Cambridge: Polity Press, 1990), p. 18.
29   David Gross, 'Temporality and the Modern State', *Theory and Society* 14, no. 1 (1985): pp. 53–82.

century that the Swedish military officer Philip-Johann von Strahlenberg proposed the Ural Mountains as marking the 'frontier' between the two continents.[30]

These shifts in the classificatory frameworks of physical geography coincided with the emergence of new ways of classifying human beings – a new 'human geography' that defined the world's population as being divided into 'races'. Colonial expansion confronted European thinkers with the awareness not only of previously unimagined expanses of territory, but also of a previously unimagined diversity of human groups and lifestyles. To reduce this bewildering diversity to manageable order, eighteenth-century thinkers (most notably the French natural historian Georges Louis de Buffon, discussed further in the following chapter) began to extend to human beings systems of taxonomy similar to those used by scientists like Linnaeus to study non-human species. The new classificatory system of 'race', further developed in the nineteenth century by writers such as Georges Cuvier and James Prichard, could then be superimposed upon the new spatial classificatory system of 'continents', producing a neatly colour-coded vision of the world. The German naturalist Johann Friedrich Blumenbach (1752–1840) helped to elaborate this colour coding by dividing the human race schematically into 'Caucasians' (white), 'Mongolians' (yellow), 'Malayans' (brown), 'Ethiopians' (black) and '[native] Americans' (red), and by the early nineteenth century Carl Ritter (1779–1859) – one of the most influential geographers of his day – was also defining each continent in racial terms: Europe was the realm of white people, Asia of yellow people, Africa of black people and America of red people – and each continent thus had its own 'special function in the progress of human culture'.[31]

This vision of the world naturally lent itself to a new way of colouring in maps of the world: as well as using colour to highlight the boundaries between one nation and another, one could also use larger blocks of colour to depict the spatial boundaries between one race and another. Jeremy Black notes that 'interest in ethnicity coincided with the greater use of colour' in mapping. Edward Grover's mid-nineteenth-century *Historic Geographical Atlas of the Middle and Modern Ages*, for example,

---

30   MW Lewis and KE Wigen, *The Myth of Continents: A Critique of Metageography* (Berkeley: University of California Press, 1997), p. 27.
31   Quoted in Lewis and Wigen, *Myth of Continents*, p. 30.

paid special attention to 'tinting and colouring the maps, by which the tribes of particular races, as the Germanic, the Hunnish, the Sclavic, the Mongol and the Turkish are represented in different colours'.[32]

Now geographical space came to be seen as divisible at two levels: first into large units – 'continents' containing 'races' – and then into the smaller units of 'nations' containing 'peoples'. Each of these levels of division, moreover, was envisaged as being an inherent part of the natural order. The graphic simplicity of this image of the world, together with its power as an instrument of colonialism, gave it great appeal: an appeal that survived despite the repeated failure of the natural sciences to reach any consensus about the meaning of the term 'race'. This paradox is vividly illustrated, for example, by Blackie's *Comprehensive Atlas and Geography of the World*, published in London in 1882. The atlas divides the world, first into continents and then into nations, and gives a description of the territory, resources and human culture of each. The written text notes that:

> attempts to classify the races of mankind have led to too little agreement among men of science to be able to present to the reader any general conclusions that have been arrived at, and we must therefore content ourselves … with a comparison based on comparisons of language, on which there is at least more agreement than on any other.[33]

Yet despite this rejection of the notion of 'race' as a reliable scientific concept, the volume is illustrated with a series of strikingly stereotypic pictures of 'races' identified with particular nations or continents: including 'the Grecian race', 'the Caucasian race', 'the Mongol race' (represented by Japanese) and a composite picture of 'The Ethiopian race, Negroes, Kaffirs'.

32   Black, *Maps and History*, p. 79.
33   WG Blackie, *The Comprehensive Atlas and Geography of the World* (London: Blackie and Sons, 1882), p. 124.

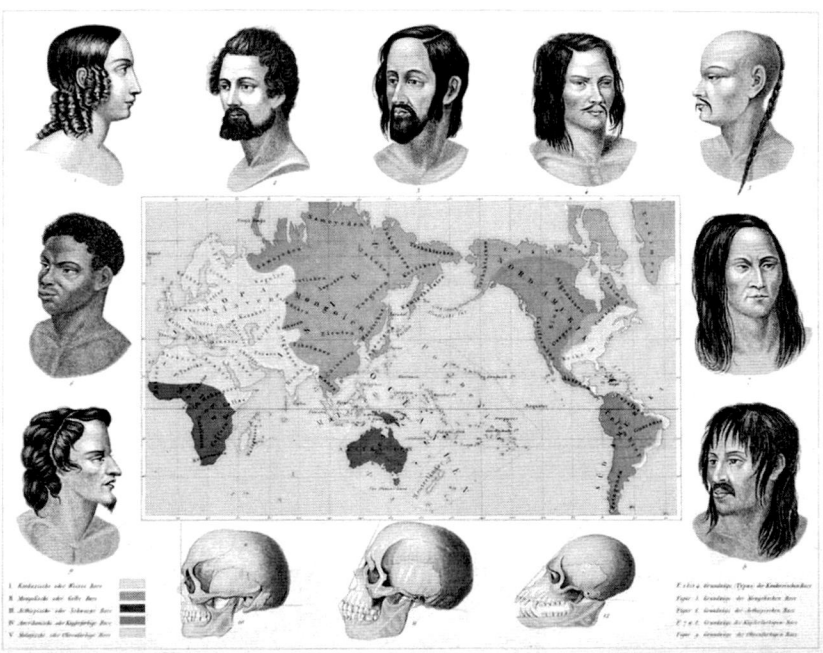

Figure 2.7. English world map based on Blumenbach's classifications, 1849.

Source: Johann Georg Heck, *Bilder-Atlas zum Conversations-Lexicon* (Tafel: Leipzig, 1849).

It was this racially coded view of the continents of the world that was imported into nineteenth-century Japan in the first popular geography text, *Account of the Countries of the World* [*Sekai Kunizukushi*], published in 1869 by the famous Meiji-era thinker Fukuzawa Yukichi. Fukuzawa followed Ritter's and Blumenbach's geographical schemes closely, dividing the world into five continents inhabited by five races: Europeans, he tells his readers, are white, Asians 'slightly yellow', Africans black, the peoples of the Pacific Islands brown and the inhabitants of 'the mountains of America' red.[34] Meanwhile, however, the parallel but separate stream of modern historical thought was producing a very different system for classifying human difference: a system where difference was a function of time rather than space. While human geographers attempted to come to terms with cultural and social diversity (and to justify colonial expansion) by deploying the concept of race, historical philosophy addressed the same problems by deploying the concepts of 'progress' and 'civilisation'.

---

34 Fukuzawa Yukichi, *Sekai Kunizukushi* (Tokyo: Keio Gijuku Shuppankyoku, 1968). Original published in 1869.

According to this view (as the French historian François Guizot put it) society was 'on the march, not in order to change its place, but to change its situation'.[35] Although the idea of progress (as we saw) goes back at least as far as the early seventeenth century, it was particularly during the eighteenth century that it was developed into a coherent taxonomy of stages of historical development. This taxonomy, as we shall see in subsequent chapters, began to be expressed very clearly in eighteenth-century Enlightenment works written around the time of the French revolution, and was later elaborated by various nineteenth- and twentieth-century theorists of civilisation. While spatial notions of the division of the world into races and nations sustained the vision of the 'nation-state' as a naturally existing social and geographical unit, temporal notions of progress and civilisation provided a justification for the ranking of nations into hierarchies reflecting their 'degrees of development'. This hierarchy in turn could be used to justify the colonial domination of more 'civilised' nations over those deemed insufficiently 'civilised' to rule themselves. The global power of this new vision of time is evident from the enthusiasm with which it was taken up in countries like Japan and China as part of the process of modern nation-building. In Japan, Fukuzawa Yukichi not only helped to introduce the spatial stream of modern European thought – the vision of the world as divided between races and nations – but also (even more famously) helped to introduce the temporal stream – the notion of a hierarchy of civilisation stages. His *Outline of a Theory of Civilization* [*Bunmeiron no gairyaku*], published in 1876, presented human history as progressing from the 'primitive' to the 'semi-developed' stage, and thence to the contemporary stage of full civilisation.[36]

Rethinking Time and Space

The emergence of the modern state thus brought with it a fundamental reordering of notions of space and time. On the one hand, geographical space came to be reimagined as divided into clearly bounded blocks of national territory. During the seventeenth and eighteenth centuries, this method of subdividing space was elaborated. The smaller territorial blocks of nation-states were envisioned as subsections of larger blocks

35   François Guizot, *Histoire de la Civilisation en Europe depuis la Chute de l'Empire Romain*, 6th ed. (Paris: Victor Masson, 1951), p. 14. Original published in 1828.
36   See Fukuzawa Yukichi, *Outline of a Theory of Civilization*, trans. David A Dilworth and G Cameron Hurst III (New York: Columbia University Press, 2008). Original published in 1876.

– 'continents' that in the popular imagination came to be commonly identified with distinct 'races'. This way of seeing space in turn gradually became naturalised – accepted as an inherent part of the natural order, rather than understood as an ideological construct. One consequence of such naturalisation was that it became common to project this division of space back in time. We now readily speak, for example, of 'medieval Spain', 'Jōmon period Japan' or 'America before the coming of Columbus', as though such entities really existed. Yet in fact all are anachronistic projections of a modern geographical vision into times and spaces where 'time' and 'space' themselves were experienced in quite different ways.

More fundamentally, modern nation-state building also brought with it a radical division between the dimensions of time and space. Geographical space came to be seen as a physical reality existing independently of time. It was the domain of an emerging professional group of geographers, surveyors and cartographers, who measured space in terms of longitude, latitude, miles and kilometres. The study of time, meanwhile, was entrusted to the historians, who divided it into decades, centuries and epochs, and debated the sequences of human stages of progress. Yet despite this conceptual and professional separation, time and space could in practice never be kept strictly separate. Spatialised notions of 'racial difference', for example, constantly merged into temporal notions of 'stages of civilisation'. Indeed, the close interconnection these two parallel, though theoretically separate, dimensions for classifying difference was repeatedly exploited in the discourses of nationalism and colonialism. Where notions of racial difference failed to provide a justification for conquest or resistance, the spatial discourse of race could readily be transposed into the temporal discourse of 'stages of progress', and vice versa.

Over the course of the twentieth century, however, the images of time and space born from the revolutions of the sixteenth and seventeenth centuries were exposed to new challenges. Particularly in the latter decades of the century, critical writings on the nation-state re-envisioned the nation, not as an enduring and natural territorial unit, but rather as an imagined and historically contingent entity.[37] As Immanuel Wallerstein suggested, it seemed as though we were being impelled to embark on the:

---

37   See, for example, Benedict Anderson, *Imagined Communities: Reflections on the Origin and Spread of Nationalism* (London: Verso, 1983); Nishikawa Nagao, *Kokkyō no koekata: Hikaku Bunkaron Josetsu* (Tokyo: Chikuma Shobō, 1992); Amino Yoshihiko, *'Nihon' to wa nani ka* (Tokyo: Kōdansha, 2000).

> very difficult, very interesting road of questioning one of the bedrocks of our intelligence, our certainties about time and space. At the end of the road lies not simplicity but complexity. But our geohistorical social systems are complex; indeed, they are the most complex structures of the universe.[38]

These bedrocks are not easily shifted. The maps of space and time that will emerge from this journey of discovery have yet to be imagined. In the chapters that follow, we will first look more closely at the way in which the European 'discovery' of East Asia shaped Enlightenment divisions of time and space, and (conversely) the way in which these divisions in turn influenced academic and popular perceptions of East Asia, before going on to point out some possible paths towards the process of questioning and reimagining time and space in the twenty-first century world.

An earlier version of this chapter appeared in Japanese in Uemura Tadao, Ōnuki Tadashi, Tsukimoto Akio, Ninomiya Hiroyuki and Sakamoto Hiroko eds, *Rekishi o Tou 3: Rekishi to Kūkan* (Tokyo: Iwanami Shoten, 2001), pp. 111–30.

---

38   Immanuel Wallerstein, *Unthinking Social Science* (Oxford: Polity Press, 1991), p. 148.

3

'TARTARY' IN THE RESHAPING OF HISTORICAL THOUGHT

In June 1643, the crews of the Dutch East India Company's ships *Castricum* and *Breskens*, under the command of Maarten Gerritszoon Vries, sailed past the north-eastern tip of the island that we now call Hokkaido (though at that time it had not yet acquired this name) and, emerging from the dense summer fog, saw the rocky outlines of the southernmost Habomai Islands. These islands in the Okhotsk Sea today mark the hotly contested frontier between Japan and Russia, but in the seventeenth century they lay at the furthermost limits of the vast region known to Europeans as 'Tartary'.

The origins of the term 'Tartary' are the subject of some debate, but it is commonly understood to be associated with the Chinese word 'Dada', used to describe pastoralist tribes to the north. This provided the origin for the term 'Tatar' (sometimes also spelled 'Tartar') applied to Turkic and Mongol peoples living on the eastern fringe of the Russian Empire. In the European imagination, that word in turn came to be associated with 'Tartarus', the Latin word for hell.[1] The narrative of Marco Polo's travels helped to popularise the image of Tartary in fourteenth-century Europe, and it appears (for example) in Geoffrey Chaucer's 'Squire's Tale', written towards the end of the century, which is set in a utopian 'land of

---

1   See Susanna Soojung Lim, *China and Japan in the Russian Imagination, 1685–1922: To the Ends of the Orient* (London and New York: Routledge, 2013), p. 22, doi.org/10.4324/9780203594506.

Tartarye'.[2] By the early seventeenth century, then, Tartary had become fixed in the European imagination as an exotic and hazily defined region stretching to the east and roughly spanning the area from the Caspian Sea and the fringes of Persia to Japan, Korea and the Pacific coast of Siberia.

Figure 3.1. Map of Tartary based on de Vries' voyage, 1682 (Original by Giacomo Cantelli da Vignola).

Source: Wikimedia commons, public domain.

---

2   Chaucer, 'Squire's Tale', *Canterbury Tales*, frag. 5, line 9.

Castricum and *Breskens* had reached the easternmost limits of 'Tartary' in their search for rich islands of gold and silver, rumoured to lie somewhere to the east of Japan.[3] The quest for treasure was unsuccessful, but the voyage brought back something else of great value: a detailed description of a community of people whose manners and customs were utterly unknown in Europe. This description, though unusual in its vivid and immediate quality, was just one of a multitude of travellers' tales that added to store of information underpinning the emergence of modern European images of world.

Western encounters with Tartary fed into evolving understandings of the world whose echoes continue to influence understandings of history to the present day.[4] If the pillaging of riches from around the world by European merchant adventurers was part of the process of 'primitive accumulation', which Marx saw as feeding the rise of European capitalism, the journals brought back from voyages like those of the *Castricum* and *Breskens* were, in a sense, part of a different kind of 'primitive accumulation': the amassing of a vast store of still raw and undigested knowledge of the world, which was to feed the intellectual revolutions of eighteenth- and nineteenth-century Europe. In this chapter, I shall explore some of the ways in which travellers' images of the (from the European perspective) remote regions of far eastern Tartary helped to shape crucial elements of modern thought: particularly ideas of civilisation, race and ethnicity.

After two weeks of wanderings through the Habomai and southern Kurile Islands, the *Castricum* and *Breskens* anchored off the north coast of the small island of Kunashir, and here Cornelius Coen, who documented the voyage, went ashore to be greeted by a group of six adults and three children dressed in fur robes. One man spread a straw mat on the sand, while the eldest of the group of islanders, taking Coen by the hand, led him to the mat and gestured to him to sit down. The Dutchman handed out tobacco, necklaces for the children, and small pieces of white linen for the women, who were 'so pleased that they could not exclaim enough', and rewarded him with slices of fresh halibut. After sharing some schnapps with the villagers, Coen 'took the eldest by the hand and went dancing with them up to the green plateau' where stood five or six houses of bark and thatch.[5]

---

3   PA Leupe, ed., *Reize van Maarten Gerritszoon Vries in 1643 naar het Norden en Oosten van Japan Volgens het Journaal Gehouden door C. J. Coen* (Amsterdam: Frederik Muller, 1858), pp. 11–31 and 45.

4   Guillaume-Thomas Reynal, *A Philosophical and Political History of the Settlements and Trade of the Europeans in the East and West Indies*, trans. J Justamond, vol. 2 (London: T. Cadell, 1777), pp. 222–23. Original published in 1770.

5   Leupe, *Reize van Maarten Gerritszoon Vries*, pp. 111–12.

The following day Coen and his companions gave the villagers some rice, which they accepted 'with great courtesy', and they in turn helped the Dutchmen to load their boats with fish in preparation for the next stage of the voyage. By now, however, the receding tide had stranded the Dutchmen's boats on the sand. 'I became aware', wrote Coen, 'that the inhabitants were very concerned for us, and they gave us all the help they could, lending us a hatchet to cut firewood and giving us smoked halibut to eat. They suggested that we should come to their huts, but we stayed on the beach warming ourselves by a great fire and waiting for the high tide'.[6]

At last the tide turned, and the explorers sailed westward towards the island of Sakhalin, arriving at Aniwa Bay on the island's southern coast on 16 July, another day of mist and rain. Here again boats came out to greet them, and the villagers helped Coen and his two assistants to go ashore. The unexpected arrival of the foreigners aroused excited curiosity, and a large crowd was on the beach to meet them. Most of the villagers wore unbleached hempen garments decorated with coloured cotton, but one old, half-blind man was resplendent in a robe of blue and gold adorned with Chinese or Japanese characters. After a feast of smoked fish served in lacquer dishes, the Dutchmen and a group of villagers settled down to the serious business of trade, exchanging furs for linen and tobacco, and haggling over relative values with an enthusiasm befitting the representatives of two mercantile peoples. Watched by the wondering eyes of a small child, the guests struggled to eat dishes of salmon and vegetables with the 'two small sticks' which served as utensils. Their hosts, seeing the Dutchmen's clumsy handling of chopstick, pointed at Coen and laughingly said 'Spanola' – 'which made me think that Spaniards must have been here before'.[7]

Discovering Tartary

Coen's introduction to the people of Okhotsk was a meeting of merchants: an encounter with people who traded widely, both southwards with Japan and westwards with China, who appeared to know about the existence of the Spaniards (although there is no evidence to suggest that any Spaniards had travelled further north than Hokkaido), and who spoke at least a smattering of several languages. As Philips de Bakker later described them:

---

6   Leupe, *Reize van Maarten Gerritszoon Vries*, pp. 112–14.
7   Leupe, *Reize van Maarten Gerritszoon Vries*, pp. 130–31.

with their shaggy beards and hair they appear very cruel, but they know how to behave towards foreigners with such honesty and simplicity that one can only judge them to be civil and refined people [*burgerlijk and beschaafde mensen*].[8]

Until the seventeenth century, European understandings of the human past and present were still confined to a narrow realm of space and time. Even Sir Walter Raleigh, the founder of Virginia and plunderer of the Orinoco, taking up his pen in the Tower of London to compose his monumental *History of the World*, perceived a world that extended no further west than Britain and no further east than Babylon, and whose temporal dividing lines were those of biblical revelation.[9] The same geographical and chronological horizons confined works such as Bossuet's *Histoire Universelle*, written in 1680 as an edifying text for the French Dauphin.[10] But by the end of the seventeenth century, as information about North and South America, Africa and East Asia accumulated, the boundaries of this narrow world were already crumbling. Voltaire's *General History*, written in the 1730s, began by pondering 'if there is nothing worthy of my attention in the other part of our hemisphere':

> struck with the lustre of [the Roman] empire, and with its growth and fall, we have in most of our universal histories treated of other men as if they had no existence. Judea, Greece and Rome have possessed all our attention; and when the celebrated Bossuet happens to mention the Mahometans, he speaks of them only as a deluge of barbarians. Yet many of these nations possessed useful arts, which we have learnt from them; their countries furnished us with commodities and things of value, which nature has refused us ...[11]

The broadening vision disturbed the intellectual certainties of European Christendom, while also bringing with it an immense hunger for knowledge of the rest of the world. Accounts of distant places, including the Okhotsk region, were translated, edited, reprinted and distributed throughout much of western Europe. Although Coen's log-book lay

---

8   Nicolaes Witsen, *Noord en Oost Tartarye, ofte Bondig Ontwrp van eenige dier Landen en Volken welke Voormaels Bekent zijn Geweest* (Amsterdam: François Halma, 1705), p. 134.

9   Walter Raleigh, *The History of the World in Five Books* (London: Robert White and Co., 1666).

10   Jacques-Bénigne Bossuet, *Discours Sur L'Histoire Universelle*, ed. Jacques Truchet (Paris: Garnier-Flammarion, 1966). Original published in 1681.

11   Voltaire (François-Marie Arouet), *The General History and State of Europe from the Time of Charlemain to Charles V with a Preliminary View of the Oriental Empire*, vol. 1 (London: J. Nourse, 1765), pp. 3–4. Original published in 1758.

neglected in the archives until the mid-nineteenth century, accounts of the voyage of the *Castricum* and *Breskens* were included by Nicolaes Witsen in his massive compilation of descriptions of the 'North and East Tartary', a book that also contains a wealth of travellers' tales about the eastern Siberian seaboard, Kamchatka, the Kurile Islands, Korea and Tibet, as well as what may be the first account of a Japanese visit to the American continent.[12]

Figure 3.2. Illustration from Witsen, showing 'Yakut, Kalmyk, Kyrgizian Ostiak and Daurian Tungus' peoples.

Source: Nicolaes Witsen, *Noord en Oost Tartarye, ofte Bondig Ontwrp van eenige dier Landen en Volken welke Voormaels Bekent zijn Geweest* (Amsterdam: François Halma, 1705).

Not all of these accounts were as humane or as endearing as Coen's. In the very week when Coen and his fellow voyagers were being welcomed by the villagers of Kunashir, a band of Cossacks led by Vasili Poyarkov had left Siberian outpost of Yakutsk on a journey in search of the eastern

---

12 The Kurile Islands are also known in Japanese as the Chishima Archipelago (千島諸島). I use the term 'Kurile' here because it is the best known name for the islands internationally. Witsen's book contains two versions of a story told by a Dutch merchant in Japan, Hendrik Obé, who claimed to have met a Japanese sailor who had been blown off course on a voyage north-east from Japan, arriving at 'a great land which seemed to be the coast of a continent', and that stretched north-westward 'in the direction of Yesso [Hokkaido]'. After spending the winter there, the sailor had managed to make his way back to Japan, and, when shown Dutch maps, estimated the place that he had been to lay on the west coast of America. Witsen, *Noord en Oost Tartarye*, pp. 138 and 149.

limits of the Asian continent.[13] They went as warriors, not as merchants, with the aim of subjecting the inhabitants to Russian rule and exacting tribute (*yasak*). Poyarkov's band was soon followed by others, including the freebooter Yerofei Khabarov, who reached the lower Amur (just across the narrow sea straits from Sakhalin) in 1651. The increasing Russian presence in the east led to conflicts, not just with the small societies along the Amur, but also with the Chinese empire, which regarded those societies as its tributaries. In 1689, after Chinese forces destroyed the main Russian outpost on the Amur, the Russians were reluctantly persuaded to sign the Treaty of Nerchinsk, creating a rather hazily defined frontier between China and Russia in the mountains to the north of the river.[14] In the decades that followed, the focus of Russian expansion shifted northward, towards the peninsula of Kamchatka, which was reached by the Cossack adventurer Vladimir Atlasov in 1698.

All of these expeditions, too, generated widely read accounts of the landscape, natural riches and human societies of the Asian north-east. The Cossack incursions into the Amur region were described by the Swedish aristocrat Philipp-Johann von Strahlenberg (1676–1747) – who had spent several years in Russia as a prisoner of war and whose writings (as we saw in Chapter 2) helped to define the border between Asia and Europe – and by the German scholar Gerhard Friedrich Muller (1705–83), and both accounts were translated into English and French within a couple of decades of their publication.[15]

The story of Atlasov's invasion of Kamchatka was included in Witsen's anthology, while another version, together with a description of the region's geography and population, was written and published in 1755 by the Russian botanist Stepan Krasheninnikov, who had himself taken part in a second expedition to Kamchatka in the 1740s. Krasheninnikov's

---

13 Gerard Muller, *Voyages et Decouvertes faites par les Russes le Long des Côtes de la Mer Glaciale et sur l'Ocean Oriental*, trans. CGF Dumas, vol. 2 (Amsterdam: Marc-Michel Rey, 1766), pp. 6–7.

14 FA Golder, *Russian Expansion on the Pacific 1641–1850* (Cleveland: Arthur H. Clark and Co., 1914), p. 64.

15 See Golder, *Russian Expansion on the Pacific*; also Gerard Muller, *Voyages from Asia to America*, trans. Thomas Jefferys (London: T. Jefferys, 1761); PJ von Strahlenberg, *Das Nord- und Östliche Theil von Europa und Asien in so Weit solches das Gantze Russische Reich mit Siberien und der Grossen Tatarey in sich Begreiffet* (Stockholm: PJ von Strahlenberg, 1730); PJ von Strahlenberg, *Description Historique de L'Empire Russien* (Amsterdam: Desaint et Saillant, 1742); Philip John von Strahlenberg, *An Historico-Geographical Description of the North and Eastern Parts of Europe and Asia, but More Particularly of Russia, Siberia and Great Tartary* (London: W. Innys and R. Manby, 1738).

account in turn was published as an English translation in 1764.[16] Russia's eastward expansion led to gradual shifts and elaborations in the vision of Tartary. Von Strahlenberg treated Russian-controlled Siberia as separate from 'Greater Tartary', and divided the latter into six separate realms, stretching from 'Lesser Tartary' in the Caucasus to 'Eastern or Chinese Tartary', which embraced Tibet and regions to the north stretching as far as what is now Inner Mongolia.[17]

Wherever they went, explorers created 'the natives' in their own image. Poyarkov's exploration of the Amur began with an unprovoked attack on the prosperous agrarian community of Daurs (Daguur), an independent Mongol-speaking group who inhabited the area around the mouth of the Zeya River, and by the time they reached the eastern seaboard his ill-equipped followers had reportedly been reduced to cannibalism, butchering both local inhabitants and their weaker comrades for food.[18] The Nivkh people whom the Cossacks found living by the mouth of the Amur (and who also lived on the island of Sakhalin) are described as being:

> bellicose. They sow no corn and live on wild animals. They know how to tame bears, and harness them, instead of horses, to pull their sleighs and carts and to ride on.[19]

(The last improbable piece of information clearly refers to the practice, shared by Nivkh, Ainu and other Okhotsk societies, of raising bears for sacrifice in the most important of their religious celebrations.)

Nivkh belligerence was not surprising. Poyarkov's techniques for extracting tribute – which succeeded in obtaining 480 furs and 16 whole pelisses of sable from the Amur Nivkhs[20] – relied heavily on murder and kidnap, and created a pattern of violence that was repeated by subsequent expeditions. In 1652, for example, a party of Cossacks sent to relieve Khabarov's expedition found their route downriver blocked by a large Nivkh community, so that they could neither advance nor retreat:

---

16   Stepan Petrovich Krasheninnikov, 'A Translation of Stepan Petrovich Krasheninnikov's Opisanie Zemli Kamchatki by EAP Crowhart Vaughan' (PhD diss., Portland State University, 1970), Portland State University Dissertations and Theses, paper 353, doi.org/10.15760/etd.353.

17   Von Strahlenberg, *An Historico-Geographical Description*, p. 13.

18   Golder, *Russian Expansion on the Pacific*, p. 36.

19   Witsen, *Noord en Oost Tartarye*, p. 106.

20   Witsen, *Noord en Oost Tartarye*, p. 15.

> In this state [says their chronicler] they remained at anchor for
> two and a half weeks, always in the middle of the river. At last
> hunger, despair and greed for a good supply of fish which they saw
> from their boat, hanging to dry in the village, gave them a more
> than heroic courage. They advanced to the village, massacred
> some thirty Gilliaeques [Nivkhs], took their fish, and continued
> to descend the Amur, whose mouth they reached three days later
> on 26th June.[21]

In the far north and Kamchatka, where the encounter between the
Russians and the local Koryak, Itelmen and Kurile Ainu inhabitants
was particularly violent, explorers' accounts were similarly unflattering.
Krasheninnikov, who visited the region after it had been ravaged by
a renegade Cossack band under the leadership of Danilo Anziforov and
Ivan Kozirevski, carefully distinguished the various cultural and linguistic
groups of the region, and reached the conclusion that the Kamchadals
or Kamchadales (Itelmen), who inhabited the southern part of the
Kamchatka Peninsula, were related neither to Japanese nor to Tatars.[22]
His accounts of the indigenous people, though, repeatedly echo the
dehumanising attitudes of conquerors towards the conquered. He wrote
that the 'Kamchadales' were uncivilised in their habits, 'their instincts are
animal instincts; and they have no conception of the spiritual aspects of
the soul',[23] and described the Koryaks as 'hot-headed, stubborn, vindictive
and cruel'.[24] He did, however, go on to observe that 'they are convinced
that they have the best way of life in the world; they consider everything
foreigners tell them as deceits, lies and untruths'.[25] Only the Ainu-speaking
inhabitants of the southern tip of Kamchatka and the Kurile Islands won
some praise. They were, said Krasheninnikov, 'gentle, loyal, upright and
honest', and as 'infinitely more civilized and polite than their neighbours',
though elsewhere he also remarked that:

> the customs of the Kuriles [i.e. Kurile Ainu] resemble those of the
> Kamchadales so much I would not here give a separate description
> of the former, if there were not some difference between these
> two peoples.[26]

---

21 Witsen, *Noord en Oost Tartarye*, pp. 50–51.
22 Krasheninnikov, 'Translation', pp. 347–48.
23 Krasheninnikov, 'Translation', p. 347.
24 Krasheninnikov, 'Translation', p. 483.
25 Krasheninnikov, 'Translation', p. 483.
26 Krasheninnikov, 'Translation', pp. 502 and 504.

Figure 3.3. Engraving of a 'Kamchadale' woman from Krasheninnikov's *Opisanie Zemli Kamchatki.*

Source: SP Krashininnikov, *Opisanie Zemli Kamchatki*, vol. 1 (St Petersburg: Imperatorskaya Akademiya Nauk, 1755), plate 3.

Whether they were regarded as bellicose and slovenly or civil and educated, the very existence of these unfamiliar societies disturbed the established categories of European thought. Within the vast, mysterious and vaguely defined realm of 'Tartary', the outlines of many different peoples – Uzbeks, Yakuts, Mongols, Koryaks – began to take shape. Von Strahlenberg wrote:

> It is evident what false conceptions we have hitherto had, in Europe, of this north-eastern part of the world, by supposing it to be entirely inhabited by Tartars, and by no other nation. Just as in the time of the Assyrian monarchy, and the Children of Israel, it was believed that all the nations which lie beyond Assyria, Greece and Persia were called Gog, Goy and Magoy, or Gojim and Magojim: These denominations were not in themselves wrong; but they were not the proper names of those nations, whereby they called themselves, but only appellatives … which were given to all remote nations, whose particular names were unknown.[27]

---

27 Von Strahlenberg, *An Historico-Geographical Description*, p. 55 (spelling and punctuation modernised).

Dawning awareness of the complexity of human populations created a new sense of Europe, not as a world unto itself, but as a small part in a wider order of things. As von Strahlenberg came to realise, the national divisions and rivalries that dominated the politics of seventeenth-century Europe faded into insignificance from the perspective of some Asian observers who 'call us Europeans, in general, Frangs or Franks, without distinction'.[28]

Organising Difference: Herder's Visions of Spatial Diversity

This realisation had profound implications for the European understanding both of past and present. The medieval vision of 'world history' had been shaped by manageable geographical bounds. The flow of human destiny (as we have seen) moved from Israel, Egypt and Babylon through Greece and Rome to the Holy Roman Empire and its European neighbours; and, since the narrative of history was made up of the deeds of kings and princes, the rise and fall of royal houses provided a natural phrasing to the rhythms of historical time. But widening European knowledge of global geography coincided with the stirrings of democratic sentiments in which 'the people' themselves claimed a place as the subjects of history.

> While we read history, it seems as if the earth was only made for a few sovereigns, and for those who have flattered their passions. Historians, like kings, sacrifice the human race to a single man. Have there been none but princes on the earth? And must almost all the inventors of arts be unknown, while we have chronological accounts of such numbers of men, who have done a great deal of mischief, or at least have been of very little service to society?[29]

If the people were as important as the princes, then even obscure and distant societies without kings might become participants in the narrative of world history. The spatial and temporal frontiers that had made sense of the past melted away into air, and new lines through time and space were needed to give structure and meaning to the history of the world. From this intellectual ferment emerged the geographical and chronological taxonomies that formed the basis of modern historical understanding,

---

28 Von Strahlenberg, *An Historico-Geographical Description*, pp. 55, 192–93.
29 Voltaire, *General History*, p. 2.

not only in Europe itself but, ultimately, throughout the world. The shifts, the tensions and the controversies in Enlightenment historical thought are themselves the subject of a vast amount of historical research, and it would be impossible to do justice to their richness and complexity here. By looking a little more closely at the way in which travellers' tales of Tartary were incorporated into European knowledge, though, we can further illuminate the way in which the new borderlines through time and space discussed in the previous chapter were developed and became fixed in the modern imagination.

The redefining of spatial boundaries found its clearest and most poetic expression in the work of Johann Gottfried von Herder (1744–1803). Herder, whose voracious reading of travellers' tales encompassed numerous accounts of 'Tartary', was particularly intrigued by the almost endless diversity of human customs and beliefs described by the writings of European explorers. In his *Reflections on the Philosophy of the History of Mankind* (1784–91), Herder argued that all shared a common human nature, but that each society, moulded by its natural environment and its inherited traditions, manifested that human nature in a particular way. Climate and geography exerted a particularly powerful influence. Extreme temperatures, he believed, induced physical insensitivity, while temperate climates promoted balanced and harmonious temperaments. Even the inhabitants of Kamchatka, whose way of life (as revealed by the writings of Krasheninnikov) contradicted this thesis, were incorporated into his theorising as an exception which proved the rule:

> I was astonished, for instance, to observe in the mythology of the Kamtschadales, dwelling so far to the north, a lasciviousness, that might have been more naturally expected from a southern nation: but their climate and genetic character afford us some explanation of this anomaly. Their cold land is not without burning mountains and hot springs: benumbing cold and melting heat there contend against each other; and their dissolute manners, as well as their gross mythological tales, are natural offspring of the two.[30]

The influence of natural environment was deepened, Herder argued, by becoming embedded in the traditions and customs passed down through the generations. So each society adapted to its particular place in what we would now call the ecosystem, and the transportation of people to

---

30 JG von Herder, *Reflections on the Philosophy of the History of Mankind*, ed. FE Manuel (Chicago and London: University of Chicago Press, 1968), p. 46.

radically new environments, or sudden human efforts to transform the natural landscape, were doomed to disaster. Herder's reflections on the past, indeed, have a curious resonance in our own time of environmental concerns:

> Nature is everywhere a living whole, and will be gently followed and improved, not mastered by force … All newcomers from a foreign land, who have submitted to naturalise themselves with the inhabitants, have not only enjoyed their love and friendship, but have ultimately found, that their mode of life was not altogether unsuitable to the climate: but how few such there are! How seldom does a European hear from the native of any country the praise, 'he is a rational man like us!' And does not nature revenge every insult offered her?[31]

From these speculations Herder sketched a picture of a world divided between a multitude of clearly defined 'peoples' or 'nations' (*Völker*), each with its own distinctive traditions, beliefs and ways of life. The sense of national identity, such a potent force in late eighteenth-century European thought, was not (to Herder) a product of local political or social forces, but an innate part of the human heritage, engraved on every soul by the relationship between community and natural environment. Every Volk had its own social integrity and its own historical trajectory:

> thus nations modify themselves, according to time, place and their internal character: each bears in itself the standard of its perfection, totally independent of comparison with that of all others.[32]

Here, for an instant, one can almost glimpse an image of a global history without hierarchies of development; where each Volk, in working out its own destiny, is equal to every other. But Herder was also the child of an age of European expansion, which made such radical cultural relativism almost impossible. So concepts of scientific and moral superiority creep back into his comparisons between historical trajectories, and certain 'standards of perfection' – particularly those of the 'temperate middle region' of the world – turn out to be more perfect than others.[33] And, despite the accumulating knowledge that had challenged the image of a vast, undifferentiated 'Tartary', Herder's vision of the world suggests how tenacious and enduring that vision was, for his interpretations of

---

31 Von Herder, *Reflections on the Philosophy*, p. 33.
32 Von Herder, *Reflections on the Philosophy*, p. 98.
33 Von Herder, *Reflections on the Philosophy*, p. 85.

European civilisation repeatedly fall back on contrasts with Tartary perceived as a place of 'erratic hordes' and 'wandering people' whose barbarism poses an eternal threat to European stability and enlightenment:

> Eastwards, on the right hand, observe that vast elevated region, Asiatic Tartary; and in reading of the troubles that threw Europe into confusion in the middle ages, exclaim with Tristram Shandy, 'this was the source of all our misfortunes'.[34]

Herder represents a broadly spatial concept of difference, in which the bewildering diversity of humanity becomes a matter of place on the map, of climate and geography. The opposite extreme, in which difference was understood as a product of time, is perhaps best represented by Herder's French contemporary, Marie-Jean Antoine de Caritat, Marquis de Condorcet (1743–94): a passionate believer in the perfectibility of humanity, who died, probably by his own hand, after being arrested by the forces of a revolution he had hailed as the dawn of the coming utopia.

Condorcet's *Sketch for a Historical Picture of the Progress of the Human Mind*, composed in the weeks before his death, follows a course not unlike that of many medieval histories, from Greece to Rome to Western Europe. Now, however, the story to be told is not a story of the revelation of divine providence, but of the gradual unfolding of human reason. The path is not always smooth: at times knowledge is lost and the wise sink back into superstition. But eventually, with the growing size and complexity of human societies, the increasing division of labour, and the development of ever more sophisticated methods of classifying and storing knowledge, a door is opened to a world in which everything can be understood by all:

> Since, as the number of known facts increases, the human mind learns how to classify them and subsume them under more general facts, and, at the same time, the instruments and methods employed in their observation and their exact measurement acquire a new precision ... so truths that were discovered only by great effort, that could at first only be understood by men capable of profound thought, are soon developed and proven by methods that are not beyond the reach of common intelligence.[35]

---

34 Johann Gottfried von Herder, *Outlines of the Philosophy of a History of Man*, trans. T Churchill (New York: Bergmann Publishers, 1800), p. 487.
35 Antoine-Nicolas de Condorcet, *Sketch for a Historical Picture of the Progress of the Human Mind*, trans. J Barraclough (London: Weidenfeld and Nicolson, 1955), p. 185. Original published in 1795.

While British contemporaries like Adam Smith saw human economies as evolving through hunting, pastoral, agricultural and commercial stages of development, Condorcet proposed a more elaborate 10-stage hierarchy from a tribal existence focused on the satisfaction of 'simple needs' to a modern civilisation inspired by 'the doctrine of the indefinite perfectibility of the human race'.[36] Each of these stages marked the emergence of a more complex division of labour, allowing knowledge itself to be divided up between a growing number of specialist groups, and thus to expand into a perfect system of human omniscience.

In this scheme of things, the multiplicity of social forms beyond the fringes of Europe represent various stages of the development of the human race. 'All peoples whose history is recorded fall somewhere between our present degree of civilization and that which we still see amongst primitive tribes.'[37] Like Rousseau and Montesquieu before him, Condorcet derived his image of the earliest ages, the dark times before the light of written records, from 'the tales that our travellers bring back to us about the state of the human race among the less civilized peoples'.[38] But, living in an age of revolution, Condorcet (far more than his predecessors) saw the history of the world in terms of revolutionary changes that carved the past into stages, as sharply bounded in temporal terms as Herder's Volk were in spatial terms.

Far from possessing their own internal standards of perfection, therefore, remote societies represented for Condorcet distinct steps along a single evolutionary path. First came the stage where humans lived in tribes and subsisted by hunting and gathering, occasionally supplementing wild food with a few edible plants grown around their huts.[39] Next, animals were domesticated, tribes grew in size and differences of wealth appeared. Up to this point, societies everywhere shared a primeval cultural uniformity, but in the third stage, with the coming of fully fledged agriculture, the story 'loses its uniformity'.[40] The division of labour becomes more complex; tribes form themselves into kingdoms; alphabets are created and wise men begin to study the heavens and lay the foundations of mathematics and chemistry. The way is now open for the beginning of recorded history and the rise of Greece in stage four.

---

36 De Condorcet, *Sketch for a Historical Picture*, pp. 14 and 142.
37 De Condorcet, *Sketch for a Historical Picture*, p. 8.
38 De Condorcet, *Sketch for a Historical Picture*, p. 8.
39 De Condorcet, *Sketch for a Historical Picture*, pp. 14–18.
40 De Condorcet, *Sketch for a Historical Picture*, p. 25.

For those societies that, through indolence, conservatism or timidity, had been stranded in the earliest phases of development, Condorcet foresaw only two possible futures. Most – those 'large tribes … who wait only to find brothers amongst the European nations to become their friends and pupils' – would be caught up in the great wave of freedom and enlightenment spreading outward from Europe. The rest, 'driven back by civilized nations, … will finally disappear perceptibly before them or merge into them'.[41] The worldwide triumph of reason was irresistible. Only one event could have the power to block its course: a new invasion of Asia by the Tartars, and this, says Condorcet firmly and without elaboration, 'is now impossible'.[42]

Condorcet's model of human progress, in other words, had two key features. One was that it assumed the existence of a *single* vision of the truth: a vision to which human understanding gradually but unfailingly draws closer. Second, and most importantly, Condorcet's vision identified the accumulation of knowledge with the creation of ever larger and more centralised knowledge systems, held together by ever more comprehensive generalisations about the truth. In Herder and Condorcet we can see the emerging skeletal shape of an intellectual construct that sustained understanding of small, non-state societies almost until the present day. The kaleidoscopic diversity of social forms, described by the explorers of America, Africa and the eastern limits of 'Tartary', was arranged into comprehensible patterns within two hierarchies that were conceptually distinct but always in practice interrelated in complex ways. Spatially, each society could be seen as a unique Volk, carrying within itself a Platonic essence formed by environment and tradition. Temporally, each could be placed in a long sequence of human development – a sequence divided by unmistakable revolutionary markers that separated one stage of history from another.

In the nineteenth century, as philosophies of the past dispersed into the narrower disciplinary channels of history, archaeology and anthropology, these two dimensions of understanding were reworked and combined in many different ways. Some scholars placed greater emphasis on spatial and cultural difference, others on developmental stages, but most used some combination of both dimensions to explain the cultural diversity of the modern world.

41 De Condorcet, *Sketch for a Historical Picture*, p. 177.
42 De Condorcet, *Sketch for a Historical Picture*, p. 178.

The Rise of Racial Thinking

Herder's mosaic of autonomous Volk was given harsher dividing lines by the idea of biologically distinct races. In the early stages of European expansion, physical difference had commonly been understood in Biblical terms, a heritage of descent from separate branches of Noah's family after the flood. But the Linnaean classification of the natural world into scientifically defined species and subspecies suggested the possibility of extension to the human world. In 1749, just 14 years after the appearance of Linnaeus's great taxonomy of nature, the French scientist Georges Buffon published his *Histoire Naturelle, Général et Particulier*, an encyclopedic overview of the living world, which began with the formation of the earth and worked its way down the chain of being from humans to moulds and mushrooms. The section entitled 'Of the Varieties of the Human Species' begins with a description of 'a race of men of uncouth figure, and small stature' inhabiting Lapland and the northern coasts of Tartary: a group described as being:

> so different from all others, that it seems to constitute a distinct species; for if there be among them any distinction, it arises only from a greater or less degree of deformity.[43]

This was the first time that the word 'race' had been applied specifically to subdivisions of the human species. As Bronwen Douglas has emphasised, in Buffon's work 'race' was still a vague and malleable term, in which human variation was still seen as being shaped by climate and nutrition.[44] In its initial formulation, it referred loosely to '1. The colour; 2. The figure and stature; and 3. The dispositions of different peoples'.[45] Here travellers' tales of dwarves and monstrosities, and Renaissance ideas of the relationship between physical beauty and the state of the soul, jostle with the search for unifying scientific principles, and with speculations about the historical migration of peoples from Asia to the Americas. But by the early nineteenth century, 'race' was rapidly hardening into a fixed hereditary boundary, and French naturalist Georges Cuvier (1769–1832), English physician James Cowles Prichard (1786–1848) and Scottish anatomist

---

43   Georges Buffon, *A Natural History: General and Particular*, trans. W Smellie, vol. 1 (London: Thomas Kelly and Co., 1866), p. 252.

44   Bronwen Douglas, 'Climate to Crania: Science and Racialization of Human Difference', in *Foreign Bodies: Oceania and the Science of Race, 1750–1940*, ed. Bronwen Douglas and Chris Ballard (Canberra: ANU E Press, 2008), pp. 33–96, doi.org/10.22459/fb.11.2008.02.

45   Buffon, *Natural History*, p. 252.

Robert Knox (1791–1862) were earnestly debating whether all humans had evolved from a single common stock, or whether the various races were products of separate acts of divine creation.[46] So writers like Gustav Kossina (1858–1931) were able to redefine Herder's 'culture' groups as products, less of environment than of distinct and eternal genetic types, and to identify the shared features of European culture and language as a legacy of characteristics inherited from a common 'Aryan' ancestry.[47]

Condorcet's historical stages, meanwhile, were redefined from a materialist and archaeological perspective by the nineteenth-century Danish scholars Christian Jürgensen Thomsen (1788–1865) and JJA Worsaae (1821–85), who divided the past into Stone, Bronze and Iron Ages. From a social and anthropological viewpoint, the stages of development were also rewritten by the American scholar Lewis Morgan (1818–81), who perceived a past divided into a stage of 'Savagery' (subdivided into Lower, Middle, and Upper Savagery), a stage of 'Barbarism' (similarly subdivided) and a stage of 'Civilization'. Morgan, like Condorcet, read the past from the present:

> The remote ancestors of the Aryan nations presumptively passed through an experience similar to that of existing barbarous and savage tribes. Though the experience of these nations embodies all the information necessary to illustrate the periods of civilization, both ancient and modern, together with a part of that in the later period of barbarism, their anterior experience must be deduced, in the main, from the traceable connection between the elements of their existing institutions and inventions, and similar elements still preserved in those of savage and barbarous tribes.[48]

Morgan's stages, in turn, were borrowed by Karl Marx and (more systematically) by Friedrich Engels, who described their author as 'the first person with expert knowledge to attempt to introduce a definite order into the prehistory of man',[49] and who used the savagery–barbarism–civilisation sequence as the framework for his analysis of the evolution of the human family from random promiscuity to monogamous household.

46 Douglas, 'Climate to Crania', pp. 40–44; Nancy Stepan, *The Idea of Race in Science: Great Britain 1800–1960* (London: Macmillan, 1982), pp. 29–46, doi.org/10.1007/978-1-349-05452-7.
47 See BG Trigger, *A History of Archaeological Thought* (Cambridge: Cambridge University Press, 1989), pp. 163–67.
48 Lewis Morgan, *Ancient Society or Researches in the Lines of Human Progress from Savagery Through Barbarism to Civilization* (Calcutta: Bharati Library, 1896), pp. 7–8, doi.org/10.1522/030110918.
49 Friedrich Engels, *The Origin of the Family, Private Property and the State in the Light of the Researches of Lewis H. Morgan*, ed. EB Leacock (New York: International Publishers, 1975), p. 87. Original published in 1891.

Figure 3.4. Thomsen expounding the 'three age' system, illustration by P Marquardt, 1846.

Source: Wikimedia commons, public domain.

Theory influenced the angle of vision of the practical ethnographer, and ethnographic fieldwork fed back into the refinement of theory: Lev Shternberg, the pioneering ethnographer of Eastern Siberia and Sakhalin (whose work is discussed further in Chapter 6), was profoundly influenced by his reading of the first edition of Engels's *Origin of the Family* (which he encountered while he was in prison as punishment for his involvement with the Russian revolutionary group Narodnaya Vol'ya [The Will of the People].[50] Engels suggested that the earliest forms of primitive communal society had practised group marriage, in which individuals do not form sexual partnerships, but members of the group may have sexual relations with any adults of the opposite sex within the group. Later, when he started to research the social patterns of the Nivkh of Sakhalin, Shternberg used Engels's theory to explain the complex patterns of sexual relationship that he found in Nivkh communities (though this interpretation was later to be challenged by others). Then, in the 1890s, Engels discovered Shternberg's Sakhalin research, and used its conclusions as a vindication of his theory of group marriage in the revised version of his *Origin of the Family*, arguing that Shternberg's findings reaffirmed his own vision of 'the similarity, even the identity in their main characteristics, of the social institutions of primitive peoples at approximately the same stage of development'. For:

> most of what [Shternberg's] report says about the Mongoloids on the island of Sakhalin also holds for the Dravidian tribes of India, the South Sea Islanders at the time of their discovery, and the American Indians.[51]

Even in the mid-twentieth century, theorising on the global past was deeply marked by the influence of Herderian notions of Volk and of stage theories reminiscent of Condorcet's notions of progress. The immensely popular writings of the Australian-born archaeologist Vere Gordon Childe (1892–1957), for example, presented a picture of a world divided into 'culture groups', each possessing its own 'national character'. 'Culture groups' were separated by environment and tradition, not biology (Childe was a trenchant critic of scientific racism); yet every group could also be placed on a broad single stairway of progress whose steps were separated

---

50   YP Al'kor, 'L. Y. Shternberg kak Issledovatel' Narodov Dal'nevo Vostoka', in *Gilyaki, Orochi, Gol'dy, Negidal'tsy, Ainy*, ed. LY Shternberg (Tokyo: Nauka Reprint, 1991); see also Bruce Grant, *In the Soviet House of Culture: A Century of Perestroikas* (Princeton: Princeton University Press, 1995), pp. 55–57.

51   Engels, *The Origin of the Family*, p. 239; see also Grant, *In the Soviet House of Culture*, pp. 55–57.

by successive revolutions. Childe's historical stages are fewer and simpler than those set out in the *Sketch for a Historical Picture of the Progress of the Human Mind*, but they closely follow the schema suggested by Condorcet's Stages One to Four. First came a hunter-gatherer phase, succeeded by a Neolithic or agricultural revolution. The resulting agricultural society was then transformed by an urban revolution, which gave rise to the development of specialist craft production, complex social hierarchies, large-scale monumental architecture and permanent systems of recorded information.[52] Each revolution was, of course, implicitly analogous to the Industrial Revolution (a historical landmark first conceived by the elder Arnold Toynbee[53] in the late nineteenth century).

In these stages, once again, the image of small societies in remote regions like the Okhotsk area was invoked to represent the remote human past. The patterns of bones and skulls from bears found in some of the earliest European cave dwellings, for example, were equated with:

> the rituals still performed by hunting tribes in Siberia to avert the wrath of the bear spirit and ensure the multiplication of bears to hunt. Perhaps, then, we have here proof of hunting magic, if not worship, before the last ice age. In any case even the rude Neanderthaler had an ideology.[54]

Childe's map of the past was particularly schematically satisfying because it could be superimposed upon Lewis Morgan's chart of human evolution. The agricultural revolution marked the threshold between 'savagery' and 'barbarism', and the urban revolution the threshold between 'barbarism' and 'civilisation'.[55] Childe was more sensitive to spatial difference than Morgan: no one civilisation was quite like another, and some had disappeared leaving little trace of their achievements. Each, however, contributed to a current that moved irresistibly onward:

> progress is real if discontinuous. The upward curve resolves itself into a series of troughs and crests. But ... no trough ever declines to the low level of the preceding one, and each crest out-tops its last precursor.[56]

---

52   Vere Gordon Childe, *New Light on the Most Ancient East* (London: Routledge and Kegan Paul, 1934).
53   Arnold Toynbee (1852–83) was the uncle of Arnold Joseph Toynbee (1889–1975), the author of *A Study of History*.
54   Vere Gordon Childe, *What Happened in History*, rev. ed. (London: Penguin Books, 1954), p. 35.
55   See particularly Childe, *What Happened in History*.
56   Childe, *What Happened in History*, p. 252.

For Childe, like Condorcet, possessed a profound faith in human progress, even though, like Condorcet, he died by his own his own hand. His utopia was not the liberal utopia of the French revolution, but the socialist millennium promised by the Russian Revolution: a vision that was shattered as the clouds of Cold War gathered in the 1950s.[57]

Race and Progress in Modern Thought

Scientific racism – which saw humans as divided into subgroups, with culture and character irrevocably tied to physical appearance – was of course comprehensively criticised and discredited by scholars in the early to mid-twentieth century;[58] but the popular imagery generated by nineteenth-century racial theorising proved much more difficult to exorcise from the social landscape, and persists into the twenty-first century, where it remains an enduring source of human conflict. Meanwhile, the vision of unilinear human progress through a series of defined stages from 'primitive society' to 'civilisation' came to permeate our language so deeply that its vocabulary continues to lay traps for our thought despite the extensive academic criticism to which this vision has been exposed. The words 'savagery' and 'barbarism' may have been banished from the academic vocabulary, but the term 'civilisation' with all its positive connotations – and still commonly attached to large state-structured societies and the monuments they build – survives, and continues to be actively promoted in some quarters. In its shadows still lurk the 'others': those who failed to achieve linear history's standards of civilisation.

'North and East Tartary' (to use Witsen's phrase) played an important part in the shaping of these yet-to-be-exorcised visions of the world. As the furthermost limit of the Eurasian landmass (from the Western European point of view), it provided a rich and malleable source of images of 'others' through which the European place in global culture and world history could be defined and confirmed. Can we use the history of an area like the Okhotsk Sea region, which was turned into a 'frontier zone' by the expansion of nation-states (Russia and Japan in particular), to develop

---

57   See Sally Green, *Prehistorian: A Biography of V. Gordon Childe* (Bradford-on-Avon: Moonraker Press, 1981).

58   See, for example, Ashley Montagu, *Man's Most Dangerous Myth: The Fallacy of Race* (New York: Columbia University Press, 1942); Elazar Barkan, *The Retreat of Scientific Racism: Changing Concepts of Race in Britain and the United States Between the Wars* (Cambridge: Cambridge University Press, 1992).

other vocabularies and foster other ways of imagining the past? The area around the Okhotsk Sea has tended to escape the historical gaze precisely because it is, from the viewpoint of nation-state and civilisation history, liminal – a place on the fringes of nations and empires, occupied by a multitude of small societies (Ainu, Nivkh, Uilta, Itelmen and others) that never formed nation-states and had few written records of their past. It is seen as a remote frontier zone on the boundary between Russia and Japan, and thus (in area studies terms) on the boundary between Russian or Eastern European studies and (East) Asian studies. If we place this region not at the fringes of vision but at the centre, how might that change the way we see history as a whole?

Some indirect answers to that question can perhaps be found by revisiting John Smail's well-known 1961 essay on 'the Problem of an Autonomous History of Southeast Asia'.[59] Smail set out to consider the vexed question of whether it is possible for a 'Western' historian to write history from an 'Asian' perspective. In doing this, Smail made very clear that the very categories of 'Western' and 'Asian' perspective are deeply fraught by historical and cultural complexities, and that the notion of 'perspective' itself also needs to be unpacked. Writing history from the perspective of a particular society might, Smail observed, mean several things. It could mean that the historian tries to adopt the worldview of the people whose history is being written. The people of the Okhotsk region, of course, had a multitude of indigenous histories. The stories passed on around smoky fires in the long northern winters told of origins and becomings, of human societies in relation to the flow of time. There were also more recent retold memories, not yet rounded into the mellow forms of myth: 'before the Russians came there were plenty of bears, sables and reindeer, but since they arrived and burnt the woods the rich [have] become poor'.[60] Even the contemporary descendants of those storytellers, though, are probably too far removed to be able to immerse their imaginations fully in the circle around the hearth of an eighteenth-century *aundau* or *torakh takh* (Uilta or Nivkh winter house). There is certainly no way that a foreign historian, schooled in the more sharply bounded discipline of modern historiography, could enter into the world of such imagined pasts.

59   John RW Smail, 'On the Possibility of an Autonomous History of Modern Southeast Asia', *Journal of Southeast Asian History* 2, no. 2 (1961): pp. 72–102.
60   Charles Hawes, *In the Uttermost East* (London and New York: Harper and Brothers, 1903), p. 275.

There are, though, two other possible meanings of historical perspective. As Smail put it, '"perspective" might be used either in the sense of angle of vision (standpoint, looking over someone's shoulder) or in the sense of evaluation of relative importance'.[61] There is nothing to stop historians from looking over any shoulder they choose. In doing this, we have to recognise that all history writing is a matter of imagination as well as fact, and that imagination has profound limitations, particularly when twenty-first-century academics attempt to think their way back into a world vastly different from anything that they have experienced. But this act of imagination, used with caution and a consciousness of its limitations, may, I think, open up angles of vision that can give us new insights into historical events far beyond the limits of the locality from whose perspective we try to imagine the world. In the process, it can open up fresh perceptions of 'perspective' in its second sense: 'evaluation of relative importance'. In other words, the attempt to imagine the past from unexpected standpoints can provide a way of reassessing our senses of importance, and of recognising that the neglected histories of very small non-state communities have crucial importance to the way that we understand the human past as a whole. In the next two chapters, I shall attempt to use such a shift in perspective as a means of challenging some common assumptions about the relative historical importance of the societies of the Okhotsk region, and of shedding some new light, not only on the histories of the region's small indigenous societies, but also of the neighbouring and more distant large states which sought to subject and subsume them.

---

61 Smail, 'On the Possibility of an Autonomous History', p. 82.

4

UNTHINKING CIVILISATION: AN IMBRICATED HISTORY OF THE OKHOTSK REGION

Spring comes late to the Okhotsk Sea. In March, and into April in many places, ice grinds in wide sheets across the surface of the waters. Along the sea's western shores, and on the island of Sakhalin which extends parallel with these shores, winds still whip gusts of snow through the larch forests, where the first green is barely starting to appear on the tips of branches. In May, the temperature may still fall below freezing in Sakhalin and on the northern Kurile Islands to the east. But by June the short warm summer is beginning to spread from the southern shores of the sea as far north as the Kamchatka Peninsula. As the subsoil thaws to marsh, plants grow with startling speed – giant golden Amur lilies, umbrella plants whose stems will soon be as tall as a human being. Wild roses cover the sand dunes.

With the unfurling of plants comes a profusion of other life. Migrating birds fly back to the region across the Soya and Kunashir Straits. Bears, mink and squirrels emerge from hibernation, and mosquitoes and other insects that haunt the summer forests rise in clouds from the mossy earth. Until the early twentieth century, in April to May and again in June, two species of salmon used to swarm back in millions to their spawning grounds, and the rivers of the region would fill so full of fish that it was possible to scoop them out by hand. In September the forests turn golden, and cranberries appear in abundance between the trees. But already the snow is beginning to creep down from the higher slopes of the mountains, and by November it will cover the region again as the days grow short and the night-time temperatures fall below minus 30 degrees Celsius.

This environment, with its bitter cold and extreme seasonal variations, sustains only a sparse population of people able to adjust to its rigours. But, just as it contains great natural diversity, so too it has contained great human diversity. It has been, and still is, home to many small societies and language groups. The names by which these groups defined themselves, and the ways in which they drew their own boundaries, have changed over time, but today we know them as the Ainu, who inhabit its southern shores, and at times in the past extended their range as far as the southern tip of Kamchatka and the lower reaches of the Amur River; the Itelmen of the Kamchatka Peninsula, and the Chukchee of the northern Okhotsk; the Nivkh, whose territory extends from the region around the mouth of the Amur across the north of the island of Sakhalin; the Uilta who herded reindeer in the forests of central and northern Sakhalin; the Evenk and Saha herders who moved into the region from the west in the nineteenth and early twentieth centuries; and many others. Among them, in the past three centuries, have lived migrants and colonisers from larger societies: the Manchu officials and Cossack adventurers who collected furs from the local communities in the seventeenth, eighteenth and early nineteenth centuries; Chinese and Korean farmers and hunters who moved into the Lower Amur region in growing numbers in the late nineteenth and early twentieth centuries; Japanese colonial settlers, hundreds of thousands of whom arrived in Hokkaido from the Meiji period onwards (and who also moved into southern Sakhalin and the southern Kurile Islands, only to be evicted again after Japan's defeat in war in 1945); the convicts and colonists who moved east from Russia and later from all parts of the Soviet Union; and the Korean workers brought (often forcibly) to Sakhalin by the Japanese colonial authorities during the 1930s and early 1940s.

Conventional history writing, which subdivides the region into national entities labelled 'Russia' and 'Japan', has often tended to obscure this diversity. Yet the human diversity of the region has been maintained, in constantly changing configurations, throughout modern history, and still survives in the twenty-first century, as the region is reshaped by new forces of inward and outward migration, global investment and cross-border flows of people, goods and ideas. The distinctive character of the Okhotsk Sea region – its harsh climate, low population density and human diversity – makes it a particularly appropriate place to elaborate a particular approach to the past: an approach I refer to as 'imbricated history'.

'Imbricated history' explores the historical connections between a variety of different social groups (both large and small, state and non-state) inhabiting an area whose environment encourages human interaction, but whose territory is transected by political or cultural frontier lines. In this way, it aims to illuminate some of the human connections and confluences that are obscured by conventional spatial frameworks of history writing: the framework of the nation-state and the framework of civilisation. All writers of history must draw horizons around their subject, and all horizons obscure parts of the world from view. Nation-states have had a decisive influence on the history of the world for the past several centuries, and will continue to have a decisive impact upon its future. It therefore remains important to write histories that operate within a national framework. It is also valuable to consider how the sharing of particular belief systems or material practices influence the past and present of societies. Provided that such categories are treated with care and reflection – not treated as eternal verities – there is surely a place for histories of (for example) the Japanese or Thai nations, the Islamic world, or the East Asian societies that shared a stock of political and social ideas originating in the Chinese empire.

But in taking a different – imbricated – standpoint for looking at past and present, I want to try to expose some issues that are obscured by the blind spots of national histories and histories of civilisations, and to draw attention to some deep-seated and debatable assumptions that implicitly underlie many national and civilisational narratives. Most importantly, imbricated history focuses, not just on interaction across national or 'civilisational' boundaries, but also on the long history of interaction *between different social forms*: large states and empires, small non-state societies, and migrant communities created (directly or indirectly) through the processes of imperial expansion.

The Mediterranean and the Okhotsk

In this sense, imbricated history differs from 'inter-civilisational' histories like Fernand Braudel's classic study of the Mediterranean in the age of Philip II. Braudel envisaged the Mediterranean – that sunlit sea whose 'history can no more be separated from that of the lands surrounding it than the clay can be separated from the hands of the potter who shapes it' – and as a meeting place of 'Greek', 'Latin' and 'Islamic' civilisations (and an area infused by the less visible presence of a diasporic 'Jewish civilisation').[1] Although he was intrigued by the interchange of ideas and material culture between these civilisations, Braudel also repeatedly stressed their underlying durability:

> civilizations are transformed only over very long periods of time, by imperceptible processes, for all their apparent changeability. Light travels to them as it were from very distant stars, relayed with sometimes unbelievable delays on the way: from China to the Mediterranean, from the Mediterranean to China, or from India and Persia to the inland sea.[2]

Braudel's civilisations are spatial units – large regions distinguished by allegiance to a supposedly common set of values. But, like all civilisation theories, his view of the past also implicitly rests on a temporal vision of 'civilisation' as the highest in a series of stages of human progress. In this sense, it draws on a tradition (explored in earlier chapters) according to which 'civilisation' is distinguished from earlier phases of 'savagery' or 'barbarism' by the presence of urban settlements, social stratification, centralised organs of government and various technologies such as the art of writing, pottery making, metalworking, etc.

This idea of civilisation has had profound effects on modern historical and social thought. Above all, it focused the attention of the historian on the large states and empires that possess cities and the other hallmarks of the 'civilised'. Civilisation theory thus tended to banish the many small societies that have existed throughout human history to the spatial margins or to the temporal mists of 'prehistory'. Stage theories of history – which assumed a succession of human progress from small hunter-gatherer communities to agrarian-based tribes, kingdoms and empires and ultimately to industrial modernity – implied that the large number of small-scale, non-agrarian societies still existing in the sixteenth, seventeenth or eighteenth centuries (or more recently) were survivals from the remote past, fossils preserving into modernity the social forms of stone-age 'prehistory'. This view of the world defined such communities as societies without history, whose study (in the modern division of academic labour) was the territory of the anthropologist or prehistorian, not the historian. 'Historical time' thus came to be occupied exclusively

---

1   Fernand Braudel, *The Mediterranean and the Mediterranean World in the Age of Philip II*, trans. Sian Reynolds, vol. 1 (London: Collins, 1972), p. 18.
2   Braudel, *Mediterranean*, p. 773.

by large-scale, state-organised societies, and small non-state societies appeared on the horizon only when they were conquered or exterminated by expanding nations and civilisations, or when they themselves expanded to the scale of nations.

Braudel's approach to the history of civilisations derived inspiration from these intellectual traditions but developed them in distinctive ways. His vision of the Mediterranean was by no means a narrowly Eurocentric one. He paid great attention to the history and influence of the Turkish empire, as well as to the histories of Spain, France and the Italian city states. But at the same time, his history focused much more on the northern than on the southern shores of the Mediterranean. In particular, the small-scale nomadic societies of North Africa tended to be confined to the fringes of his narrative. This reflected, not only Braudel's interest in the history of 'civilisations', but also his particular (and profoundly influential) understanding of the structure of historical time.

For Braudel, all of historical time was stratified into three levels, simultaneously flowing at three distinct speeds. In the lower depths of history (as it were) lay the stratum of the *longue durée*, that very slow-moving current of change that shaped landscape, environment and the fundamental elements of human culture. Superimposed upon this was the structural stratum: the stream of time that shaped the political and social order, and in which change could be measured in units of centuries or decades, rather than of millennia. Finally, on the surface of history were the ephemeral waves and eddies of the conjunctural, that stratum of time inhabited by all the crises, triumphs, conflicts, victories and defeats that occupied the attention of most historians, and where change was measured in months and years.

Within this framework, discussion of the small nomadic societies of the southern shores of the Mediterranean is largely limited to chapters dealing with the *longue durée* – the 'almost timeless' realm of environment – and this discussion is couched in terms that repeatedly evoke the forces of nature. Seen from the inside, Braudel acknowledged, the nomadic societies of the sparsely populated desert areas 'reveal their complicated organisations, hierarchies, customs and astonishing legal structures'. But 'seen from the outside, they seem like a handful of human dust blowing in the wind'. The migrations of these peoples from desert to coast are described, like tides, as 'one of the rhythms of Mediterranean history', although unfortunately for the historian they lack 'the regularity of the tides of the seas'.[3] So, while he describes the vibrant power of sixteenth-century Algiers as one of the corsair capitals of the Mediterranean, Braudel depicts the city as an oasis of civilisation disconnected from its surrounding timeless, cultureless hinterland: during the sixteenth century,

> the central Mahgreb, as far as Tiemcen (a city both of Morocco and the Sahara) was amazingly uncivilised. Algiers was to grow up in a country as yet without a leavening of culture, a virgin land, peopled by camel-drovers, shepherds and goatherds.[4]

But dividing time into separate strata inhabited by separate groups of people has curious effects on the way we view history. When the history of indigenous small societies is consigned by the historical imagination to a distinct 'time zone', whether the time zone of prehistory or that of the *longue durée*, it becomes difficult to conceive of these societies as possessing their own 'structural' and 'conjunctural' history, their own dynamics of change. It also becomes difficult to visualise them as existing *simultaneously* with spatially contiguous 'historical' states and empires, and indeed as interacting in important ways with these states and empires. Yet it seems fair to suggest that the Mediterranean's small nomadic communities of camel-drovers, shepherds and goatherds existed not only in the slow-moving depths of the *longue durée*, but also possessed their own 'structural' and 'conjunctural' pasts. Those pasts may be far less easily accessible to the modern historian than the pasts of the Ottoman empire of the Spain of Philip II, but they coexisted with them in that span of time that (for example) modern English-language history labels 'the sixteenth century'.

This issue becomes much more obvious when one turns from the history of a region like the Mediterranean to the history of a region like the Okhotsk Sea. Like the Mediterranean, of course, the Okhotsk is a sea that links as much as it separates human communities: an expanse of water that, in the past, was crossed by complex routes of trade and social communication. But unlike the shores of the Mediterranean, the lands around the Okhotsk Sea are not suited to monocultural agriculture and therefore did not (until very recent times) sustain the dense populations that gave rise to urban life. Most of the communities of the region were small and decentralised, consisting of little self-governing settlements linked to

---

3   Braudel, *Mediterranean*, pp. 176–77.
4   Braudel, *Mediterranean*, p. 772.

one another by bonds of kinship and ritual, rather than of centralised states. From time to time the power of expanding empires (the Mongol Empire in the thirteenth century, the Qing Empire in the seventeenth and eighteenth centuries, the Russian and Japanese Empires in modern times) exerted an influence over the communities of the region. But the presence of states and empires was more remote, and the part played by small, non-state societies more important, than in the history of the Mediterranean. To study the history of the Okhotsk region, therefore, it becomes essential to address the history of these small non-state communities.

What might happen if we put this 'hinterland' in the foreground? What would happen if we tried to write an imbricated history from the point of view of the small societies – seeing them always as active participants in history, moving through time alongside their larger neighbours, and interacting with those neighbours and with one another. The picture of history that would emerge would be a very different one: not necessarily a more 'correct' picture, since history always needs to be seen through multiple lenses, but a history in which certain long-neglected features of the past might begin to become visible. The conventional image of human evolution as progressing step by step through stages of hunter-gatherer, herder or agricultural, urban and industrial society would be of little guidance to us, since the societies in question have (as we shall see) not followed such a simple path. Many were based on hunting and gathering or herding, but some (as we shall see) also had histories of crop growing and livestock rearing, and most were engaged in trade of various forms. The societies of Eastern Siberia and the Okhotsk, in other words, have histories in which there is abundant evidence of major social, economic and cultural changes over recent centuries. It is just that this change does not follow the prescribed patterns of stage theories of progress.

Hedgehogs and Foxes

This view of the past, in other words, brings us face to face with key assumptions that underpinned much modern historical and social thought. In the previous chapters, we have explored some of these assumptions, particularly notions of historical progress and of the emergence of civilisations. Here let us look at some ways in which the history of the Okhotsk region challenges those assumptions, and consider why these challenges may be particularly important in the light of profound problems faced by twenty-first-century global society. In the previous chapter we saw how Condorcet's *Sketch for a Historical Picture of the Progress of the Human Mind* (1795) depicted human knowledge as cumulatively expanding with the growing size and complexity of society. The vision of progress as the creation of ever larger and more centralised knowledge systems was already taking hesitant shape in the axiom of Giambattista Vico (1668–1744) 'first the forests, after that the huts, then the villages, next the cities, and finally the academies',[5] and persisted in the writings of twentieth-century civilisational theorists from Vere Gordon Childe (1892–1957) to Norbert Elias (1897–1990), and through them exerted a profound influence on modern social theory.

Childe followed Enlightenment thinkers like Condorcet in seeing social progress in terms of ever-expanding human knowledge systems, positing a series of epoch-making technological 'revolutions' – the Neolithic (or agricultural) revolution, the urban revolution and the Industrial Revolution: a schema that provides the basis for many versions of civilisation theory.[6] Elias's study of the 'civilizing process', meanwhile, focused initially on the impact of social structures on customs and manners.[7] But in his later years Elias turned increasingly to the role of knowledge, language and symbol in social organisation, for, he observed, one of the most ancient human terrors is:

> the horror of not-knowing, the encounter with events for which [we] have no name. Human beings cannot survive if they cannot place events by giving them a name, by fitting them into their fund of communal symbols.[8]

Civilisation thus becomes an exorcism of the unknown by the unending process of naming and classifying. Elias's view of history, like Condorcet's, was one of ever-growing social units with ever more complex knowledge structures:

---

5   Giambattista Vico, *The New Science*, ed. TG Bergin and M Fisch (Ithaca and London: Cornell University Press, 1968), p. 78. Original published in 1725.

6   Vere Gordon Childe, *New Light on the Most Ancient East* (London: Routledge and Kegan Paul, 1934); Vere Gordon Childe, *What Happened in History*, rev. ed. (London: Penguin Books, 1954).

7   Norbert Elias, *The Civilizing Process*, trans. E Jephcott (Oxford: Blackwell, 1990). Original published in 1939.

8   Norbert Elias, 'The Retreat of Sociologists into the Present', *Theory, Culture and Society* 4, no. 2–3 (1987): pp. 223–47, quotation from p. 237, doi.org/10.1177/026327687004002003.

from small bands of twenty-five to fifty members, perhaps living in caves, humans coalesced into tribes of several hundred or several thousand members, and nowadays more and more into states of millions of people.[9]

This was accompanied first by the emergence of specialised priesthoods who held power through their control of esoteric knowledge, and then by the much wider diffusion of scientific knowledge among many specialist groups.[10]

Elias recognised, of course, that human history did not run in a straight line: large, complex societies sometimes dissolved into fragments, as happened in Europe after the fall of the Roman empire. In the long run, though, the 'trend towards bigger survival units is clear'.[11] Moments of social fragmentation are essentially troughs in the uneven process of social progression – regroupings that prepare the ground for more extensive and complex social integration – and human adaptation to life in ever larger centralised societies becomes the central theme of the social history of the world. Stephen Mennell and others have used Elias's social theories as a basis for understanding the emergence of contemporary global culture. Paraphrasing Elias, Mennell traced the development of humanity from small-scale survival units, in which there could be no specialisation of knowledge, through an ineluctable 'trend ... towards survival units larger and larger both in population and geographical extent' to 'the factual integration of humanity as a whole into a world-wide system of tensions'.[12]

This mapping of expanding knowledge systems, though, overlooks the fact that knowledge may be accumulated in a variety of different ways, which might be imagined as suspended along a range of possibilities between two polar archetypes. One archetype involves the creation of large, centralised knowledge systems of the type sketched by Condorcet, while the other involves the creation of many small decentralised knowledge systems. In the first case, social knowledge comes to be divided between an increasingly complex hierarchy of specialists, and held together by an increasingly formalised system of general axioms. Centralised knowledge

9   Elias, 'Retreat of Sociologists', p. 225.
10   Elias, 'Retreat of Sociologists', p. 225.
11   Stephen Mennell, *Norbert Elias: An Introduction* (Oxford: Basil Blackwell, 1992).
12   Stephen Mennell, 'The Globalisation of Human Society as a Very Long-Term Social Process: Elias' Theory', in *Global Culture: Nationalism, Globalisation and Modernity*, ed. Mike Featherstone (London: Sage Books, 1990), pp. 359–71, quotation from pp. 361–62.

systems are potentially extremely powerful in that they allow very large masses of information to be sorted and classified, allowing the generation of generalised theories of science or social science that may have high levels of predictive accuracy. In the second case – the accumulation of knowledge in small decentralised knowledge systems – there may be relatively little hierarchical division of knowledge or creation of universal rules; instead, human societies divide horizontally into many different small groups that acquire their own intimate experiential knowledge of particular and varied small-scale environments. Here knowledge acquired from neighbouring groups is shaped and deployed precisely in ways that separate and distinguish each group from its neighbours, creating endlessly replicated honeycomb patterns of small-scale difference: endless variations on common themes.

The distinction, in other words, is a little like that suggested by Stephen Marglin, who drew a line between the forms of knowledge he called 'episteme' and 'techne'. 'Episteme', according to Marglin, is analytical, articulate, cerebral, theoretical and professionalised, and it claims to be universally valid. 'Techne', by contrast, is holistic, often implicit, practical and personal; it involves the eye, hand and heart as well as the brain, is derived from tradition and intuition as much as from logical reasoning, and makes no claim to universality. Marglin identified 'episteme' with the aggressively colonising knowledge system of the modern West, and 'techne' with the colonised and rapidly disappearing knowledge systems of 'the Rest' (particularly Asia).[13] A different and perhaps more productive way of looking at things, though, is to suggest that all societies rely on a combination of episteme and techne, but that epistemic knowledge, in one form or another, is a particularly crucial feature of all large-scale, centralised knowledge systems, while small decentralised systems tend to rely more on techne.

In small knowledge systems, where there is relatively little division of knowledge between specialist groups, the relationship between the parts and the whole can remain implicit, to be reimagined and renegotiated

---

13 Stephen Marglin, 'Losing Touch: The Cultural Conditions of Worker Accommodation and Resistance', in *Dominating Knowledge: Development, Culture and Resistance*, ed. Frédérique Apfel Marglin and Stephen Marglin (Oxford: Clarendon Press, 1990), pp. 217–82, doi.org/10.1093/acprof:oso/9780198286943.003.0007; Stephen Marglin, 'Farmers, Seedsmen and Scientists: Systems of Agriculture and Systems of Knowledge', in *Decolonizing Knowledge: From Development to Dialogue*, ed. Frédérique Apfel Marglin and Stephen Marglin (Oxford: Clarendon Press, 1996), pp. 185–248, doi.org/10.1093/acprof:oso/9780198288848.003.0006; see particularly pp. 226–38.

through continuous face-to-face contact between the members of the group, and through continuous interaction between people and their lived environment.

> Direct experience, generation by generation, feeds back into the tale told. Part of that direct experience is the group context itself, a circle of listeners who murmur the burden back or voice approval, or snore. Meaning flashes from mind to mind, and young eyes sparkle.[14]

There is little need for the recording of formal axioms, or for that generalising of relationships so lovingly described by Condorcet. The strength of such small, techne-based systems lies precisely in their deep perception of the interrelationships within a relatively small surrounding cosmos, and in their sensitivity to the unpredictable, the irregular and the uncertain.

At the opposite end of the imaginary scale, large centralised knowledge systems rely on epistemic knowledge to maintain their coherence. Where knowledge is divided among a large number of specialist groups (priests, philosophers, bureaucrats, craftspeople, scientists) in societies whose size precludes regular face-to-face contact, formal methods of recording, classifying, storing and transmitting knowledge become increasingly important. This is not simply a characteristic of the Greek or Judaeo-Christian tradition, but can be seen to some extent in many other large systems. Classical Chinese scientific thought, for example, demonstrates a passion for recording, classifying, labelling and ordering the phenomena of the natural world. Its analytic urge may not entirely coincide with modern concepts of 'rationality' – dragons may be classified with as much care as snakes or bamboos – but it is unmistakably 'epistemic' in Marglin's sense of the word. The strength of such epistemic knowledge systems lies (as Condorcet perceived) in their ability to handle a large number of facts, and to extract from them generalisations about the natural and human world, and therefore above all in their power to comprehend the regular, the repeated and the certain. Metaphorically, we can represent this distinction between episteme and techne in terms of the now famous

---

14 Gary Snyder, foreword to *Songs of Gods, Songs of Humans*, by DL Philippi (Tokyo: University of Tokyo Press, 1979), p. vii.

saying of the poet Archilocus about the wisdom of the hedgehog and the wisdom of the fox: the hedgehog knows one big truth but the fox knows many small truths.[15]

From this point of view, human history (at least until the emergence of the modern global system) can be seen, not simply as the one-way march of 'civilisation', but as a far more complex two-way pull between the creation of centralised and decentralised knowledge systems, and an intricate interplay between the many resulting social forms, in which a multiplicity of knowledge systems coexisted and interacted. Kingdoms and empires expanded, imposing unifying orthodoxies on neighbouring societies. Smaller societies separated themselves from the crumbling edges of imperial systems, domesticating inherited ideas in divergent ways. Migration produced fissures within already small social groups, allowing the separated parts to develop different beliefs and techniques. Large and small societies interacted with one another, exchanging words, stories, rituals and secrets.

The disproportionate attention historians have paid to the growth of large centralised systems has much to do with the fact that these are the systems most likely to leave the monuments and written records whose texts the historian reads. Small societies, lacking these records, tend to be filtered out of the historical vision. Since a number of centralised systems have indeed evolved through a series of roughly comparable (though certainly not identical) technological stages, the tendency has been to generalise these stages into a law of development for all humanity, and consequently to depict smaller societies as remnants of the past, deposited in the frozen realms of an eternal 'prehistory'. As I shall try to show in the sections that follow, an imbricated history approach to the societies of the Okhotsk region can help us to appreciate the historical and contemporary significance of the techne-centred knowledge systems of small societies that operate without centralised state structures.

---

15   See Isaiah Berlin, *The Hedgehog and the Fox: An Essay on Tolstoy's View of History* (London: Weidenfeld and Nicolson, 1953).

Multiple Paths to the Present: The Case of the Okhotsk Region

The archaeological record shows that this region had experienced many waves of change as communities adapted to climatic shifts, as migrations brought new populations into the Okhotsk seaboard, and as the rise and collapse of states on the fringes of the region altered balances of power. Few of these changes, though, can readily be mapped on the conventional itinerary of social evolution. Instead, shifts between hunting and fishing, herding and crop growing seem to have pursued a meandering course in response to intersecting environmental, social and political forces.

From the fourth to the early first millennium BCE, the lower reaches of the Amur River were inhabited by people who lived in villages close to rivers, lakes or the sea shore, alternating between above-ground summer dwellings and semi-subterranean winter houses. They combined fishing with marine hunting and the raising of dogs, and may also have raised domesticated boars, though evidence for this is controversial.[16] They made pottery in styles that changed over time. Similar patterns of subsistence existed on Sakhalin Island, and in the south of the island distinctively decorated pottery indicates trade links to Japan during the early Jōmon period (c. 5000–2500 BCE).[17] Excavations of shell-mounds from the region also show that, 3,000 years ago, the inhabitants of its shoreline were venturing far into the Okhotsk Sea to hunt marine mammals, using harpoons identical to those of the circumpolar peoples of far northern Siberia.[18] By the early centuries of the common era, new patterns of social activity were becoming evident in the region. In the maritime area, there is evidence that reindeer-herding groups from the west were migrating to the Amur region where they settled and adopted many of the economic and cultural patterns of the local fishing communities. Bronze and later iron implements were becoming common, and crop-growing and pig-raising communities spread though many parts of the region, extending as far as the vicinity of today's Vladivostok.[19] Between the late seventh and

---

16   Richard Zgusta, *The Peoples of Northeast Asia Through Time: Precolonial Ethnic and Cultural Processes Along the Coast Between Hokkaido and the Bering Straits* (Leiden: Brill, 2015), pp. 122–24.

17   Zgusta, *The Peoples of Northeast Asia*, p. 82.

18   MG Levin and LP Potapov, *The Peoples of Siberia*, trans. S Dunn (Chicago: University of Chicago Press, 1964), pp. 67–68.

19   Hokkaidō Kaitaku Kinenkan, *Rosshia Kyokutō Shominzoku no Rekishi to Bunka* (Sapporo: Hokkaidō Kaitaku Kinenkan, 1995), p. 4; Zgusta, *The Peoples of Northeast Asia*, pp. 137–39.

tenth centuries CE, the southern parts of this region were incorporated into the Balhae (or Bohai) kingdom, a state covering the area that now straddles the frontier between far north-eastern China, North Korea and the Maritime Province of Russia. After incursions by Khitans from the west in 926, the Balhae kingdom collapsed, but in its eastern regions a new centralised state emerged: the Jurchen Jin Empire, which flourished in the twelfth and early thirteenth centuries.

The Balhae kingdom and Jin Empire coexisted with the realm of social and economic interaction now known as 'Okhotsk culture', extending across the southern Okhotsk Sea from the Kurile Islands along the northern coast of Hokkaido to Sakhalin and the mouth of the Amur River between about the third and thirteenth centuries. If you go to the northern Hokkaido city of Abashiri today and walk along the river embankment towards the sea you will find, tucked away between the public library and the fish-processing factories that line the shore, a small park surrounded by high metal railings. Within the park, thick greenery half conceals a complex maze of hummocks and mounds, the remains of the large semi-subterranean houses the people of this place once built to shelter themselves from the intense winter cold. This site, the Mayoro shell-mound, contains one of the most complete remaining villages from the Okhotsk culture era. The Okhotsk peoples, sometimes romantically (and Eurocentrically) referred to as 'Asian Vikings', lived largely from fishing and hunting marine mammals. A glimpse of their long-vanished beliefs is revealed in their graves, each one topped with an inverted pottery vase, and in their beautiful miniature carvings of bears and of human figures with strange pointed headdresses, excavated from this Abashiri site. They were also traders. Their closest mercantile contacts to the south were with the hunting, fishing and farming communities that inhabited all but the northern fringe of Hokkaido, and whose culture is labelled by archaeologists Epi-Jōmon (lasting roughly from the third to the seventh century CE), followed by Satsumon (roughly seventh to thirteenth century CE). To the north the trade routes of Okhotsk culture extended as far as the Kamchatka Peninsula.[20]

---

20 Kikuchi Toshio, 'Ohōtsuka bunka to Nibufu minzoku', *Kan Ohōtsuku* 1 (1993): pp. 1–27; Utagawa Hiroshi, *Ainu Bunka Seiritsushi* (Sapporo: Hokkaido Shuppan Kikaku Senta, 1988), pp. 274–76.

Figure 4.1. Okhotsk culture grave, Abashiri.
Source: Photograph by author.

Okhotsk culture is commonly seen as reflecting a coming together of long-standing indigenous hunting and fishing traditions, forms of marine hunting (including the hunting of whales), which spread throughout the region from the north, and influences from the Amur region and beyond, which included the raising of pigs and the introduction of new designs of pottery.[21] Within Okhotsk culture itself, though, regional differences existed; for example, archaeological evidence shows that pigs were raised in Okhotsk culture areas in Sakhalin and western Hokkaido, but not in sites on the eastern seaboard of Hokkaido.[22] Trading links connected the Okhotsk culture area to the coastal societies of mainland Asia, and it seems likely that it was this area to which a Tang Dynasty Chinese chronicler referred when he described the arrival at the imperial court of an emissary from a land where:

---

21   Zgusta, *The Peoples of Northeast Asia*, pp. 83–84.
22   Mark J Hudson, 'The Perverse Realities of Change: World System Incorporation and the Okhotsk Culture of Hokkaido', *Journal of Anthropological Archaeology* 23 (2004): p. 296, doi.org/10.1016/j.jaa.2004.05.002.

the people live scattered on the various isles. There are many moors and marshes. The land is favoured with plenty of fish and salt. It grows cold quite early and is frequently visited by a heavy frost and snow. With their feet strapped to the wooden pieces 6 inches wide and 7 feet long [i.e. skis], the people walk on the ice and chase running animals. The land abounds in dogs whose skins are made into skin-garments. It is a custom to wear long hair.[23]

The extensive trading networks that spanned the Okhotsk Sea, linking its southern inhabitants to China and also to the fishing and marine-hunting communities to the north, are evident from the fact that Chinese coins of this period have been found not only at sites in northern Hokkaido but even as far afield as Sredniya, near the northern end of the Kamchatka Peninsula.[24] On the northern and eastern shores of the sea, meanwhile (as the researches of Il'ia Gurvich showed), the peoples of Kamchatka, Chukotka and Alaska came into contact through hunting expeditions, and developed trading links which enabled them to exchange valuable resources and artefacts.[25]

From about the thirteenth century onwards, patterns of daily life and cultural interaction in the Okhotsk region were transformed. The reasons for the historical shift are not obvious, but it is likely that important triggers included Mongol incursions into the Lower Amur region and Sakhalin in the late thirteenth century.[26] Climatic change may also have had a part to play, along with the northward expansion of Japanese influence into the south of Hokkaido.[27] Whatever the causes, some economic activities (like the keeping of domestic pigs) disappeared from most of the region, while others (like inland hunting) became more important. Throughout Hokkaido, the production of pottery began to disappear, and the pattern of life archaeologists and anthropologists describe as 'Ainu culture', in which fishing and forest hunting played a particularly important role, took shape, influenced by a confluence of the legacies of Okhotsk and Satsumon cultures.

23   Quoted in S Wada, 'The Natives of the Lower Reaches of the Amur River as Represented in Chinese Records', *Memoirs of the Toyo Bunko* 10 (1938): pp. 41–102, quotation from p. 52.
24   Kikuchi Toshio, 'Ohōtsuka bunka'.
25   Il'ia S Gurvich, 'Interethnic Ties in Far Northeastern Siberia', in *Anthropology of the North Pacific Rim*, ed. William W Fitzhugh and Valerie Chaussonnet (Washington DC and London: Smithsonian Institution Press, 1994), pp. 309–20.
26   John Stephan, *Sakhalin: A History* (Oxford: Clarendon Press, 1971), pp. 20–21.
27   Ben Fitzhugh, E Gjesfjeld, W Brown, MJ Hudson and Jennie D Shaw, 'Resilience and the Population History of the Kuril Islands, Northwest Pacific: A Study in Complex Human Ecodynamics', *Quaternary International* 419 (2016): pp. 165–93, doi.org/10.1016/j.quaint.2016.02.003.

'Ainu culture' is sometimes seen as being characterised by an absence of ceramics, but in fact archaeological evidence shows that pottery making continued in some areas until quite recent times. Excavations in southern Sakhalin reveal large amounts of pottery fragments mixed with the remains of tobacco pipes, showing that these date to a period after the introduction of tobacco to the region in the sixteenth century.[28] One prewar excavation also yielded pottery fragments decorated with the imprint of bears' feet alongside fragments decorated with a pattern clearly made by the cog-wheel of a clock.[29] Another characteristic of Ainu culture in both Hokkaido and Karafuto was the development of weaving techniques using looms, which the French explorer La Pérouse described in the 1780s as looking 'absolutely similar to ours'.[30]

During this period, connections across the Okhotsk Sea seem to have diminished, but links between the north-west of Hokkaido, western Sakhalin and the Amur River region intensified. It was also perhaps around this time that reindeer herding was introduced to Sakhalin by migrants from the Siberian mainland (ancestors of the people later known as Uilta).[31] The Qing Dynasty established a series of trading posts along the Amur, and by the 1730s were extending their influence across the Tartar Straits into Sakhalin, appointing prominent villagers on the west coast to the positions of 'clan chief' (*hala i da*) and 'village chief' (*gasan da*), in which capacity they were responsible for collecting furs to be taken as tribute to the Amur trading posts (discussed further in the following chapter). This system encouraged the close interaction between the Ainu and Nivkh-speaking villagers of western Sakhalin and the indigenous communities of the Amur region, which lasted into the early nineteenth century.[32]

---

28 Saharin Kōkogaku Kenkyūkai, ed., *Karafuto Nishikaigan no Kōko Shiryō* (Obihiro: Saharin Kōkogaku Kenkyūkai, 1995).

29 Oka Masao and Baba Osamu, 'Kita Chishima Shumushutō oyobi Karafuto Taraika Chihō ni okeru Kōkogakuteki Chōsa Hōkoku', *Minzokugaku Kenkyū* 4, no. 3 (1938): pp. 489–552.

30 Jean-François de Galaup de La Pérouse, *The Journal of Jean-François de Galaup de La Pérouse*, trans. and ed. John Dunmore, vol. 2 (London: The Hakluyt Society, 1995), p. 292.

31 Zgusta, *The Peoples of Northeast Asia*, p. 156; Yoshiko Yamada, 'A Preliminary Study of Language Contacts around Uilta in Sakhalin', *Hoppō Bunka Kenkyū* 3 (2010): pp. 59–74, reference from pp. 62–63.

32 Sasaki Shirō, 'Amūru-gawa Shimoryūiki Shominzoku no Shakai, Bunka ni okeru Shinchō Shihai no Eikyō ni tsuite', *Kokuritsu Minzoku Hakubutsukan Kenkyū Hōkoku* 14, no. 3 (1989): pp. 671–771.

None of this suggests the stagnation of societies trapped in the timeless mists of prehistory. On the contrary, the picture is one of rather rapid economic change and dynamic interaction between many small social groups. At the same time, though, this change does not readily fit the image of 'progress' depicted by nineteenth-century theory. Some aspects of change – the diffusion of techniques like reindeer herding and weaving, the development of new trading links and specialised centres of boat production, etc. – match definitions of 'progress', while others – the disappearance of pig farming and the decline of pottery production – could in conventional terms be seen as a 'relapse' towards a lower stage of development. To put it another way, the story of Okhotsk history raises questions about the usefulness of conventional trajectories of social and economic 'progress' in charting the long pre-modern experiences of small-scale communities living in areas unsuited to dense settlement and intensive agriculture.

An area like the Okhotsk seaboard, with its extreme climate where temperatures regularly fall below minus 20 degrees Celsius in the winter and where land that is hard in winter turns to impassable marsh in summer, is ill-adapted to large-scale monoculture. Survival in this environment requires patterns of settlement and economic activity that shift with the seasons, and the deep knowledge of small local environments that enables humans to make the best use of scarce food resources.[33] Small climatic variations are likely to have had a very large impact on patterns of human existence. Climate variation not only affected the frontiers of crop growing and the availability of fodder for domestic animals like pigs and reindeer; it also had a dramatic effect on human communications. In much of the region, the quickest form of transport was by ski or dog sled over snow or frozen sea. The cold months of the year were the main time for trading journeys or for travelling to arrange marriages with distant clans. Every winter, small islands ceased to be islands and places like Sakhalin 'became' part of the Asian continent. A slight rise in winter temperatures could make a large difference to the area of sea or river that could be traversed in winter, drastically affecting regular travel routes. In this environment, the ability of societies to adapt swiftly from one form of subsistence to another, and to reorganise their social interrelationships, was at a premium.

---

33   See, for example, Tat'yana Roon, *Uil'ta Sakhalina: Istoriko-Etnografucheskoe Issledovanie Traditsionnovo Khozyaistva* i *Material'noi Kul'tury XVIII – Serediny-XX Vekov* (Yuzhno-Sakhalinsk: Sakhalinskoe Oblastnoe Knizhnoe Izdatelstvo, 1996).

The societies of the Okhotsk, then, needed to adapt both to environmental change and to fluctuating relationships with large, centralised societies to the south and west. Existing on the very outermost fringes of the Chinese world, they were subject to the waxing and waning pull of mainland Asian states, as kingdoms and dynasties rose and fell. When the Balhae kingdom, Jurchen Jin Empire, the Mongol Empire or the Manchu Qing Dynasty were at their most powerful, communities along the fringes of the Okhotsk Sea were drawn into trading and tributary relationships that were sometimes exploitative, but at times also allowed them to exchange the rare products of their region (particularly furs) at high prices. As these centralised kingdoms declined, on the other hand, trade links to the mainland atrophied, and the Okhotsk societies were forced to rely more on production for subsistence (fishing, dog farming, reindeer herding, craft production, etc.), or on trade among the small, non-state societies of the region. Recent research on the archaeology of the Kurile Islands, for example, suggests that, while the fourteenth-century onset of the so-called Little Ice Age may have been a factor in the decline of the islands' population around the end of the Okhotsk culture era, another factor was probably the erosion of trade contacts with neighbouring societies as a result of shifts in the East Asian international order.[34] Surviving such changes required the flexibility to shift emphasis from one part of the productive system to another – in some eras, devoting more time to hunting and long-distance trade, in others spending more energy on fishing, local trade, craft production and (in certain areas) crop growing.

Complex patterns of overlapping social networks probably helped to sustain this economic flexibility. In areas like the central parts of Sakhalin, for example, Nivkh and Uilta villages were often close to one another, and some villages were made up of inhabitants belonging to more than one language group.[35] The language groups developed cultural practices that allowed both sharing of some forms of knowledge and economic differentiation, enabling different groups to make use of different parts of the natural environment. Uilta, for example, hunted marine mammals in summer and forest animals in winter, but also made use of forest resources

---

34   Fitzhugh et al., 'Resilience'.
35   See, for example, Bronislaw Piłsudski, 'B. O. Pilsudski's Report on his Expedition to the Ainu and Oroks of the Island of Sakhalin in the Years 1903 to 1905', in *The Collected Works of Bronislaw Piłsudski*, vol. 1, *The Aborigines of Sakhalin*, ed. Alfred F Majewicz, Trends in Linguistics Documentation 15-1 (Berlin and New York: Mouton de Gruyter, 1998), pp. 192–221, doi.org/10.1515/9783110820768-013.

such as summer grass, mosses and lichens as food for their reindeer herds, while Nivkh living in neighbouring areas focused more intensively on fishing.

Although there was oral history evidence of past conflicts between these groups – particularly between the Ainu and Uilta – a modus vivendi developed over time that allowed diverse language groups to share the same ecological space while adopting and adapting techniques from one another. An interesting example of the continuous processes of technological innovation and interaction was cited by the Polish scholar Bronislaw Piłsudski, who noted in the early twentieth century that, as whaling expanded in Sakhalin, Ainu communities started to use whalebone as runners for their dog sleighs. This practice was then taken up by the Uilta neighbours for their reindeer sleighs, but the Uilta soon found that reindeer appeared to have a negative reaction to the smell of whalebone, so they reverted to the use of wooden sleigh runners.[36]

Marriage between members of different language groups seems to have been common. In these multilingual communities, villagers cooperated in productive tasks and also probably shared some ritual activities. But members of each language group also possessed ritual and kinship ties that linked them to other members of their own language community, often in distant parts of the island, or as far away as the Siberian mainland. Russian naturalist and geographer Leopold von Schrenck, for example, described the scene on the Tymy (or Tym) River in central Sakhalin, which he visited in 1856:

> The Gilyaks [Nivkh] of the Tymy collect immense stores of frozen fish, not only as food for themselves and their dogs during the winter, but also as an object of trade with the Ainos, Oronchons [Uilta], the Gilyaks [Nivkh] of the coast, the mainland, the Ainan and the Manguns on the Amur. The Ainos bring to the valley of the Tymy Japanese goods, the Oroke furs, the others copper, seals, Russian and Manchu merchandise.[37]

---

36 See Bronislaw Piłsudski, 'From the Report on the Expedition to the Orok in 1904', in *The Collected Works of Bronislaw Piłsudski*, pp. 618–77, reference from pp. 642–43, doi.org/10.1515/9783110820768.

37 Quoted in EG Ravenstein, *The Russians on the Amur* (London: Trübner and Co., 1861), p. 273.

Figure 4.2. Nivkh drying fish, early twentieth century.
Source: Wikimedia commons, public domain.

By mobilising intersecting and often geographically extended social networks, the people of the region would more readily have been able to adjust to a world where repeated realignments of trading patterns and subsistence activities were needed.

A Problem of Progress

I have described imbricated history as dealing with the intersections between large and small societies, but of course the distinction between large- and small-scale social systems is itself a matter of ideal types. In the real world, the picture has been one of infinitely complicated local particularities, hybridities, imperial expansions and interactions. In times of Chinese imperial expansion some groups on the fringes of the empire were fairly thoroughly absorbed into the North Chinese or Manchu social and cultural world, while other societies were more loosely drawn into the imperial orbit – as in the seventeenth century, the Nanai, Ul'chi, Nivkh and Ainu peoples of the Lower Amur and Sakhalin were subjected to a tributary relationship with China. This link exposed the societies of the region to the influence of Chinese and Manchu goods, techniques, designs and social systems (including the creation of new village power structures), but left much of the underlying substructure of local knowledge unaltered.

On the other hand, the centralising pull of the Chinese empire was balanced by the fragmenting pull of human migration. Small groups repeatedly split off from established settlements, moving into new territory where they gradually developed distinctive dialects, legends and ways of life. So the reindeer-herding community now known as the Uilta who probably migrated to Sakhalin from Eastern Siberia sometime before the seventeenth century were, by the nineteenth century, far enough removed from their continental roots to be classified by anthropologists as a distinct 'ethnic group'. These processes of dispersal continued until quite recent times: the social group known as the Even, living mostly along the western shores of the Okhotsk Sea, seem to have developed the dialect and myths that distinguish them from their neighbours, the Evenk, in the period since the early eighteenth century.

Meanwhile, of course, many of the peoples of the region had begun to be exposed to the technological and social influences of newly emerging imperial systems: Russia in the west and Japan in the south. The Japanese influence became particularly powerful from the eighteenth century onward. Throughout the Tokugawa period (1603–1868), the island then known as Ezo (Hokkaido) was divided, with a small region to the south-west (the peninsula in the lower left corner of the map in Figure 4.3, known as Wajin-Chi or Matsumae-Chi[38]) being placed under the direct control of the Japanese Matsumae Domain and settled by migrants from other parts of Japan, while in the remainder of the island (Ezo-chi), Ainu continued to live a more or less independent existence. In the second half of the eighteenth century, though, Ainu society was increasingly affected by influences from Matsumae Domain, as Japanese fishing concerns were licensed to set up ventures along the shores of Ezo-chi as far as southern Sakhalin and the southern Kurile Islands. Meanwhile, the Matsumae domain lords were also placing increasing demands for 'tribute' on the indigenous population.[39]

---

38   Literally 'Matsumae Territory' or 'Japanese Territory'.

39   See, for example, David L Howell, *Capitalism from Within: Economy, Society and the State in a Japanese Fishery* (Berkeley and London: University of California Press, 1995); Brett Walker, *The Conquest of Ainu Lands, 1590–1800* (Berkeley and London: University of California Press, 2001).

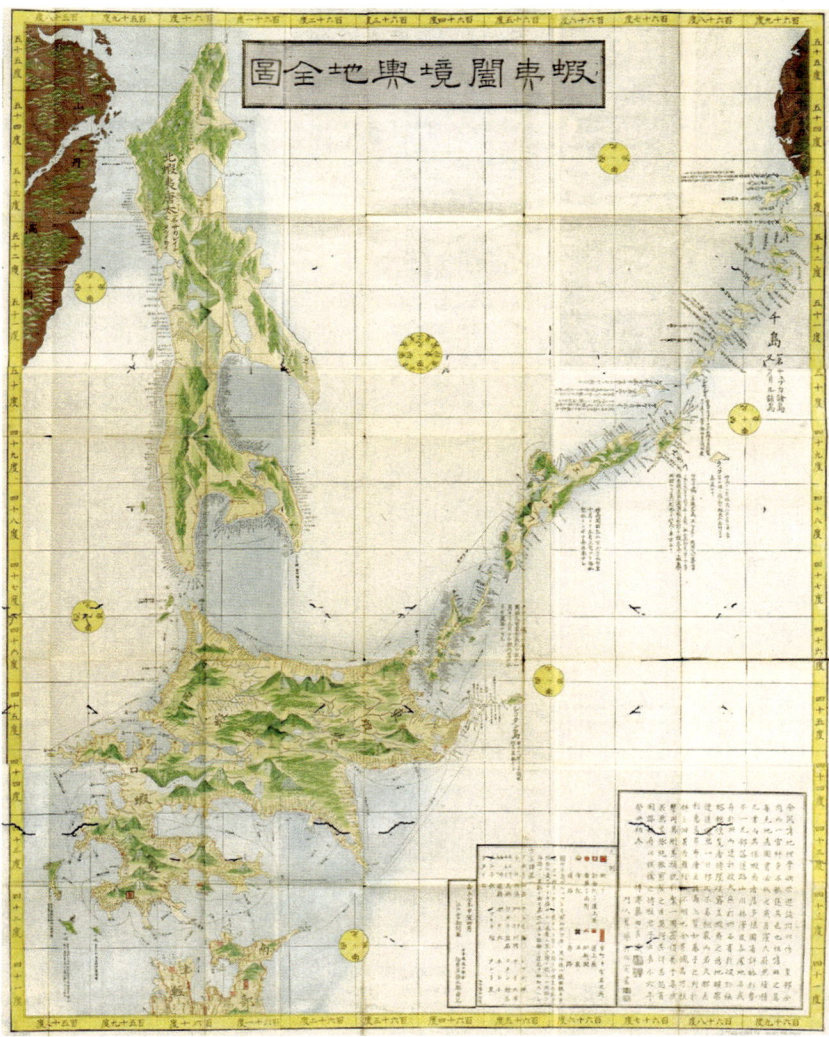

Figure 4.3. 1807 map of Ezo.

Source: Fujita Tonsai and Hashimoto Ransai, 'Ezo Kōkyō Yochi Zenzu', Library of Congress Geography and Map Division, Washington DC.

The violence that is done to the history of this region by trying to fit it in to stage theories of human development is well illustrated by the vexed question of the place of farming in Ainu society. In historical times, Ainu societies relied on hunting, fishing and the collection of shellfish and plants for a large part of their diet, but there is also abundant archaeological, documentary and ethnographic evidence to show that they practised at least two forms of farming. The first was dog farming, an activity that formed the basis of the Sakhalin Ainu economy (and also seems to have been practised on a smaller scale in other parts of Ainu territory). Perhaps because dogs play a very different role both in European and the Japanese society, the Ainu techniques of dog breeding are seldom recognised as 'farming', yet all the available information suggests that for the Sakhalin Ainu dogs played very much the same role that cows or camels play in other societies; in other words, they provided food and clothing and acted as draft animals. In addition, of course, they were important companions in the hunt.[40]

Japanese official Mamiya Rinzō, who travelled through Sakhalin in 1807–09, describes each well-to-do Ainu family as owning between five and 13 dogs, who were selectively bred, and fed and trained with great care. Small and weak dogs were killed for their meat and hides, while the stronger dogs were used to pull sleds and boats. Sakhalin Ainu had well-developed veterinary techniques, which were used, for example, when castrating sled dogs – a practice said to make them stronger. Good-quality dogs were greatly valued and traded for high prices.[41] As well as their use as food and beasts of burden, Cornelis Coen records that the dogs were trained to catch salmon from the rivers, and that they would tear off and eat the fish head and carry the rest of the carcass back to their owner's house.[42]

40   Takakura Shinichirō. *Shinpan Ainu Seisakushi* (Tokyo: San-Ichi Shobō, 1972), p. 31; see also Chuner M Taksami, 'Traditional Culture of the Peoples of the Russian Pacific Coast', in Fitzhugh and Chaussonnet, *Anthropology of the North Pacific Rim*, pp. 275–80 (particularly p. 278).
41   Mamiya Rinzō, 'Kita Ezo Zusetsu or a Description of the Island of Northern Yezo by Mamiya Rinsō', trans. John A Harrison, *Proceedings of the American Philosophical Society* 99, no. 2 (1955): pp. 93–115, reference from pp. 104–06. Original published in 1855.
42   PA Leupe, ed., *Reize van Maarten Gerritszoon Vries in 1643 naar het Norden en Oosten van Japan Volgens het Journaal Gehouden door C. J. Coen* (Amsterdam: Frederik Muller, 1858), p. 131.

Figure 4.4. Ainu with dog sleigh.

Source: Mamiya Rinzō, 'Kita Ezo Zusetsu or a Description of the Island of Northern Yezo by Mamiya Rinsō', trans. John A Harrison, *Proceedings of the American Philosophical Society* 99, no. 2 (1955). Originally published in 1855.

The second form of farming involved the more familiar activities of cultivating grains and vegetables. Crops seem to have included barley, wheat, sorghum, millet and beans; some rice was also found, though this was probably imported. A number of Tokugawa texts include references to Ainu crop production, and the subject has also been researched in some detail by scholars like Takakura Shinichirō and Hayashi Yoshishige.[43] Work in the fields was generally carried out by women, who, throughout the summer months, would rise early and spend the morning tending their crops. Small fields were cleared along the banks of rivers, with the cut grasses and weeds being burnt to provide ash as fertiliser. These fields would be cultivated for two or three years, and then allowed to return to forest. Once the seeds had been sown no fertiliser was used and fields

---

43 Takakura, *Shinpan Ainu Seisakushi*; Hayashi Yoshishige, *Ainu no Nōkō Bunka* (Tokyo: Keiyūsha, 1969).

were only occasionally weeded, but before planting seeds were sometimes soaked in a mixture of bird's egg and extracts of various plants, which was believed to encourage germination.[44]

Over the past two decades, archaeologists have recognised and researched the role of crop growing in a historically dynamic and changing Ainu culture.[45] This shift in perspectives is part of a broader rethinking of the vision of the 'Neolithic revolution', and a growing acknowledgement of more complex and diverse historical processes of change from one pattern of subsistence to another.[46] Yet standard accounts of Japanese society still quite frequently present Ainu primarily in terms of immutable genetic connections to Japan's earliest population, as embodiments of 'the Jōmon origins of Japan'[47] and being 'on the brink of extinction'.[48] This interpretation blurs the important distinction between genetics and culture: the fact that people who identify themselves as Ainu today may have DNA links to Jōmon ancestors (as well as to peoples of Eastern Siberia) does not make Ainu culture a survival of Jōmon culture, any more than the Scandinavian DNA found in many British people today makes contemporary British culture a survival of Viking culture. Part of the reason why this image of the Ainu has been so hard to shift, I believe, lies in the fact that the history of Ainu farming radically contradicts various deeply rooted modern intellectual paradigms that have sometimes become entirely invisible to observers.

In the first place, the very existence of Ainu farming upsets the attempts that a number of Japanese scholars have made to construct the Ainu as preservers of the most ancient known form of Japanese culture. This view, for example, was energetically proposed by philosopher Umehara Takeshi, who saw Jōmon as being the crucible of Japanese culture, and argued that

---

44   Hayashi, *Ainu no Nōkō Bunka*; Matsuura Takeshirō, *Sankō Ezo Nisshi*, vol. 2 (Tokyo: Yoshikawa Kōbunkan, 1971), pp. 51–52. Original written in 1850.

45   See, for example, Yuriko Fukasawa, *Ainu Archaeology as Ethnohistory: Iron technology among the Saru Ainu of Hokkaido, Japan, in the 17th century* (Oxford: British Archaeological Reports, 1998); Gary W Crawford, 'The Jomon in Early Agriculture Discourse: Issues Arising from Matsui, Kanehara and Perason', *World Archaeology* 40, no. 4 (2008): pp. 445–65, doi.org/10.1080/00438240802451181; Hideyuki Ōnishi, 'The Formation of the Ainu Cultural Landscape: Landscape Shift in a Hunter-Gatherer Society in the Northern Part of the Japanese Archipelago', *Journal of World Prehistory* 27, no. 3–4 (2014): pp. 277–93, doi.org/10.1007/s10963-014-9080-2.

46   Junzo Uchiyama, JC Gillam, LA Hosoya, K Lindström and Peter Jordan, 'Investigating Neolithization of Cultural Landscapes in East Asia: The NEOMAP Project', *Journal of World Prehistory* 27, no. 3–4 (2014): pp. 197–223, doi.org/10.1007/s10963-014-9079-8.

47   Ken Henshall, *A History of Japan: From Stone Age to Superpower*, 3rd ed. (Basingstoke and New York: Palgrave Macmillan, 2012), p. 12.

48   Roger J Davis, *Japanese Culture: The Religious and Philosophical Foundations* (Tokyo: Tuttle Publishing, 2016), p. 16.

the Ainu had preserved Jōmon hunter-gatherer culture into the modern era in a particularly pure form.[49] An alternative version, put forward by Hayashi Yoshishige (one of the first Japanese scholars to write extensively about Ainu crop-growing practices) suggests that Ainu society was a survival not of Jōmon hunter-gatherer culture, but of the very earliest form of Japanese agricultural society, associated with the Yayoi to Kofun periods (around 200–500 CE). Hayashi wrote:

> It is recognized … that Ainu material culture was influenced to no small degree by Japanese Yayoi and Kofun period culture. One typical example is the impact of farming. The Ainu being a static hunter-gatherer people, we can say that they preserved this Yayoi and Kofun period Japanese farming almost unchanged until modern times.[50]

So, having provided a careful and fascinating description of the nature of Ainu farming techniques, Hayashi then felt impelled to go on to demonstrate that these techniques were similar to techniques found in Japan, but – since the Ainu were a 'static hunter-gatherer people' – always more primitive than anything to be found in historical Japanese society.[51]

But this picture of Ainu society as a culture trapped forever on the brink of an 'agricultural revolution' presents problems. For one thing, despite Hayashi's emphasis on differences between Ainu farming and modern Japanese techniques, Ainu farm practices were remarkably like forms of farming practised in certain parts of Japan at least until the late eighteenth century. For example, Japanese Tokugawa-period settlers in Matsumae-Chi, whose small-scale farming activities were described by Mogami Tokunai in the 1780s, also practised shifting cultivation. They too cleared small fields, abandoning them after three to five years, and like Ainu farmers did not fertilise the soil (despite the abundance of locally produced fertiliser) or devote effort to weeding. These farming practices, besides, were not unique to the far north, for one farmer whom Mogami interviewed in Ezo came from the island of Sado off the western coast of Japan, and said that the same techniques were used in his home district.[52] Indeed, similar forms of shifting cultivation are known to have existed in many parts of Japan until relatively recent times.

---

49 See, for example, Umehara Takeshi and Hanihara Kazurō, *Ainu wa Gen-Nihonjin ka* (Tokyo: Shōgakukan, 1982).
50 Hayashi, *Ainu no Nōkō Bunka*, p. 3.
51 Hayashi, *Ainu no Nōkō Bunka*, pp. 175–88.
52 Mogami Tokunai, *Ezo Sōshi*, reprinted in *Hokumon Sōsho*, ed. Ōtomo Kisaku, vol. 1 (Tokyo: Kokusho Kankōkai, 1972), pp. 326–27. Original written in 1790.

Japanese farmers in Matsumae-Chi and Sado would surely have known about the more intensive farming techniques used in other parts of Japan, and the fact that their crop production was similar to that of the Ainu suggests a rather different interpretation of this form of shifting cultivation: an interpretation that is borne out by Japanese official Sakakura Genjirō's observations of the region in the 1730s. Sakakura commented that farming was uncommon in even in the Japanese-settled area of Ezo, not because the soil was poor, but because the main farm season coincided with the summer months when herring swarmed in vast shoals off the coast. The lucrative herring fisheries drew labour away from farming, and made the very labour-intensive forms of farm production employed in most other parts of Japan impractical. In fact, Sakakura implied that farming had at one stage been attempted on a larger scale in region, but that, because of the wealth to be won from the fisheries 'the people have long since ceased to attempt farming'.[53] In the light of these comments, it seems likely that the types of crop production practised by the Ainu and by Japanese communities in Ezo and Sado were not simply a primitive survival of the past, but were techniques specifically developed to suit societies where a large amount of time was taken up with fishing or hunting activities. Small-scale, shifting cultivation with very little weeding, fertilising and irrigation would have made good sense in area where land was abundant and labour scarce.

This close interrelationship between farming and fishing activities had crucial implications for the fate of Ainu farming during the Tokugawa period. For the fact is that, as the archaeologist Fukasawa Yuriko puts it 'Ainu culture is defined rather by the disappearance of cultivation than by its existence'.[54] While there is substantial archaeological evidence for farming in earlier centuries, signs of crop growing seem to become more and more elusive in the middle to late Tokugawa period. The increasing incorporation of Ainu labour (both male and female) into the herring fisheries almost certainly had much to do with this disappearance. When Sakakura Genjirō visited the region in the 1730s, he remarked that farming was carried out by Ainu living in the mountain areas, but not by

---

53 Sakakura Genjirō, *Ezo Zuihitsu*, reprinted in *Hoppō Mikōkai Komonjo Shūsei*, ed. Terasawa Hajime et al., vol. 10 (Tokyo: Sōbunsha, 1979), p. 77. Original written in 1739.
54 Yuriko Fukasawa, 'Emishi and the Ainu' (paper presented at the international symposium *Japanese Archaeology in Protohistoric and Early Historic Period: Yamato and its Relations to Surrounding Populations*, University of Bonn, 1992).

those on the coast. The extent of farming by coastal Ainu in earlier periods is not clear, but the penetration of Japanese fishing activities into the area undoubtedly discouraged cultivation.

At times, this may have been a simple question of 'comparative advantage': catching fish for the Japanese may indeed have been more profitable than the uncertain process of producing a small harvest of grain or vegetables. But, as is often the case in economic history, comparative advantage was, where necessary, backed up by force. As Matsumae's revenue became increasingly dependent on Ainu labour in the herring fisheries, so it became essential for Ainu farming activities to be discouraged. Mogami Tokunai noted that by the late eighteenth century the import of seeds from Matsumae to Ainu territory was prohibited,[55] while another Edo text provides a fascinating comment on the reason why Ainu farming was carried out in remote mountain valleys rather than near to their villages: it was '(1) so that they [the farm fields] are not troubled by thieves; (2) *because when the Japanese come to trade they object that [crop growing] prevents fishing and suppress it*'.[56] The same story is told by Matsuura Takeshirō, an unusually observant and sympathetic Japanese traveller who visited the remoted parts of Ezo-chi in the mid-nineteenth century. Matsuura heard complaints from local village leaders that efforts to cultivate crops – particularly crops such as tobacco and hemp – invariably evoked reprisals by officials from Japanese trading posts, who feared that farming might reduce the reliance of Ainu on imported Japanese products and on wage labour in the Japanese fisheries.[57] Anthropologist Deriha Kōji has also pointed out that Ainu hunting activities were intensified by growing pressure from Matsumae Domain, which demanded that Ainu communities provide 'tribute' in the form of animal pelts. In particular, after 1812, Matsumae strictly enforced its demands for small animal pelts from the Ainu, and used these for its own trading activities with indigenous communities of the Lower Amur region.[58]

---

55 Mogami, *Ezo Sōshi*, p. 315.
56 Quoted in Hayashi, *Ainu no Nōkō Bunka*, p. 26, emphasis added.
57 See Hanasaki Kōhei, *Shizuka na Taichi* (Tokyo: Iwanami Shoten, 1993), p. 79.
58 Deriha Kōji, 'Kinsei Makki ni okeru Ainu no Kegawajū Shuryō ni tsuite: Kegawa Kōeki no Shiten kara', *Senri Ethnological Reports* 34 (2002): pp. 97–163; Deriha Kōji, 'Trade and Paradigm Shift in Research on Ainu Hunting Practices', in *Beyond Ainu Studies: Changing Academic and Public Perspectives*, ed. Mark J Hudson, Ann-Elise Lewallen and Mark K Watson (Honolulu: University of Hawai'i Press, 2014), pp. 136–49, doi.org/10.21313/hawaii/9780824836979.003.0009. For further discussion of the impact of Matsumae's economic policies on the Ainu population, see Howell, *Capitalism from Within*, particularly Chapter 2.

De-agrarianisation was also caused by other, less obvious factors. Inland Ainu communities depended on a complex and interrelated web of food-gathering activities, one of the most important being salmon fishing. In autumn, cherry and dog salmon would swim up the rivers of Ainu territory to spawn, and villagers in the mountain valleys would catch the salmon using spears or bag-nets.[59] During the Ainu salmon fishing season, relatively small numbers of fish were taken, and these were often caught after they had spawned. By contrast, the Japanese fishing enterprises, which entered the region in growing numbers during the late Tokugawa period, used large nets to catch the fish as they entered the river mouth. The result was a drastic drop in salmon stocks, which caused hardship and even famine in some inland Ainu settlements. Driven by hunger, villagers left the inland districts for the coast, where they often found employment as fishery workers.[60] The drift of population away from the mountains further undermined the balance of hunting, fishing and crop growing that had characterised the inland Ainu economy.

In other words, the incorporation of Ainu society into an increasingly close economic relationship with Japan encouraged a shift from a relatively diversified, self-sufficient economy to one that concentrated on the areas of particular Ainu 'comparative advantage': hunting and fishing. This led not only to a diminution of farming, but also to the disappearance of other activities for which Japan was more advantageously placed. One of the most important examples was metalworking. When Mamiya Rinzō reached Sakhalin in the early nineteenth century, he found Ainu blacksmiths using techniques quite different from those that existed in Tokugawa Japan.[61] This type of metalworking, he noted, had existed until recently in other parts of Ainu territory (including the north of modern Hokkaido), but had gradually vanished in the face of Japanese imports of metal goods. Many modern texts on Ainu culture deny that they ever possessed the ability to make metal tools.[62] The process of declining self-sufficiency in early modern Ainu society is also emphasised by the historian Kaiho Mineo, who focuses particularly on the disappearance of Ainu pottery and on growing Ainu dependence of Japanese-made tools.[63]

59   Hiroshi Watanabe, *The Ainu Ecosystem* (Seattle and London: University of Washington Press. 1972) p. 31.
60   Uemura Hideaki, *Kita no Umi no Kōekishatachi: Ainu Minzoku no Shakai Keizaishi* (Tokyo: Dōbunkan Shuppan. 1990), pp. 230–32.
61   Mamiya, 'Kita Ezo Zusetsu', pp. 338–42.
62   For example, Hayashi, *Ainu no Nōkō Bunka*, p. 31; Takakura, *Shinpan Ainu Seisakushi*, p. 31.
63   Kaiho Mineo, *Kinsei no Hokkaidō* (Tokyo: Kyōikusha, 1979), pp. 96–97.

Figure 4.5. Sakhalin Ainu blacksmiths.
Source: Mamiya Rinzō, 'Kita Ezo Zusetsu or a Description of the Island of Northern Yezo by Mamiya Rinsō', trans. John A Harrison, *Proceedings of the American Philosophical Society* 99, no. 2 (1955). Originally published in 1855.

It seems probable, then, that it was the very process of increasing trade with an evolving and expanding Japanese economy that tended to reconstitute Ainu society as an archetypal 'hunter-gatherer' society. The growth of trade promoted a more sharply defined division of labour between Japan and the Land of the Ainu: a division in which the latter specialised in fishing and hunting while the former specialised in farming and metalworking. Such patterns of change are not unique to the Okhotsk region. In the North American context, for example, Stephen Cornell has documented the way in which the colonial fur trade transformed the life patterns of Native American peoples. Cornell points out that the fur trade did not simply mean that increasing amounts of time were spent in hunting and trapping animals, but also that new techniques for skinning and processing had to be developed or acquired from the European colonists. As the fur trade expanded:

hunting grew in importance, to the detriment of agriculture. Crucially, it was hunting on an increasingly commercial, instead of subsistence, basis. The purpose of the hunt was no longer simply to secure food, hides and other products for home consumption, but to sustain trade relationships with Europeans.[64]

This commercialisation of life had other lasting effects:

> As Indian material goods were replaced by European ones, some traditional crafts fell into disuse. Eventually some were forgotten. Trade items once considered luxuries or conveniences became necessities. At the same time new wants emerged that could be satisfied only by European products.[65]

Imbricated History in an Age of Climate Change

The story told here, then, highlights the importance of re-examining the historical importance and dynamics of small, decentralised knowledge systems; and the significance of their history has recently been highlighted by twenty-first-century environmental challenges, particularly the challenge of global warming. In recent years, there has been a growing interest in 'Big History',[66] and a growing acceptance of the view that the macro-history of our planet has entered a new era – the Anthropocene – in which 'humankind has become a global geological force in its own right'.[67] A core characteristic of Big History, in the words of its pioneer David Christian, is:

> its interdisciplinary nature and its search for an underlying unity beneath the various accounts of the past told in different historically oriented disciplines. Big History studies the past across physics, astronomy, geology, biology and human history.[68]

---

64   Stephen Cornell, *The Return of the Native: American Indian Political Resurgence* (Oxford: Oxford University Press, 1988), p. 23.
65   Cornell, *Return of the Native*, p. 22.
66   See, for example, David Christian, *Maps of Time: An Introduction to Big History* (Berkeley: University of California Press, 2004); Fred Spier, *Big History and the Future of Humanity* (Oxford: Wiley-Blackwell, 2010); David Christian, *Origin Story: A Big History of Everything* (Harmondsworth: Penguin Books, 2018).
67   Will Steffen, J Grinevald, P Crutzen and John McNeill, 'The Anthropocene: Conceptual and Historical Perspectives', *Philosophical Transactions of the Royal Society A: Mathematical, Physical and Engineering Sciences* 369 (2011): pp. 842–67, quotation from p. 843, doi.org/10.1098/rsta.2010.0327.
68   David Christian, 'Preface to the 2011 Edition', in *Maps of Time: An Introduction to Big History*, rev. ed. (Berkeley: University of California Press, 2011), p. xxiv.

To achieve this grand synthesis, Big History, as it were, takes a step back from the human past, allowing us to observe human history as just one part of the much bigger processes of becoming that begin from the Big Bang. The result is in some ways a radically new approach to thinking and writing about history. Dipesh Chakrabarty has similarly advocated a fundamental transformation of the timescale of history, creating a view of the past that embraces the vast and slow movement of planetary time. He sees the subject of history not as individuals, nations, ethnic groups, social classes etc., but as the planetary system itself, of which the human race is just one small part.[69]

Historian of Japan Julia Adeney Thomas, whose work is deeply influenced by Chakrabarty's, argues that the study of the diverse historical trajectories of past societies around the world is crucial to enable us to find alternative historical futures that diverge from the endless pursuit of material wealth and power. She emphasises the urgency of developing a different sort of history writing, which might enable us to appreciate how the human body is inseparably embedded in its environment, and which might thus make it possible for us to conceive of a new economic and political order to counter 'neoliberalism's naturalization of infinite economic expansion'.[70] One important historical experience in this context, she suggests, is the story of Tokugawa Japan, which (according to the accounts of historians like Geoffrey Parker) appears to have weathered the climatic changes of the Little Ice Age with relatively little social disruption.[71] Thomas argues that, in the search for a different vision of past and future, we may find hope in the resilience of Tokugawa Japan, which 'was fairly isolated from the rest of the world and did not export its human population and did not import food, and managed to live for 250 years in peace'.[72]

Here I would like to suggest a somewhat different way of thinking about this profound problem – one that moves not up to the grand scale of geological history, but down to the small scale of decentralised knowledge

---

69   Dipesh Chakrabarty, 'Anthropocene Time', *History and Theory: Studies in the Philosophy of History* 51, no. 1 (2018): pp. 5–32.

70   Julia Adeney Thomas, 'History and Biology in the Anthropocene: Problems of Scale, Problems of Value', *The American Historical Review* 119, no. 5 (2014): pp. 1587–607, quotation from p. 1606, doi.org/10.1093/ahr/119.5.1587.

71   See Geoffrey Parker, *The Global Crisis: War, Climate Change and Catastrophe in the Seventeenth Century* (New Haven: Yale University Press, 2013), particularly Chapter 16.

72   John McNeill and Julia Adeney Thomas, 'Historians and the Anthropocene' (lecture, Woodrow Wilson Center History and Public Policy Program, 17 November 2017, www.youtube.com/watch?v=xhrP1hZuW0M (accessed 17 December 2018)).

systems and their imbricated history. Viewed from the perspective of the Okhotsk region, the history of Tokugawa Japan does not look much like a story of peace and isolation, but rather like one of northward expansion and of the exploitation both of human and natural resources. The tendency to see Tokugawa Japan as self-contained and non-expansionist is largely a product of a projection of Japan's contemporary national boundaries back onto the past, obscuring the story of the eighteenth- and early nineteenth-century Japanese state's economic encroachments both to the south and to the north. What comes to the fore when we look at the history of the Okhotsk, rather, is a striking picture of the drastic destruction of small-scale knowledge systems as the borders of Japanese state power moved northwards and those of Russian state power moved eastwards from the late eighteenth century onwards. Japan was able to maintain its high population density despite limited trade with other nation-states partly because it was able to exploit the resources of Ezo – particularly the region's rich fish resources, which were converted to fertiliser and used to enrich the soil for Japanese rice agriculture.

The very success and material might of the centralised and globalised knowledge system that took shape from the sixteenth century onward allowed it to subordinate and displace a multitude of small-scale knowledge systems around the world. Although (as we shall see) this did not necessarily mean that the ideas and traditions generated by such systems disappeared altogether, it did profoundly erode their integrity and autonomy. Some of the consequences of this process are now all too apparent as we face the challenge of anthropogenic climate change. It is, of course, a profound irony that the globalised system of modern science and technology, which unleashed the forces that create climate change, also plays an essential role in providing the scientific tools that allow us to track and predict global warming. But the centralised knowledge system that is so effective in calculating aggregate patterns of climate change is notoriously bad at predicting the impacts that these patterns will have on specific local environments and their inhabitants (including their vast diversity of animal and plant inhabitants). The complexity of the way that global trends like climate change play out in specific places demands the kind of intricate local knowledge of geology, weather, living creatures and their interactions in which small-scale knowledge systems like those of the Okhotsk excelled. But much of that knowledge has now been lost or deliberately destroyed; and we have also lost the flexibility and adaptability that was created by the existence of the wide diversity of distinct but interrelated social forms and systems of knowledge and subsistence.

This is not to suggest, of course, that we can find a solution to contemporary global problems in nostalgia for indigenous pasts, or in attempting to recreate long-vanished social systems. We are now, to varying degrees, all embedded in a centralised global knowledge system, and must find our way out of our present predicaments from within that system. But an attempt to understand the diversity of, and interaction between, the knowledge systems of the past may help us at least to glimpse what Julia Thomas calls 'multiple viable ways of life' – the many possibilities that exist within the human historical experience.[73] One important part of this discovery of the history of interaction between diverse knowledge systems is an exploration of the way in which small-scale knowledge systems like those of the Okhotsk responded to the overwhelming arrival of a globalised order armed with science, modern weaponry and an unshakable faith in its own civilisational superiority. In fact, despite great inequalities of material and military power, the outcome of the interaction between global and national knowledge systems (on the one hand) and the local systems of colonised small societies (on the other) proved complex. It is true that in some places existing small societies were totally destroyed by the processes of world expansion, and that everywhere their ways of life were changed forever. In some cases, though, the interaction produced more subtle and surprising results. In the three chapters that follow, we shall examine some aspects of this interaction and its historical legacies.

---

73 Thomas, 'History and Biology', p. 1606.

5

THE TELESCOPE AND THE TINDERBOX: REDISCOVERING LA PÉROUSE IN THE NORTH PACIFIC

It was late on a summer's day, and the wind had dropped, when the two ships entered the bay. They remained quite still, some distance offshore from the place where the river flowed into the sea. The villagers of Tomarioro had seen foreign vessels, of course. The canoes of the mainland people whom they knew as Sandā were regular visitors: one had arrived just a few days earlier.[1] The junks of Sisam (Japanese) from the south occasionally sailed close to the shore, and there were darker stories of other, unknown visitors who came from the north and west.[2] But these two ships were unlike anything they had seen before.

---

1   Except where otherwise indicated, the details in this account (including the presence of the Sandā canoe) are derived from Jean-François de Galaup de La Pérouse, *The Journal of Jean-François de Galaup de La Pérouse*, trans. and ed. John Dunmore, vol. 2 (London: The Hakluyt Society, 1995), pp. 286–95; 'Sandā' or 'Santa' was the Ainu word used to refer to traders from the Amur river region; see Kojima Kyōko, '18, 19 Seiki ni Okeru Karafuto no Jūmin: "Santan" o Megutte', in *Minzoku Sesshoku: Kita no shiten kara*, ed. Hoppō Gengo Bunka Kenkyūkai (Tokyo: Rokkō Shuppan, 1989), pp. 31–47, particularly p. 35.
2   On Manchu officials and other visitors to the west coast of Sakhalin, see Mamiya Rinzō, 'Kita Ezo Zusetsu or a Description of the Island of Northern Yezo by Mamiya Rinsō', trans. John A Harrison, *Proceedings of the American Philosophical Society* 99, no. 2 (1955): pp. 93–117, particularly pp. 116–17, original published in 1855; Mogami Tokunai, 'Ezo Sōshi Gohen', in *Ezo Sōshi*, by Mogami Tokunai, ed. Yoshida Tsunekichi (Tokyo: Jiji Tsūshinsha, 1965), pp. 189–90.

One by one, small boats crossed the water between the two ships and the shore, and by the time the villagers had returned from fishing, a group of strangers had gathered on the beach. They spoke a language that no one understood, but they seemed harmless, and left gifts of axes, pieces of metal, beads and cloth at the entrance to one of the village houses. The next morning, the ships were still there, and the strangers came back to the shore. As though performing magic, out of their bags they produced a seemingly endless stream of objects: lumps of precious metal; pieces of cotton and silk; coloured glass rings; red, white and yellow feathers; flasks of vile-smelling liquid ...[3] Once again, they set out their gifts and began to speak in their unknown language. All the men of Tomarioro gathered round, and tried to help the visitors by pointing out different objects – boat, house, sun, and so on – and saying the word for each object. The strangers appeared to understand, for they took out paper and writing implements and tried to write each word down.

Then, through pointing and sign language, they gestured that they wanted to go to land of the Manchus: a promising sign that, having left their gifts, they would soon sail away. One of the *henke* (elders) drew a map for them on the sand, showing the coastline and the way to the mouth of the Segalien River. The strangers recognised the name of the river, and were delighted by the map, but by now the tide was coming in and washing away the traces on the sand, so a young man took a piece of paper from the visitors and drew the map for them again, using sign language to add information about the distance to each stopping point and the depth of the sea along the coast.[4]

The strangers remained all day, poking and staring at everything, and always making notes on paper, but they did no serious damage. There were just a few worrying moments when one of them produced some strange instruments and tried to press them against the body of an *henke*, to measure the size of his torso. The *henke* recoiled, gesturing his refusal with his hands, and the stranger understood and put the instruments away.

---

3   See 'Catalogue of Goods and Merchandize Put on Board the Vessels Under the Order of Mr. de la Pérouse , for the Purpose of Barter and Making Presents', in Jean-François de Galaup de La Pérouse, *A Voyage Round the World Performed in the Years 1785, 1786, 1787 and 1788 by the Boussole and the Astrolabe*, vol. 1, 1969 reprint (Amsterdam: N. Israel; New York: Da Capo Press, 1969), pp. 182–86, doi.org/10.1017/cbo9781139056519.004; also La Pérouse, *Journal*, p. 294.

4   La Pérouse, *Journal*, pp. 289–91.

Next morning, soon after dawn, the two strange ships sailed out of the bay and were never seen again. But after that, foreign ships came more frequently, some from the south and some from the west. The Sisam started to build houses on the shore and catch fish in vast nets, and then the Nuća (Russians) came with cows and pigs, cutting the forests and killing the dogs that were the Tomarioro villagers' most precious possessions.[5] The people of the villages up and down the coast began to fall ill and die of strange diseases. The landscape changed, and language with it. The villagers of Tomarioro became Russian, and then Japanese. Four generations on, their descendants no longer remembered the two tall ships and strangers with their bazaar of gifts. All they remembered were the dark stories of dangerous white-skinned people who had hideous faces and held their heads in a strange way.[6] Then a huge Japanese pulp mill was built on the banks of the river, polluting the waters of Tomarioro Bay; and then the Russians came back again …

Today, the descendants of the Tomarioro villagers, if any survive, are far away in Hokkaido. There are few, if any, Ainu/Enchiw[7] left in the little Russian town of Tomari today.[8]

The Floating Enlightenment

The story I have just retold is a famous one: it is the tale of the arrival in July 1787 of French explorer Jean-François de Galaup de La Pérouse and his two ships, the *Boussole* and the *Astrolabe* on the shores of the island of Sakhalin, at the place that La Pérouse named De Langle Bay. This is a story that has been recounted in many ways, for there is something strangely compelling about narrative of the La Pérouse voyage.

---

5   See Alfred F Madjewicz, ed., *The Collected Works of Bronislaw Piłsudski*, vol. 3, *Materials for the Study of the Ainu Language and Folklore 2* (Berlin: Mouton de Gruyter, 2004), p. 214.
6   Bronislaw Piłsudski, who investigated the story in the first years of the twentieth century, wrote: 'I knew of the Sakhalin visits of La Pérouse and Khruzenstern, and kept enquiring about them with many elderly Ainu. Nobody, however, was in a position to quote descriptions of just those encounters. Remembered were certain hostile encounters probably with some seamen from Kamchatka who touched the Sakhalin shores, and tales about them later assumed the shape of obscure legends about terrifying men with ugly faces and a strange, non-Ainu, way of carrying one's head.' See Madjewicz, *Collected Works of Bronislaw Piłsudski*, p. 227.
7   Sakhalin Ainu used both the 'Ainu' and the word 'Enchiw' to describe themselves. The descendants of Sakhalin Ainu living in Japan today generally use the word Enchiw as their preferred term.
8   See, for example, Tjeerd de Graaf, 'The Ethnolinguistic Situation on the Island of Sakhalin', in *Ethnic Minorities in Sakhalin*, ed. Kyoko Murasaki (Yokohama: Yokohama Kokuritsu Daigaku Education Department, 1993), pp. 13–29, particularly p. 15.

Not simply a European journey in search of the contours of distant lands, the expedition was a floating pageant of the Enlightenment. La Pérouse's crew set off around the world with their ships filled to the gunwales with the latest scientific instruments and learned texts. They had three types of telescope, hydrometers, aerometers, mathematical instruments, 'a great number of barometers, thermometers, and hygrometers, of different kinds, for various experiments', a reverberatory furnace, a portable mineralogical chest and veritable cocktail cabinet of chemicals, as well as an extraordinary emporium of gifts, which could be used to assess the cultural inclinations of the various 'natives' they met along the way.[9] Tracing this seaborne microcosm of Enlightenment Europe as it tracked its way slowly across the Atlantic, round Cape Horn, to Alaska and California, to Macao, Manila, Sakhalin, Kamchatka, Samoa, Australia, and then into oblivion, we can observe the sparks generated as it reacted with a multitude of differing societies along the route.

Figure 5.1. The *Astrolabe* and *Boussole* at anchor off the island of Maui.
Source: Wikimedia commons, public domain.

---

9   'Summary of the Instruments of Astronomy, Navigation, Natural Philosophy, Chemistry, etc. etc. for the Use of the Men of Science and Artists Employed in the Voyage of Discovery', in La Pérouse, *Voyage*, pp. 182–86.

Figure 5.2. People of Tomarioro as seen by La Pérouse's expedition.
Source: Illustration by Gaspard de Vancy and LJ Cathelin from Jean-François de Galaup de La Pérouse, *Atlas du Voyage de La Pérouse autour du Monde* (Paris: 1797).

The mystery and tragedy of its ending makes the story more compelling still. The ships sailed into the unknown, and it took more than two centuries to unravel the details of their fate. The voyage ended in shipwreck in the South Pacific, the marvels of Enlightenment science scattered like broken toys across Vanikoro reef. The men who had set off to probe the mysteries of global geography and humanity spent their final months and years struggling unsuccessfully for bare physical survival, overwhelmed by the forces of alien culture and nature.[10]

But it is the moments of direct encounter in their journey to the Pacific that particularly stir the imagination: those moments when an islander of Sakhalin or Hawai'i looks into the eyes of a man from France, and each wonders if he can trust the other. In recent years, the meeting on the beach between La Pérouse and the people of 'De Langle Bay' (Tomarioro) – where the native elder drew a map of the region on the sand, and the younger man then copied it onto paper for the explorers – has in particular been read as an encounter replete with the meaning of Enlightenment knowledge. For sociologist of science Bruno Latour, this coming together of native map-maker and European cartographer provides the key to explaining what is distinctive about modern science.

10   John Dunmore, *Where Fate Beckons: The Life of Jean-François de Galaup de la Pérouse* (Sydney: ABC Books, 2006), pp. 259–64.

Latour acknowledges the mapping skills of the De Langle Bay natives (whom he describes, with a surprisingly cavalier approach to geography and ethnography, as 'Chinese'). There is nothing in the mapping itself, he suggests, to separate the Sakhalin 'Chinese' from the European explorer. What differentiates them is the fact that the explorers form part of a network of Enlightenment knowledge, in which geographical, biological, mechanical and other know-how can all be represented on paper in schematic form. These schematic representations – charts, diagrams, architectural and mechanical blueprints, and so on – are mobile: they can be taken anywhere. Because they are standardised, they can be compared, superimposed and combined. The French expedition can turn knowledge acquired from the local people into mobile inscriptions to be brought back to the European centre, adding to the growing store of Western scientific knowledge, and thus of Western power.[11]

In Latour's telling of the story, the 'bringing back' is crucial.

> The Chinese have lived here as long as one can remember whereas the French fleet remains with them for a day. These families of Chinese, as far as one can tell, will remain around for years, maybe centuries; *L'Astrolabe* and *La Boussole* have to reach Russia before the end of summer.[12]

The explorers' haste reflects the fact that they are 'not so much interested in this place as they are in bringing this place *back*, first to their ship and then to Versailles'.[13] The visual inscriptions of Enlightenment science are mobile, whereas the things they inscribe – 'Chinese, planets, microbes' – are not.[14] 'Bringing back' is the key that turns knowledge into power. In a process that mirrors the accumulation of capital in the metropolises of Europe, this results in a steady accumulation of knowledge at the centre – one map superimposed upon another until the whole globe is known. So the European explorers, who on the first voyage are weak and at the

---

11   Bruno Latour, *Science in Action: How to Follow Scientists and Engineers Through Society* (Cambridge, Mass.: Harvard University Press, 1987), ch. 6; Bruno Latour, 'Visualization and Cognition: Drawing Things Together', in *Knowledge and Society: Studies in the Sociology of Culture Past and Present*, ed. Henricka Kuklick and Elizabeth Long, vol. 6 (Greenwich, CT: JAI Press, 1986), pp. 1–40.
12   Latour, *Science in Action*, p. 217.
13   Latour, *Science in Action*, p. 217.
14   Latour, 'Visualization and Cognition', p. 18.

mercy of the native, gradually become strong, and the cartographer who remains fixed in the centre of the Enlightenment world, reading and studying the maps, becomes the most powerful of all.[15]

Latour views the scene on the beach at Tomarioro as through a telescope from the metropolis. Indeed, his depiction of the 'Chinese' islanders is more distant and exoticised than La Pérouse's own account. (La Pérouse distinguishes the Tomarioro villagers from Chinese, and makes clear that they are linked into their own networks of trade and travel.) Michael Bravo, drawing on but revising Latour, retells the story of La Pérouse and the Tomarioro map-makers in ethnographic terms and 'from the perspective of the field encounter'.[16] Rather than isolating the map-drawing episode, Bravo places it in the broader context of La Pérouse's circuitous journey round the Amur-Okhotsk region – the region from the north-eastern stretch of the Asian mainland in the west, to the shores of Sakhalin, past the north of Hokkaido, and to the Kurile archipelago, and the Kamchatka Peninsula in the east. It is only by looking in detail at the dynamics of various encounters along the route, Bravo suggests, that we can understand how knowledge is 'displaced' from the local informant to the explorer, and how 'enlightened navigators impose or distill time and space in the course of their encounters'.[17]

In this retelling of the narrative, La Pérouse does not arrive with fully formed scientific constructs for understanding the world already charted in his brain. His expedition's ethnographic classifications emerge only from a gradual process of description and comparison – a tentative generation of categories and boundaries. A key element in this 'ethnographic navigation' is the 'geographic gift'.[18] The process of creating ethnographic knowledge begins with the giving of gifts to the locals – an act designed to evoke words of response from the 'native'. This opens the way to a search for forms of commensurable language, which in turn will make it possible for the explorers to gather the elements that enable them to draw ethnographic comparisons and boundaries.

---

15   Latour, *Science in Action*, pp. 219–24.
16   Michael Bravo, 'Ethnographic Navigation and the Geographical Gift', in *Geography and Enlightenment*, ed. David N Livingston and Charles WJ Withers (Chicago: University of Chicago Press, 1999), pp. 199–235, quotation from p. 205.
17   Bravo, 'Ethnographic Navigation', p. 203.
18   Bravo, 'Ethnographic Navigation', p. 204.

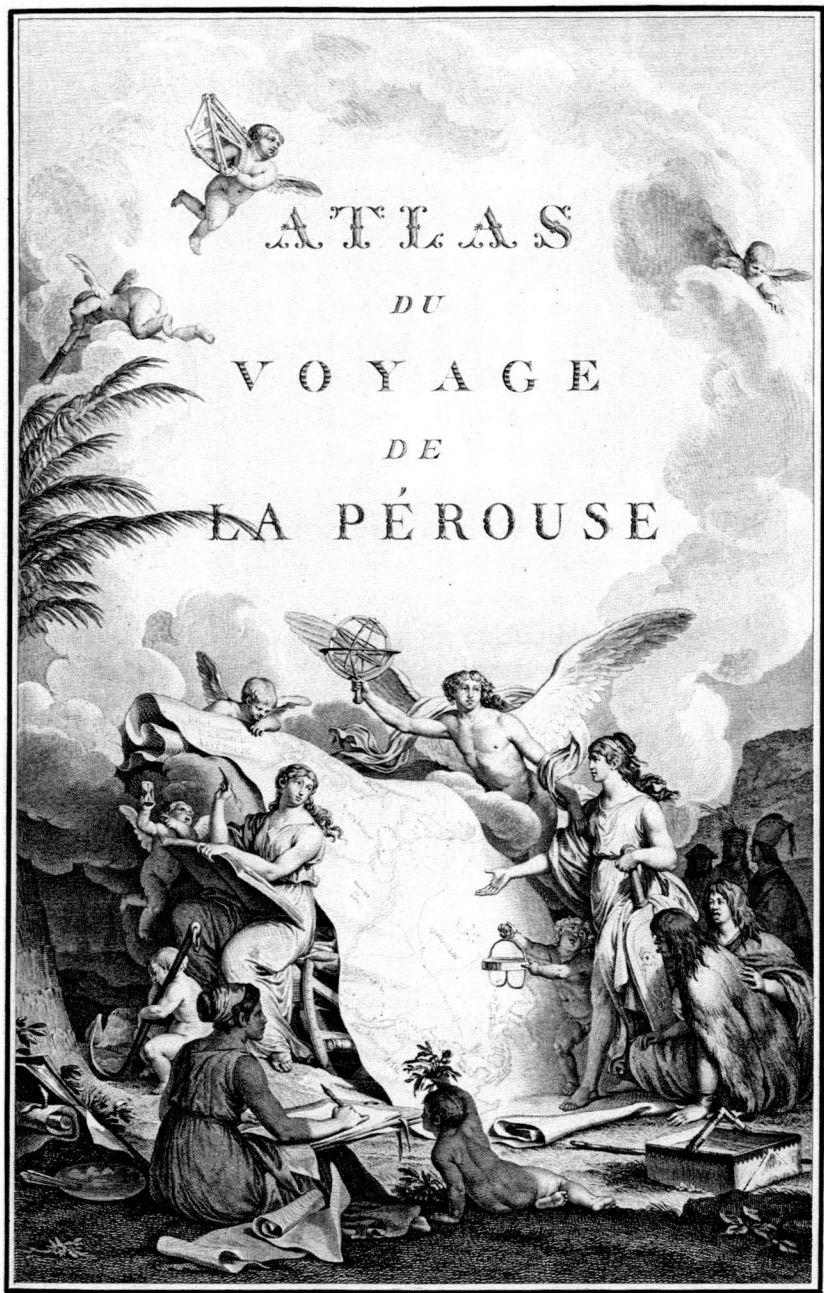

Figure 5.3. Frontispiece from La Pérouse's atlas.

Source: Image by JM Moreau and P Trière, from Jean-François de Galaup de La Pérouse, *Atlas du Voyage de La Pérouse autour du Monde* (Paris: 1797).

Bravo's view from 'the field' is more nuanced and less schematic than Latour's telescopic view from the metropolis. It recognises the complex interactions between the Tomarioro villagers and other neighbouring societies, including those of the Amur region and Japan. Bravo correctly identifies the villagers as Ainu rather than as 'Chinese', and reminds us that we should not 'ignore the importance of trade, travel and migration in their ways of life'.[19] His account, though, conveys some misconceptions of its own. He identifies the 'Orotchy' people of the place La Pérouse named 'De Castries Bay' with the reindeer-herding Uilta people of Sakhalin (known to their neighbours as 'Orok'), and he draws conclusions about the Orotchy way of life based on observations of the Uilta relationship with reindeer. But the people whom La Pérouse called Orotchy were clearly a different group from the Sakhalin Uilta, and did not herd reindeer. Bravo also depicts the Ainu communities that La Pérouse visited as being subject to a mixture of government assimilationism and merchant exploitation from Japan, but this is anachronistic.[20] At the time of La Pérouse's arrival, the creeping spread of Japanese mercantile and fishing interests had barely reached the areas that he visited. Though officials and fishermen from Matsumae Domain, and even officials of the Japanese shogunate, had travelled to Sakhalin, the first permanent Japanese fishing base, in the village of Shiranushi at the far south of the island, was not established until 1790.[21]

What is particularly fascinating about La Pérouse's account, indeed, is the fact that it captures a glimpse of western Sakhalin and the Lower Amur on the eve of momentous historical change. In 1787, Russian and Japanese nation/empire-building was seeping into the region from north and south like a relentlessly rising tide, but there was still a space between, in which multiple connections among the newly arriving powers and longer established communities were being forged. This space between allowed room for the presence of the Chinese empire, whose force continued to be faintly felt on the western shores of Sakhalin as late as the 1780s, but which was soon to be driven out of the Amur-Okhotsk region.

---

19   Bravo, 'Ethnographic Navigation', p. 207.
20   Bravo, 'Ethnographic Navigation', pp. 208–09.
21   See Hora Tomio, *Karafuto shi Kenkyū: Karafuto to Santan* (Tokyo: Shinjusha, 1956), p. 66; Akizuki Toshiyuki, *Nichirō Kankei to Saharintō: Bakumatsu Meiji Shoki no Ryōdo Mondai* (Tokyo: Chikuma Shobō, 1994), p. 36; on Japanese settlement in Karafuto, see also David L Howell, *Capitalism from Within: Economy, Society and the State in a Japanese Fishery* (Berkeley and London: University of California Press, 1995), pp. 40–41.

Latour's and Bravo's interpretations of La Pérouse's visit to Sakhalin and the Amur have been widely cited by other scholars,[22] and it is important both to acknowledge the value of their visions of the knowledge-creating process, and to address the inaccuracies of detail that their accounts perpetuate. But the more important point is that the perspective from the metropolis and the perspective from the field leave one crucial perspective still invisible: the perspective from the region explored by La Pérouse, seen not as a 'field of enquiry' but as a place in its own right – a place with its own past, present and future. I am not, of course, suggesting that we can actually find out exactly how the Ainu of Tomarioro and other Sakhalin villages saw the arrival of La Pérouse's ships. The account with which I began this chapter is obviously an act of imagination, though one based as closely as possible on the written record. But what I do want to suggest is that traces in written and other records provide a wealth of information on the history of this region in the 1780s, including some elusive but intriguing glimpses of indigenous perspectives on the coming of Europeans; and if we see La Pérouse's voyage as an event in that regional history, as well as an event in the history of the European Enlightenment, several neglected but significant dimensions of the formation of modern knowledge become visible.

The view from the region allows us to compare diverse but roughly contemporary descriptions of the same place. This in turn enables us to develop an imbricated history of the interactions between diverse groups, which in turn sheds some important light on the processes of communication and miscommunication between Enlightenment explorers and local people. Looking at La Pérouse's voyage within the context of the late eighteenth-century history of the Amur-Okhotsk region makes it easier to see the source of one of the explorer's most significant cartographical mistakes – and understanding processes of miscommunication and the making of scientific mistakes is, I shall argue, as important as (indeed, an inseparable part of) understanding processes

22 Works which cite both Latour's and Bravo's versions of the map drawing story include: David N Livingstone, *Putting Science in its Place: Geographies of Scientific Knowledge* (Chicago: University of Chicago Press, 2003); Brett L Walker, 'Mamiya Rinzō and the Japanese Exploration of Sakhalin Island: Geography and Empire', *Journal of Historical Geography* 33, no. 2 (2007): pp. 283–313, doi.org/ 10.1016/j.jhg.2006.05.007; James Delbourgo and Nicholas Dew, 'Introduction: The Far Side of the Ocean', in *Science and Empire in the Atlantic World*, ed. James Delbourgo and Nicholas Dew (London and New York: Routledge, 2008), pp. 1–28; Simon Schaffer, 'The Asiatic Enlightenments of British Astronomy', in *Brokered Worlds: Go-Betweens and Global Intelligence, 1770–1820*, ed. Simon Schaffer, Lissa Roberts, Kapil Raj and James Delbourgo (Sagamore Beach: Science History Publications, 2009), pp. 49–104.

of communication and the discovery of scientific truth. A perspective from the region also reminds us that European explorers were not only observers but also observed. This complicates our perception of the flows of information that generated the modern knowledge system. When we probe the multidirectional, overlapping flows of knowledge about 'alien' people and places that intersected in the Amur-Okhotsk region in the eighteenth century, it becomes more difficult to accept simple visions of a scientific circuit that endlessly sucks global knowledge into the academies and laboratories of enlightened Europe. Instead, the creation of modern cartographic and ethnographic knowledge of the world begins to look more untidy and multipolar, and the relationship between science and empire more random, contingent and violent.

From the Amur to the Okhotsk: Retracing La Pérouse's Route

Let us begin, then, by retracing the course of the *Astrolabe* and the *Boussole* through the northern Pacific between July and August 1787, placing their journey more firmly in the historical landscape of the region itself. The two ships arrived from the south: they had left Manila in April, and sailed past the Ryukyu Kingdom (now known as Okinawa) and the west coast of Japan and Hokkaido, before arriving in the Tartar Strait in July. Off the southern islands of the Ryukyus, La Pérouse observed the local people in boats, labelled them 'Kumi' and depicted them as a group intermediate to the Japanese and Chinese; a rather astute observation, as the Ryukyu Kingdom was at that time semi-independent, but paid tribute both to the Chinese empire and (via the Domain of Satsuma) to Japan.

La Pérouse did not attempt to land on the coast of Japan. Advisedly, he was much more afraid of the Japanese than of the small societies to their north, since the Japanese shogunate exerted very tight control on the arrival of foreign vessels, and an unauthorised landing might have been severely punished. For the same reason, he was wary of landing on the shores of Hokkaido (referred to in La Pérouse's journal as Yeso). His first landfall in the region was at the place he named De Langle Bay, after the captain of the *Astrolabe*. From the coordinates given by La Pérouse and later travellers, we can identify this as the Ainu village of Tomarioro, which, appropriately enough, meant 'anchorage' or 'place for stopping boats'.[23] Tomarioro was a relatively small village, less significant in the life of the region than settlements like Nayoro, some 10 miles to the north, or Ushiyoro, which La Pérouse later visited and named D'Estin Bay. The Ainu of Tomarioro and surrounding areas fished, gathered food plants and hunted for various animals in the nearby forests, and kept dogs (who assisted with hunting and fishing, pulled boats and sleds). La Pérouse noticed signs of trade between the village and the Asian mainland, including the presence of two visitors from the mainland, who had (he guessed) come to buy fish.

In fact, the coastal villages of Sakhalin were engaged in a complex web of trade routes that spread in many directions. Ainu from Hokkaido sometimes travelled to Sakhalin, and the Nivkh and Uilta people who lived in the north and east of the island traded with the Ainu who lived in the south. Members of the various mainland communities who lived along the lower reaches of the Amur (and whom the Ainu collectively referred to as 'Sandā' or 'Santa' and the Japanese as 'Santan') travelled to Sakhalin to trade furs for goods that reached the region both from Japan in the south and China in the west. Chinese brocades were traded via the Amur to the Ainu of Sakhalin and Hokkaido, and some even reached the metropolitan centres of Japan, where they were known as 'Ezo brocade' (*Ezo nishiki*). Nivkh populations lived not only in northern Sakhalin but also on the Lower Amur, and regularly travelled back and forth between mainland and island. Ainu from Sakhalin also travelled to the mainland and down the Amur to the Manchu trading post of Deren.[24] This helps to explain the ease with which the Tomarioro villagers were able to draw maps of the western Sakhalin coast and the Amur (Segalien) River for La Pérouse and his crew.

23   On the location of De Langle Bay, see also EG Ravenstein, *The Russians on the Amur* (London: Trübner and Co., 1861), p. 269. La Pérouse's measurements of longitude in the Amur-Okhotsk region are known to have been inaccurate by about 1 degree, but his measurements of latitude were generally accurate; see La Pérouse, *Journal*, p. 305.
24   For further discussion, see Tessa Morris-Suzuki, *Henkyō kara Nagameru: Ainu ga Keiken suru Kindai* (Tokyo: Misuzu Shobō, 2001); see also Hokkaidō Kaitaku Kinenkan, ed., *Santan Kōeki to Ezo Nishiki* (Sapporo: Hokkaidō Kaitaku Kinenkan, 1996); Hora Tomio, *Karafuto shi Kenkyū*; Kojima, '18, 19 Seiki ni Okeru Karafuto no Jūmin'.

Figure 5.4. Tsukinoe, an Ainu elder from Kunashir, wearing a brocade robe, painting by Kakizaki Hakyo.

Source: Wikimedia commons, public domain.

La Pérouse arrived in Sakhalin at a time when two other groups of people were also becoming increasingly visible in the Amur-Okhosk region. The Russian empire by now extended as far as the Kamchatka Peninsula and the northern Kurile Islands, but Russian settlement had not yet expanded to the mouth of the Amur or Sakhalin, though some Cossack adventurers had reached these regions in the seventeenth century.[25] By the end of the eighteenth century, Imperial Russia was interested in commercial and strategic expansion to the east, and a series of expeditions were sent to Amur-Okhotsk. In 1791, Adam Laxman was commissioned to return two Japanese castaways to their homeland, and at the same time observed and brought back reports on Japan and Hokkaido to St Petersburg; 13 years later, Russian Admiral Adam von Krusenstern also visited Hokkaido and Sakhalin during his circumnavigation of the globe. Krusenstern borrowed much preliminary geographical knowledge from La Pérouse, but sought to revise and expand that knowledge with his own observations. Because he made contact with Japanese in northern Hokkaido and southern Sakhalin, and had an interpreter who spoke some Japanese, Krusenstern could identify the mountain peak off northern Hokkaido that La Pérouse had named De Langle Peak by its Japanised Ainu name, Rishiri (Krusenstern calls it 'Rii-schery').[26] In 1811, Russian navigator and cartographer Vasily Golovnin also arrived on Kunashir Island to map the southern Kurile and the northern coast of Hokkaido, but was captured by the Japanese and held as a prisoner for two years before being returned to Russia. The local inhabitants played an important role as intermediaries in these interactions between Russia and Japan. For example, when Golovnin first arrived on the island of Iturup in the southern Kuriles, he was able to gather substantial amounts of information from Ainu who came from the northern Kuriles and could speak Russian. One of them served as an interpreter in Golovnin's discussions with the Japanese officials he encountered on Iturup, translating Russian into Ainu, which was then retranslated into Japanese by one of the locally based Japanese officials.[27]

---

25   See, for example, GP Muller, *Voyages et Découvertes Faites par les Russes le Long des Côtes de la Mer Glaciale et sur l'Ocean Oriental, tant vers le Japon que vers l'Amerique*, trans. CGF Dumas, vol. 1 (Amsterdam: Marc-Michel Rey, 1766).

26   AJ von Krusenstern, *Voyage Round the World in the Years 1803, 1804, 1805 and 1806*, vol. 2 (London: John Murray, 1813), p. 48.

27   VM Golownin, *Memoirs of a Captivity in Japan*, ed. J McMaster, vol. 1 (Oxford: Oxford University Press, 1973). Here I have used the standard modern transliteration of Golovnin's name; see also Watanabe Kyōji, *Kurofune Zenya: Roshia, Ainu, Nihon no Sangokushi* (Tokyo: Yōsensha, 2010), pp. 292–93.

Meanwhile, both the Japanese shogunate and Matsumae Domain were becoming increasingly aware of the presence of foreigners ('Red Ezo', as they were known, after the colour of their hair – *Furesisam* in Ainu) on the northern fringes of Japan. In the early 1780s, Kudō Heisuke, a Japanese doctor and scholar of Western learning had discovered, via information that trickled into Japan through the Dutch trading post in Nagasaki, that these foreigners were the people known as Russians, who belonged to a large empire stretching from Europe to Kamchatka. This prompted the shogunate to dispatch five officials to the northern regions in 1785, to learn more about its inhabitants and particularly to discover the extent of foreign incursions.[28] In the search for knowledge about Russians and other 'Red Ezo', Japanese explorers relied heavily on information from the indigenous people, particularly from the Ainu of the Kurile archipelago, who frequently encountered Russian settlers on Kamchatka and on the northern islands of the archipelago. The lords of Matsumae had sent officials to survey the south of Sakhalin as early as the 1630s, but the decades from the 1780s on were a time of particularly active Japanese exploration of the region. Scholar-officials Ōishi Ippei and Mogami Tokunai were sent to explore the Kurile Islands and Sakhalin in 1786, and Mogami made many subsequent visits to the region. Nakamura Shōshirō and Takahashi Jidayū were sent to Sakhalin in 1801 to find out more about the island and its connections to the lands beyond. In 1808 Mamiya Rinzō and Matsuda Denjūrō made an extensive survey of the coast of Sakhalin, and the following year Mamiya travelled via Sakhalin to the Asian mainland and as far as the Amur trading post of Deren.[29]

French, Russian and Japanese explorers shared a number of common objectives. As Brett Walker observes, Japanese officials like Mamiya Rinzō and Matsuda Denjūrō saw Sakhalin with 'cartographic' and 'imperial' eyes. Mamiya in particular compiled intricate accounts of the indigenous peoples in which, like La Pérouse, he used careful description and comparison in an effort to define ethnic boundaries.[30] But there are also some significant differences between the European and Japanese explorers, so their diverse but overlapping accounts of Sakhalin and the

28   Yoshida Tsunekichi, 'Kaisetsu', in Mogami, *Ezo Sōshi*, p. 269; see also Robert Liss, 'Frontier Tales: Tokugawa Japan in Translation', in Schaffer et al., *Brokered World*, pp. 1–47, reference from pp. 37–38.
29   See Mogami, *Ezo Sōshi*; Nakamura Shōshirō, 'Karafuto zakki', reprinted in *Saisenkai Shiryō*, ed. Takakura Shinichirō (Sapporo: Hokkaidō Shuppan Kikaku Sentā, 1982), pp. 599–650; Mamiya, 'Kita Ezo Zusetsu'; Walker, 'Mamiya Rinzō and the Japanese Exploration of Sakhalin Island'.
30   Walker, 'Mamiya Rinzō and the Japanese Exploration of Sakhalin Island', p. 299.

Amur region offer some fascinatingly complementary images. La Pérouse arrived in large ships, with very little prior knowledge of the region. His first task was to find a safe place of anchorage, and this determined where he made landfall. Like most Western explorers of the day, he named natural features – bays, mountains, headlands – on his maps. Villages, although marked on the maps, are not given names. With rare exceptions, communication was conducted by sign language.

Conversely, Japanese explorers of Sakhalin in the same period travelled, usually in small boats, with Japanese-speaking Ainu or Nivkh guides and interpreters who led them from one village to the next. Their travel accounts are generally litanies of the names of villages, often including estimates of the distance between them. From their accounts we know that Tomarioro was a relatively small place – it is mentioned but rarely described in detail. By contrast, Nayoro, a little further north, was larger and also more politically significant. At some time around the middle of the eighteenth century, apparently after a conflict between locals and visitors from the mainland, two sons of a Nayoro Ainu elder had been captured by Manchus and taken to the mainland, where they lived for several years. Eventually they were allowed to return, and one was given an official Manchu document appointing him to the position of *hala i da* or clan headman – the only Sakhalin islander to be awarded this rank. When Mogami Tokunai and Mamiya Rinzō visited Sakhalin, the position had passed to Yayenkur, a son of the original *hala i da*.[31]

After leaving Tomarioro, La Pérouse sailed up the west coast of Sakhalin until he reached another good anchorage, which he named D'Estin Bay. His description and measurements of latitude indicate that this was the Ainu village of Ushiyoro (or Ushoro), a larger settlement that also had close links to the mainland. Two of its villagers, Senbakur and Ikonaranke, had been given the Manchu title of *gasan da* or village chief (the rank below *hala i da*).[32] When La Pérouse arrived, he found a large canoe from the mainland just leaving after a trading visit. In Ushiyoro, Fleuriot de Langle, the captain of the *Astrolabe*, also described stakes surmounted by bears' heads – signs of the bear ceremony or *iyomante*, which was a vital element of the spiritual practice of Ainu, Nivkh and other indigenous groups of the region.[33]

---

31   See Mamiya, 'Kita Ezo Zusetsu', pp. 116–17; Mogami, 'Ezo Sōshi Gohen', pp. 189–90.
32   Mamiya, 'Kita Ezo Zusetsu', p. 117.
33   La Pérouse, *Journal*, pp. 295–97.

From Ushiyoro, the French expedition continued northwards, trying to determine whether there was indeed (as the Tomarioro elder had indicated) a navigable passage separating the entire length of Sakhalin Island from the Asian mainland. But the weather was worsening, and their depth soundings revealed the presence of dangerous shoals. At last, with evident disappointment, they were forced to turn back, and anchored in a bay to the south of the mouth of the Amur River, which they named De Castries Bay (now known as Kastri Bay). Here they found a village of people who, according to La Pérouse, called themselves 'Orotchys', and a boat with traders whom the 'Orotchys' called 'Bitchys, a name indicating that these people came from further south'.[34] La Pérouse describes the Orotchy as living by the coast for salmon fishing in the summer, but also having inland underground houses which they used during the winter months.

The area stretching southward from the mouth of the Amur was inhabited by a complex mixture of peoples, including the groups now known to ethnographers as Nivkh, Ul'chi, Nanai and Oroch. As the eminent Russian scholar Lev Shternberg was to discover in the late nineteenth century, attaching appropriate ethnic labels to these groups was a very difficult process. The Nivkh were relatively easy to identify, because they spoke a language quite distinct from that of other groups; but the groups now known as Ul'chi, Nanai and Oroch, as well as the Uilta of Sakhalin and a number of other Eastern Siberian groups, all spoke languages belonging to the so-called 'Tungusic' language family. As a result, the word that they used amongst themselves to designate their own group was more or less identical – 'Nani' (or a close variant), meaning 'people'. Each group also had a variety of terms that they used when describing their own group to outsiders, and when referring to neighbouring groups. It seems most likely that the people whom La Pérouse met belonged to the fishing and hunting group whom Shternberg calls the 'Oroch' or 'Southeastern Nani': when speaking amongst themselves they referred to themselves as 'Nani' or 'Nane', but when speaking to Russians (says Shternberg) they called themselves 'Orocha' or 'Orochon'. The term 'Bitchy' is probably Le Pérouse's rendering of the place name 'Botchy', which, according to Shternberg, was a village on the borderline between the regions of the northern and southern clans that constituted the Oroch/ Southeastern Nani.[35]

---

34 La Pérouse, *Journal*, p. 306.
35 L Ya Shternberg, *Gilyaki, Orochi, Gol'diy Negidal'tsiy, Ainy* (Moscow: Nauka reprint, 1991), pp. 6–9.

At that time, as La Pérouse's account indicates, the Oroch people were an integral part of the complex trade networks that linked the Amur-Okhotsk region via Manchuria to the Chinese empire:

> grain was their most precious food; they told us that it came from the country of the Manchus and we verified that they gave this name only to the people who live seven or eight days' journey upriver on the Segalien and have direct contact with the Chinese.[36]

From the mid-nineteenth century on, though, their lives were to be drastically changed by Russian colonisation. (The 2010 Russian census gives a present-day Oroch population of just under 600 people.)[37] From conversations with the inhabitants of De Castries Bay, La Pérouse received what he thought was confirmation of the fact that the Tartar Straits to the north were impassable, because they were blocked by a shallow sandbank, thus justifying his decision to abandon the attempt to travel further north.[38]

Leaving De Castries Bay, the expedition returned to Sakhalin, and anchored on the west coast of its southern tip, which La Pérouse named Cape Crillon. The expedition's measurements of latitude suggest that their stopping point was just north of the Ainu village and port of Shiranushi (close to the spot on Sakhalin where the Dutch vessels *Castricum* and *Breskens* had landed over 140 years earlier). La Pérouse himself did not go ashore here, though he met local villagers who came out in small boats to meet his ship. His description makes it clear that these local people were Sakhalin Ainu, but he also noticed that they were more heavily influenced by Japan than the people of Tomarioro or Ushiyoro.[39] Like the people of Tomarioro, though, these more southerly Ainu too had an intimate knowledge of the west coast of Sakhalin and the area around the mouth of the Amur. La Pérouse describes a map that they drew for him:

> they traced the part we had visited up to the Segalien River, leaving a relatively narrow pass for their canoes. They marked each resting place and gave it its name; in the end one cannot doubt that although distant from the mouth of the river by more than 150 leagues they all knew it perfectly well ...[40]

---

36   La Pérouse, *Journal*, p. 306.
37   'Natsional'nyi Sostav Haseleniya Rossiisckoi Federatsii', 2010, available online at www.perepis-2010.ru/results_of_the_census/tab5.xls (accessed 19 May 2013).
38   La Pérouse, *Journal*, pp. 312–13.
39   La Pérouse, *Journal*, p. 320.
40   La Pérouse, *Journal*, p. 321.

The *Astrolabe* and the *Boussole* then rounded the cape at the southern tip of Sakhalin, sailed through the straits between Sakhalin and Hokkaido, and turned northwards, tracking alongside the Kurile Islands. La Pérouse had intended to land on one of these islands, but was deterred by persistent fog, and so sailed on the Kamchatka Peninsula, where he landed on 6 September 1787. There he entrusted the precious journals and sketches from his voyage to diplomat and Russian-language speaker Barthélemy de Lesseps, who took them back to France, thus (as it turned out) saving them from destruction on the reefs of the South Pacific.

The Sandbank: Inscribing Scientific Mistakes

Bruno Latour traces the process by which knowledge, and thus power, accumulate in the metropolises of modern Europe. Each expedition incorporates information brought back by the last, and therefore arrives in distant lands forearmed with ever more sophisticated knowledge. But, as Latour himself recognises, the knowledge brought back by Western explorers was quite often wrong. In the long run mistakes were gradually removed: as one expedition tried to replicate or improve on earlier voyages of discovery, each deepened and refined knowledge, just as Krusenstern elaborated on the knowledge brought back by La Pérouse. In the short to medium term, though, the mistakes incorporated into explorers' maps of the world could have significant results. While much has been written about the way in which Enlightenment scholars revealed scientific truths, less has been written about the process by which they made mistakes. La Pérouse's exploration of the Amur-Okhotsk region provides one particularly interesting illustration of this process, which is worth tracing in some detail.

One of the main objectives of this part of the voyage was to discover whether Sakhalin was an island, and whether it was possible to sail between it and the Asian mainland, thus potentially opening up an alternative route to the Kamchatka Peninsula. La Pérouse, as we have seen, was told by the Tomarioro villagers that such a route existed and attempted to follow it, but was forced back by bad weather at the narrowest point between the island and mainland. When the expedition reached De Castries Bay, as La Pérouse reports:

> We used all our skill to question [the 'Bitchys'] on the country's geography; we drew the coast of Tartary with a pencil on some paper, with the Segalien River and the island of the same name

facing it ... and we left a pass between them; they took the pencil from our hands and joined by a line the island and the mainland, then pushing their canoe over the sand they explained that, after leaving the river, they had pushed their boat in this manner on the sandbank which joins the island to the mainland they had just drawn; after which, pulling up some weeds from the bottom of the sea ... they planted it on the sand to make clear that the sandbank they had crossed is also covered with seaweed.[41]

Just as vividly as the mapping incident in Tomarioro, this story shows the local familiarity with mapping processes, and also the remarkable extent to which two groups of people with no language in common were able to communicate by sign language. In this case, though, La Pérouse's interpretation of the sign language turns out to have been mistaken. He was puzzled by the discrepancy between the account of the Tomarioro villagers, who had informed him that the straits were passable, and that of the De Castries Bay people, who seemed to be saying that they were blocked by a sandbank that they could cross on foot. He had been intending to send a longboat to try once again to find a passage northward, but was anxious about the possible dangers and also eager to reach Kamchatka before winter – 'we did not have a moment to lose' – so, after further questions failed to produce any more information from the local people, he decided to reconcile the two stories by assuming that there was a weed-covered sandbank across the straits with narrow channels which could be navigated by canoe but not by ship.[42]

When Japanese explorer Mamiya Rinzō visited the region two decades later, he was able both to spend longer in northern Sakhalin and the Amur and to have conversations with local people via an interpreter. He therefore discovered a fact that surely explains the message the De Castries Bay villagers tried so hard to communicate to La Pérouse with their canoes and bunches of seaweed:

> because the width of the strait averages only fifteen to twenty-four miles and at the narrowest only five to seven miles, there is a rapid mid-stream current as violent as a river in flood. The tide ebbs so greatly that at low tide the bottom of the sea lies bare for a distance of two to five miles, and as far as one can see, there are acres of blue-green seaweed producing a sight which simply cannot be illustrated and which is never seen in Japan.[43]

---

41   La Pérouse, *Journal*, pp. 312–13.
42   La Pérouse, *Journal*, p. 314.
43   Mamiya, 'Kita Ezo Zusetsu', p. 99.

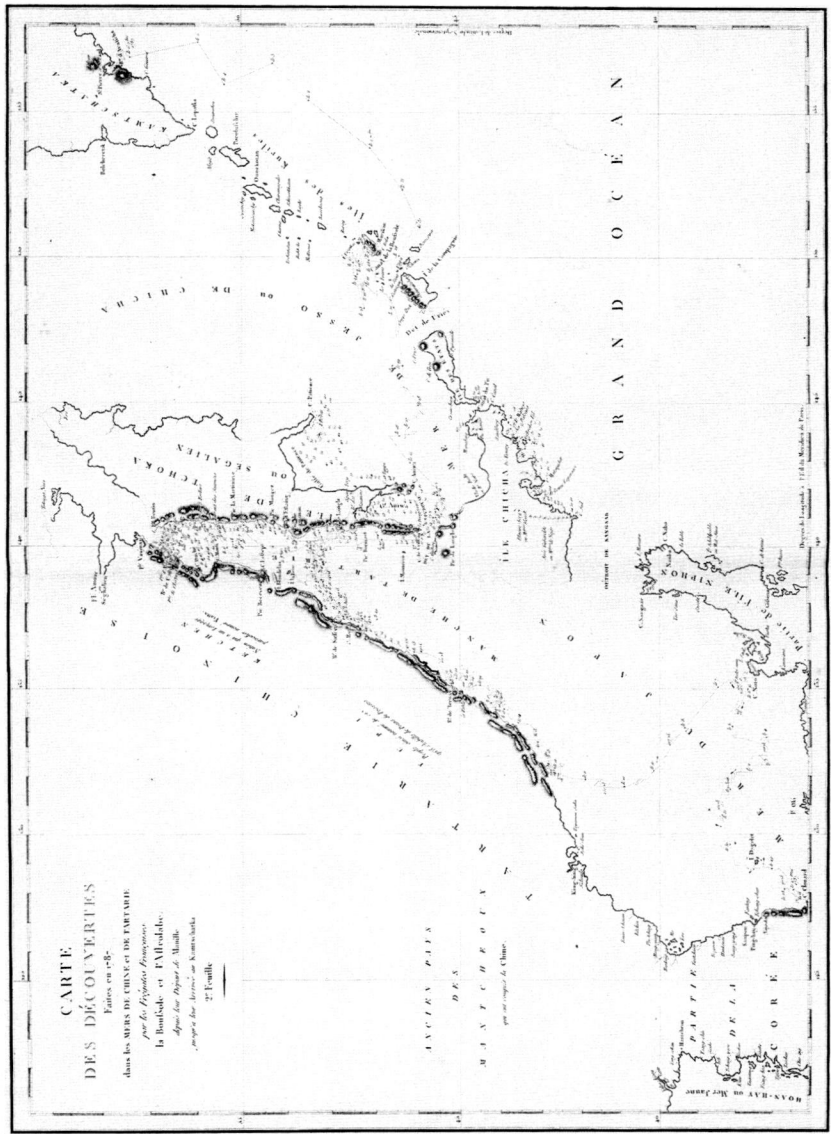

Figure 5.5. La Pérouse's map of Sakhalin.

Source: Jean-François de Galaup La Pérouse, 'Chart of the Discoveries Made in 1787, in the Seas of China and Tartary, by the Boussole and Astrolabe', Sheet II (London: G.G. and J. Robinson, 1799). David Rumsey Collection, List no. 0414.046, reproduced with kind permission of the David Rumsey Collection (www.davidrumsey.com).

In other words, the narrow neck of the straits, though dangerous, was deep enough to be navigable, but at low tide it was bordered on either side by wide, kelp-covered stretches of sand over which anyone trying to cross the straits had to drag their canoe. This was of crucial importance to the Oroch and other people of the region, for whom the narrows was a crossing point between the mainland and Sakhalin; but was at cross-purposes to La Pérouse's question, since he was interested, not in how to cross the straits, but rather how to sail through them. The readiness with which La Pérouse interpreted the villagers' sign language as meaning that the straits were impassable may in part have reflected his own anxiety to justify his decision to turn back rather than attempting to press on northwards against the odds.

In any event, the result was that the impassable sandbank La Pérouse believed he had been told about was carefully and scientifically inscribed on the map of the region, and remained on many maps until the middle of the nineteenth century. Almost 80 years later, during the Crimean War, a British naval squadron pursued their Russian opponents up the straits between Sakhalin and the mainland, but then abandoned the pursuit and waited in vain to ambush the Russians as they returned southwards, believing (on the basis of La Pérouse's cartography) that there was no means of escape to the north. But the Russians never returned: having learnt their geography from Mamiya Rinzō and others, they had sailed right through the straits, around the northern tip of Sakhalin and out into the Okhotsk Sea.[44]

The incident is a small one, but it illustrates a significant point. It was the very scientific quality of La Pérouse's research – the capacity for his illusory sandbank to be drawn by European cartographers in such persuasive technical detail – that allowed the mistake to persist for so long. The power of Enlightenment science lies in its ability to abstract and schematise, creating knowledge in forms that can be superimposed and combined into one great knowledge system. But its potential weakness lies in the fact that, through this process of abstraction, the fine-grained detail may be lost. This weakness is compounded by the very authority of the scientific inscription, which discourages the modesty that might generate (sometimes very necessary) doubt, self-questioning and acknowledgement of ambiguity.

44   FA Golder, *Russian Expansion on the Pacific, 1641–1850* (Cleveland: Arthur H. Clark and Co., 1914), pp. 264–65.

The Tinderbox: Observing the Observers

By following the voyage of La Pérouse through the Amur-Okhotsk region, we can gain insight into the Enlightenment process of observing and gathering knowledge from the field. But an exclusive focus on the ways in which European explorers perceived and extracted knowledge from local people can obscure the other side of the story: it easy to forget that the observers were also being observed.

Japanese scholar Mogami Tokunai first visited the west coast of Sakhalin in 1792, five years after La Pérouse's arrival on the same shores. By this time Mogami had already made three journeys through Hokkaido and the Kurile Islands, compiling information that was later published under the title *Ezo Sōshi* [*Notes on Ezo*]. It was on his 1792 visit, though, that the Ainu inhabitants of a village called Shōni, about 7 miles north of Shiranushi, told him a story about the coming of a ship belonging to Red People (Russians or other Europeans). In an appendix to *Ezo Sōshi* completed in 1800, Mogami retells the story as follows:

> During the Tenmei Era (1781–1788) a ship of Red People came to Karafuto (Sakhalin) and stopped at a place called Shōni, three *ri* north of Shiranushi. It was the first time those Ainu had seen a foreign [i.e. European] ship, so they were all frightened. [The foreigners] sent out a boat which landed on the shore, and summoned the Ainu, but they were reluctant to approach. At last, many Ainu gathered, and they [the foreigners] measured the Ainu from head to foot, and furthermore cut off a little of their hair with a small sword. The Ainu were absolutely astonished and alarmed, but they wanted to be helpful, so they stayed still. Then the Red People brought out an implement about two *sun*[45] in length, and made of brass. Inside it, the Ainu could see something that looked like the head of a snake. They were pressed to accept it as a present, but they refused. Then the part like the head of a snake moved, and produced a flash of fire and smoke. The Ainu people still tell the story of how fearful it was.[46]

---

45 Two *sun* is about 2.5 inches, or just over 6 centimetres.
46 Mogami, 'Ezo Sōshi Gohen', pp. 187–88.

Some Japanese commentaries on Mogami explain this as being a reference to the arrival of an anonymous Russian vessel,[47] but as Akizuki Toshiyuki has suggested, it must surely be a rare description of the La Pérouse voyage from the side of the people whom the French explorer studied: to be precise, from the perspective of a village close to the point that he called Cape Crillon.[48] The account of the measuring of bodies is too vivid and realistic to have been invented, since neither Ainu nor Japanese were at that time familiar with anthropometric ethnography. Japanese scholars such as Mamiya Rinzō certainly observed, drew and described the appearance of the various groups of people they met on their travels, but they did not measure them or remove samples of their hair. Such techniques would not be introduced into Japanese scholarship until the late nineteenth century. There is no evidence of any Russian scientific expedition to Sakhalin in the 1780s that might have undertaken scientific studies of the physique of the local people; but La Pérouse's expedition did carry out anthropometric research.

In his journal, La Pérouse writes that the Tomarioro villagers 'allowed our artists to draw them, but constantly declined the requests of Mr Rollin, our surgeon, who wanted to take measurements of their bodies'.[49] He makes no other mention of body measuring; but Rollin wrote his own separate account of the native people of Sakhalin and at De Castries Bay, and from this it is clear that he did succeed in measuring the bodies of both groups. He ends his description with a table giving comparative measurements of the inhabitants of the 'Island of Tschoka' (Sakhalin) and De Castries Bay, including such details as 'length of the upper extremities', 'ditto of the feet', 'circumference of the breast' and 'circumference of the pelvis'.[50] His detailed account of the Sakhalin islanders' physique includes the comment that:

> the hair of the head is generally black, smooth and moderately strong; but in some it is chestnut; they wear it round, about six inches long behind, and cut into a brush on the forehead and temples.[51]

---

47   See, for example, Yoshida Tsunekichi's postscript to Mogami Tokunai's *Ezo Sōshi* and 'Ezo Sōshi Gohen', pp. 225 and 227.
48   Akizuki, *Nichirō Kankei to Saharintō*, p. 41.
49   La Pérouse, *Journal*, p. 292.
50   Rollin (La Pérouse's surgeon), 'Dissertation on the Natives of Tschoka Island, and on the Eastern Tartars, by Mr. Rollin MD', in La Pérouse, *Voyage*, pp. 381–90, quotation from p. 390.
51   Rollin, 'Dissertation on the Natives of Tschoka Island', p. 382.

We can also tell from this account that Rollin went ashore at Cape Crillon, for he gives a detailed description of the 'habitations on the south of the island', which, he says are 'built with more care' than those further north (in Tomarioro and Ushiyoro), and he writes that:

> we observed in some of them vessels of Japanese porcelain, which the great value set on them by the owners led me to believe were not to be procured without considerable expense.[52]

Rollin's measurements of Ainu must have been carried out either near Cape Crillon or in Ushiyoro, or in both places.

The brass object that caused the people of Shōni such alarm sounds very much like an eighteenth European tinderbox: these commonly contained a serpentine-shaped metal hand-piece for striking sparks. The gifts for natives carried on the *Astrolabe* and *Boussole* included 1,000 'steels for striking fire'.[53] What is a little puzzling, though, is the terror this induced in the Ainu observers. Sakhalin Ainu were familiar with tinderboxes. La Pérouse's journal itself notes that the Tomarioro villagers had tinderboxes that 'came from the country of the Manchus'.[54] These, although different in design from the European versions, would have operated similarly. The object described in Mogami's account seems altogether more novel and spectacular – something closer, perhaps, to a recent and still experimental innovation that was also in the inventory of the *Astrolabe* and the *Boussole*: phosphorous matches.[55]

The story of the Shōni villagers is not, of course, an authentic eyewitness Ainu account of the coming of Western explorers: it has been filtered through the process of retelling to and by a Japanese official. It is, though, an eloquent reminder of the fact that the actions of explorers and other foreign travellers were observed, remembered, communicated over distances and, in some cases, avidly recorded and 'brought back' by both by Ainu and other people of Sakhalin and by Japanese scholars, who used them to build their own images of the world.

---

52   Rollin, 'Dissertation on the Natives of Tschoka Island', p. 383.
53   La Pérouse, *Voyage*, p. 183.
54   La Pérouse, *Journal*, p. 289.
55   La Pérouse, *Voyage*, p. 188.

Overlapping Geographies, Intersecting Ethnographies

'Modernity' tends to be envisaged as a great wave spreading outwards from Western Europe, carrying with it a burden of memories and desires that it deposits on every shore it touches. Some see the wave as the water of life that bears the floating seeds of rationality, freedom and human dignity; to others it is an annihilating flood, its arrogant, Eurocentric certainties sweeping away the variety and vitality of indigenous life. But neither simple image does justice to the complexity of the forces and traditions of thought that came together in the making of the modern world. The fate of the people of the Amur-Okhotsk region came to depend, not just on ideas of civilisation and progress accumulated and refined in Europe, but also on the confluence of those ideas with the shifting images of the world created by many non-state societies (such as those of the Ainu, Nivkh, Uilta and Oroch) and by a multitude of states (including China and Japan).

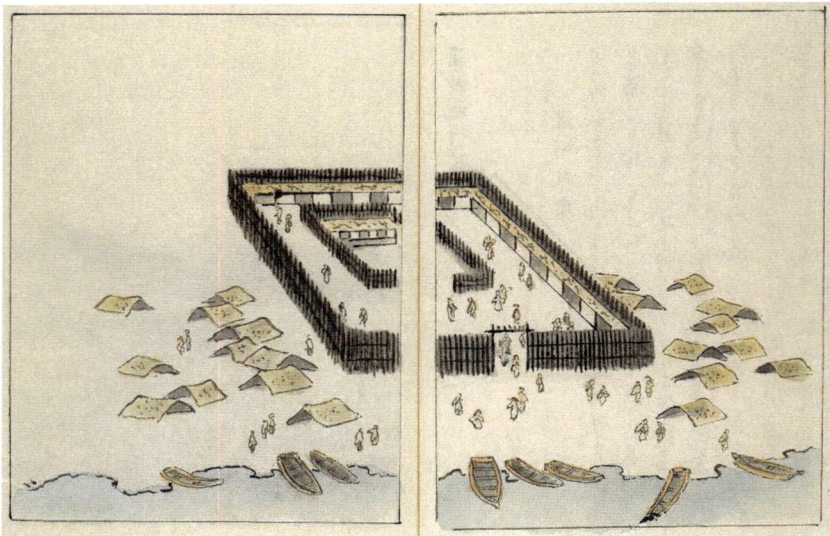

Figure 5.6. The trading post at Deren.
Source: Mamiya Rinzō, *Tōdatsu Kikō* (Dairen: Minami Manshū Tetsudō Kabushiki Kaisha, 1938) (original written in 1810 and first published in 1911), vol. 2.

When Japanese explorer Mamiya Rinzō arrived at Deren on the Amur River in the summer of 1809, he found a place whose modest appearance belied its cultural importance. It consisted only of a wooden palisade surrounding a single official building and an array of makeshift trading stalls. In winter the place was deserted, and on summer nights the candle-lit palisade shone dimly in the wide darkness of surrounding forest. But by daytime in summer, Deren was transformed. Qing officials, who arrived in spring and left in the autumn, slept in junks moored in the river, while several hundred representatives of the neighbouring Ainu, Nivkh, Ul'chi, Oroch and other societies camped in small bark shelters around the outside of the palisade.[56] Once they arrived in Deren, the tribute-bearers began by making a ceremonial visit to the junk of one of the chief officials. Then, a couple of days later, they entered the palisade bearing their tribute of furs, and waited until a minor official summoned them into the central hall. Here stood a dais, on which the representatives of Qing authority sat in a row, raised to an appropriate height above the heads of their vassals. The tribute-bearers knelt before the officials to present their gifts of sable, bowed three times to the ground, and were then rewarded with bolts of silk or other gifts from the dais.

Despite all the rigidity of its formal etiquette, Deren was a centre of thriving social interaction. The senior Qing tribute collectors were (like the emperors themselves) Manchus, but the 50 or so minor officials who helped to run the trading post were drawn from many societies, including the local Nivkh, Ul'chi and Nanai language groups. Once formalities were over, minor officials and tribute-bearers mingled around fringes of the palisade, trading goods, exchanging news, arguing, greeting old friends or long-lost relatives, playing with one another's children.[57] The Qing emperors prevented Han Chinese migration to their own original homeland, Manchuria, and left local Manchu officials to control the relationship between the many peoples on the north-eastern fringes of the empire. From the official perspective, the formalities that took place at Deren were an act of submission by the 'barbarian' peoples of the north-east to the Chinese imperial centre. Sakhalin Ainu who had been appointed to the position of *hala i da* or *gasan da* were required to

---

56   Mamiya Rinzō, *Tōdatsu Kikō* (Dairen: Minami Manshū Tetsudō Kabushiki Kaisha, 1938), pp. 31–38. Original written in 1810 and first published in 1911.
57   Mamiya, *Tōdatsu Kikō*, pp. 40–43.

travel to Deren regularly every one or two years to pay tribute.[58] From the perspective of the Ainu and other local peoples, though, visits to Deren were very probably seen more as profitable trading opportunities than as acts of political homage to the distant Chinese emperor.

Through their partial incorporation into the fringes of the Chinese empire, the people of the Amur-Okhotsk region came into closer contact both with one another and with long-standing Chinese systems for classifying the peoples of the known world, and these encounters undoubtedly exerted an influence of the ways in which they defined their own place in that world. From ancient times, Chinese scholars had attempted to describe and categorise the people to the far north-east of the empire, placing them in the order that defined the relationship between civilised centre (*hua*) and barbarian periphery (*i*). Late Ming Dynasty studies had produced a relatively detailed classification of the people of Lower Amur, including references to a group known as the 'Kuwu', generally believed to be Sakhalin Ainu.[59] When La Pérouse attempted his ethnographic mapping of the region, then, he was encountering people whose self-identification was not naïve and instinctive, but had already been influenced by encounters with the ethnographic schemas of others.

The Chinese passion for classifying and ordering the world is also reflected in the ethnographies compiled by Japanese explorers like Mamiya Rinzō. Though Mamiya had encountered some elements of Western scientific knowledge both via the Dutch and via the Russians, his conceptual framework remained much closer to that of Chinese descriptions of the empire's 'barbarian fringe'. He aimed to reorient the political and geographical order by placing Japan, rather than China, at the centre. But his ability to converse with the people of Sakhalin and the Amur via interpreters also enabled him to provide a richly detailed account of the appearance, customs and material life of the people he met on his travels.

---

58 Mamiya, 'Kita Ezo Zusetsu', p. 117.
59 See Sei Wada, 'The Natives of the Lower Reaches of the Amur River as Represented in Chinese Records', *Memoirs of the Research Department of the Toyo Bunko* 10 (1938): pp. 40–102, particularly p. 81; also Sasaki Shirō, 'Amūru-gawa Shimoryūiki Shominzoku no Shakai, Bunka ni okeru Shinchō Shihai no Eikyō ni tsuite', *Kokuritsu Minzoku Hakubutsukan Kenkyū Hōkoku* 14, no. 3 (1989): pp. 671–771; Matsuura Shigeru, *Shichō no Amūru Seisaku to Shosū Minzoku* (Kyoto: Kyoto Daigaku Shuppankai, 2006).

Figure 5.7. Portraits of Sakhalin Ainu 'Niskani, Aoucanouri and Erougantoi' of Tomarioro.

Source: Illustration by JBB Simonet, from Jean-François de Galaup de La Pérouse, *Atlas du Voyage de La Pérouse autour du Monde* (Paris: 1797).

He tells us how the Sakhalin Ainu catch sable, and how they feed their dogs (which are treated 'as though they are children'); how their blacksmiths forge metal using bellows made of fish-skin; how Uilta herd reindeer and how Ainu and Nivkh conduct funerals; and so on.[60] The illustrations to his works, which depict indigenous groups in the traditions of Japanese popular painting, draw on the experience of his prolonged stays in Sakhalin. He can draw Ainu, Nivkh and others engaged in a range of everyday tasks – fishing, nursing children, combing their hair, etc. By contrast, the visual images from La Pérouse's expedition, reproduced in a style strongly influenced by European classical images of beauty, focus on the moment of encounter between Europeans and locals (though the French explorers were unusual in attempting to produce portraits on named individuals whom they met on their travels).

Meanwhile, Ainu and other people of the Amur-Okhotsk region gathered their own knowledge of and from the peoples they encountered in their travels. Although there were as yet no Japanese settlers in Tomarioro, for example, the Ainu vocabulary assembled by La Pérouse shows that the villagers were familiar with guns, for which they used the Japanese loan word *tai-po*.[61] Their knowledge of neighbouring regions in turn was eagerly sought by Japanese scholars and explorers, as they tried to piece together a picture of the world beyond their northern and western horizons. Nakamura Shōshirō used information from local informants in Sakhalin to sketch the geography of north-eastern Manchuria, including places as far distant as the Manchu city of Ice Hoton (present-day Yilan in Northeast China) and to describe recent events (such as a famine and epidemic) in that region.[62] Mamiya Rinzō, who was unable to reach the far northern part of Sakhalin, described and mapped this part of the island on the basis of information given to him by the Ainu and Nivkh whom he met. These descriptions, too, are vivid and detailed (though he concludes them with the disclaimer that 'these above paragraphs have been set down by Rinzō from what the natives told him, so they may contain mistakes').[63] For example, of the north-western stretch of Sakhalin coast facing the mouth of the Amur, his local informants told him that:

> the water of the sea is less salty and as it is supplied by the tides of the northern sea there are ample trout, salmon and other fish upon which the [Ainu] feed, which makes for a numerous

60 Mamiya, 'Kita Ezo Zusetsu'.
61 La Pérouse, *Journal*, p. 341.
62 Nakamura Shōshirō, 'Karafuto Zakki'.
63 Mamiya, 'Kita Ezo Zusetsu', p. 101.

population. The number of *Orokko* [Uilta] and *Sumerenkur* [Nivkh] communities is about thirty-four or thirty-five. Three of these are especially large, each containing several dozen hamlets.[64]

Ainu informants also played a crucial role in enabling Japanese explorers to gather information about the Russians in the eastern Okhotsk region. Mogami Tokunai's descriptions of the Russians, which he gathered in the Kurile Islands, relied on the help of two Ainu, Haushibe and his younger brother Ivanushka. While Haushibe was an elder of the local Ainu community, Ivanushka had been converted to Christianity through his contact with Russian traders and settlers in the islands, and became a Russian interpreter, one of a quite substantial group of Ainu who acted as intermediaries in the earliest interactions between Japanese and Russians.[65]

The geographical and ethnographic information about the Amur-Okhotsk region compiled by Mogami, Mamiya and others was then eagerly consumed by early nineteenth-century European scholars and explorers. The German doctor Philipp Franz von Siebold, who was employed by the Dutch East India Company in their trading post in Nagasaki, managed to obtain a copy of Mamiya's account of Sakhalin and the Amur, and incorporated a translation of it into his monumental work *Nippon*, first published in 1832.[66] Conversely, Japanese scholars were busy translating European works such as Krusenstern's account of his voyage through the Okhotsk Sea, which they had obtained from Siebold in an unauthorised exchange of knowledge that attracted the wrath of the shogunate.[67]

Knowledge and Modernity in the Okhotsk Region

All of this suggests something more complex than a vortex that ceaselessly draws knowledge and power into the metropolitan centres of Enlightenment Europe. It is, of course, true that emerging European methods of representing and ordering global geography and ethnography made it possible to accumulate knowledge on an unprecedented scale,

---

64   Mamiya, 'Kita Ezo Zusetsu', p. 100.
65   See Shimaya Ryōkichi, *Mogami Tokunai* (Tokyo: Furukawa Kobunkan, 1977), pp. 36–37.
66   Phillipp Franz von Siebold, *Nippon: Archiv zur Beschreibung von Japan*, vol. 2 (Würzberg and Leipzig, Verlag der K U K Hofbuchhandlung von Leo Woerl, 1897), pp. 207–69.
67   Donald Keene, *The Japanese Discovery of Europe, 1720–1830*, rev. ed. (Stanford: Stanford University Press, 1969), p. 149.

but it is also important to acknowledge that the accumulation of modern knowledge was a very complex and multidirectional process, in which non-European centres including Japan and even small indigenous societies played a role, not just as sources but also as gatherers of knowledge.

This points to a need to rethink the relationship between knowledge and power. By the late nineteenth century, the small Ainu, Nivkh, Uilta, Oroch and other communities of the region found their lives overturned by the massive impact of the modern colonial world. But the role of science in the transformation of power relations was complicated and mediated by many other factors. The forces that devastated their traditional ways of life were less those of mechanised modern technology than forces of the epidemic diseases spread by settler communities, and of environmental destruction unleashed by Russian convict exiles and Japanese immigrant farmers. Colonial modernity, rather than making immobile 'natives' mobile, carved national frontiers through the Amur-Okhotsk region, severing trade routes and constricting the social horizons of the local people. In the next two chapters, we shall look more closely at the way in which these national frontiers were drawn, and how the indigenous people of the region responded and adapted to their presence.

Visiting Tomarioro in 1787, La Pérouse described the 21 villagers he met there as having 'more politeness, more gentleness, more seriousness and maybe a greater intelligence than any nation of Europe', and predicted that although 'they are a very well governed people, [they] are so poor that they will not for many years attract the cupidity of conquerors or traders'.[68] His prediction proved mistaken, but his arrival on the eve of the coming of conquerors provides a precious opportunity to explore the interweaving of many forms of knowledge that helped to form the complex texture of the modern world.

This chapter is a slightly revised version of an article that first appeared in the journal *East Asian History* 39 (2014): pp. 33–52.

---

68   La Pérouse, *Journal*, pp. 291–93.

6

LINES IN THE SNOW: THE MAKING OF THE RUSSO–JAPANESE FRONTIER

In that web of intersecting tragedies we call 'the Second World War', one of the most curious conflicts was surely the three-week war between the Soviet Union and Japan, which broke out on 8 August 1945, and ended several days after Japan's official surrender to the allied powers. Perhaps the shortest of the many wars within the war, it has created the most prolonged and intractable search for peace. Today, more than 75 years after the event, the Japanese and Russian governments have yet to sign a peace treaty. Their main stumbling block has been conflict over the Russo–Japanese frontier: specifically, over Japan's claims to the islands of Shikotan, Kunashir (or Kunashiri), Iturup (or Etorofu) and the Habomai group, seized by Soviet troops (along with the rest of the Kurile island chain and the southern half of Sakhalin) during those three weeks of fighting in August 1945. As in many border disputes, even the place names are bones of contention. The Russian government calls these islands the Southern Kuriles, while the Japanese state denies that they are part of the Kurile archipelago, and refers to the region as the Northern Territories (*Hoppō Ryōdo*).[1]

---

1   T Ishiwatari, 'The Northern Territories', in *Contested Territory: Border Disputes at the Edge of the Former Soviet Empire*, ed. T Forsberg (Aldershot: Edward Elgar, 1995), pp. 224–54.

What fascinates me about this story is not so much the glacially slow progress of international diplomacy, but rather the nature of the frontier itself: the arbitrary, moveable line that separates Russia from Japan, and now runs between Hokkaido to the south and the islands of Habomai, Kunashir and Sakhalin to the north. On the crossing from Hokkaido to Sakhalin in the summer of 1996, I encountered a man who had lived all his life in a house overlooking Wakkanai harbour. Every clear day he had looked out of his bedroom window at the dark line of the Sakhalin coast on the horizon. But for the first 30 years of his life it was as inaccessible as the moon. Now he was going to set foot on it for the first time.

This is not simply a border between nation and nation. Across the water, as guidebooks inform the small trickle of Japanese tourists who make this journey, lies 'the Europe closest to Japan'. In geographical terms, of course, Europe and Asia are separated by that other arbitrary line, drawn along the ridge of the Ural Mountains by Philip-Johann von Strahlenberg in the eighteenth century, and bisecting Russia between the two continents. But in political, social and imaginative terms, the border between Japan and Russia, which currently runs between Hokkaido and Sakhalin on its western side and between Hokkaido and the islands of Kunashir and the Habomai Group on its east, is indeed a point where Europe and Asia meet. On one side the language is Russian and the population dominated by immigrants from European Russia; on the other, the language and the vast majority of the people are Japanese. To the north, the crumbling stucco apartment blocks – their stairwells exuding smells of cool stone, musty plaster and strong cigarettes – could be buildings in St Petersburg, Kyiv or Warsaw, as could the bakeries with their displays of black bread and buns filled with sour plum jam. To the south, the huddle of shops near the harbour selling souvenir boxes of rice crackers and seaweed, the blue-roofed houses, the tangles of telephone wires and the gleaming cylinder of the All Nippon Airways Hotel are unmistakably Japanese, even though many shops now boast signs in Russian to cater to the regular influx of customers from the Sakhalin fishing fleet.

And then again, from 1945 to the end of the 1980s, this was the borderline between another sort of East and West: the two poles of the Cold War. But at that time, in defiance of Kipling's logic, it was a meeting point where (geographical) East was (political) West and vice versa. The paranoias of the Cold War period are still preserved in the almost identical arrays of enigmatic pylons, aerials and puffball domes lining both sides of the straits – a technology of espionage and early warning systems that, amongst other things, sent the crew and passengers of Korean Airlines Flight 007 to their deaths in 1983 for flying into the wrong piece of air.

Frontiers, Borders and Boundaries

National frontiers are vantage points from which to explore shifts in the world order, to rediscover 'globalisation' as a phenomenon that is neither particularly recent nor implies the disappearance of borderlines. 'Globalisation', in this sense, implies the long historical process of the ordering of human difference through the worldwide replication of common social forms: forms often imposed by conflict between unequal forces. One of these forms is the border itself. Since the eighteenth century, the boundaries between nations have acquired certain standard, internationally recognised characteristics. Yet these characteristics have changed over time, reflecting shifts in the nature of the world order. Though every frontier is unique, tracing the history of a particular frontier is a way of reflecting on some of the wider changes in the meaning, symbolism, social presence and economic influence of the lines that surround the nation-state. A focus on the boundaries between nations, rather than on the nation itself, also provides a perspective that reminds us how much nation-building is a contingent process, an uncertain interplay of forces from without as well as from within.

My purpose here is to map out the processes by which a Russo–Japanese border came into being: the way in which the area became defined as a frontier zone. I am also interested in comparing the way in which Russian and Japanese officials, colonisers and others, approaching the same region from different directions, created repertoires of imagery of the border area: images that to some degree influence the negotiation of the boundary to the present day.

Naming the Region: Siberia and Ezo

Anssi Paasi points out the importance of naming in the creation of frontier identities. Endowing a particular region with a name gathers together 'its historical development, its important events, episodes and memories and joins the personal histories of its inhabitants to this collective heritage'.[2] The names given to regions, or the unconscious decision to leave areas anonymous, influences the way in which geographical space is imagined by policymakers, colonists, merchants and diplomats, and this imagination in turn subtly influences the physical appropriation and exploitation of the frontier terrain. As the mercantile power of Russia and Japan began to penetrate the world surrounding the Okhotsk Sea from about the seventeenth century onward, the naming of the region created a framework for rival and shifting imaginative claims to the frontier.

From the Russian perspective, the Okhotsk shoreline, Sakhalin, Kamchatka and the Kurile Islands were initially the remotest limit of a vast region stretching eastward in the mind from the Ural Mountains, and known as Tartary or, in Russian from the sixteenth century onward, as *Sibir*: Siberia. Russia's foothold in the eastern fringes of this region began to be established in the middle of the seventeenth century, when (as we have seen) groups of Cossack freebooters, intent on extracting tribute (*yasak*) from the local peoples, reached the mouth of the Amur River. The Treaty of Nerchinsk, signed with the Chinese empire in 1689, confined the Russians to the areas north of the river, and in the decades that followed Russian expansion moved northward into the Kamchatka Peninsula and the northern Kurile Islands.

Mark Bassin's wonderful study of the notion of 'Siberia' reveals the multiple levels of meaning that were attached to this term by eighteenth- and nineteenth-century Russian travellers, writers, ethnographers and political activists. During the eighteenth century, Siberia or Great Tartary was seen above all as a colonial possession, rivalling the possessions of other European powers as a source of precious raw materials; but in the Siberian case, the chief resource was not gold or silver but fur – 'soft gold', as it was commonly called. This exotic imperial possession, evocatively described as 'our Peru', 'our Mexico' or 'our East India', was a source not only of material wealth but also of a rich array of images of otherness.[3]

---

2   Anssi Paasi, *Territories, Boundaries and Consciousness: The Changing Geographies of the Finnish–Russian Border* (Chichester and New York: John Wiley and Sons, 1996), p. 35.
3   Mark Bassin, 'Inventing Siberia: Visions of the Russian East in the Early Nineteenth Century', *American Historical Review* 93, no. 3 (1991): pp. 763–93, doi.org/10.2307/2162430; see also Yuri Slezkine, *Arctic Mirrors: Russia and the Small Peoples of the North* (Ithaca and London: Cornell University Press, 1994), chs 2–3.

By the early nineteenth century, however, the fur trade was in decline and Russian images of the eastern frontier region began to take on new forms. At one level, its harsh climate, and its expanding role as a place of exile for criminals and dissidents, imbued the very word 'Siberia' with overtones of darkness and terror. This vision of an icy wilderness where human hearts became as hard as the frozen soil was to survive into the twentieth century, and was reinforced, for example, in Anton Chekhov's famous account of his journey to the penal settlements of Sakhalin in 1890.[4] At the same time, though, the wide open steppes of Siberia, untainted by the legacy of serfdom, could also be imagined as Russia's equivalent to the American frontier: a region rich, not only in land and natural resources, but also in possibilities for the construction of a new society. Thus in the 1850s political and social thinker Alexander Herzen (1812–60) envisaged Russia's eastward expansion into Siberia and the United States' westward expansion to the Pacific as two flanks of a single great movement towards freedom and human prosperity: both Russia and the United States, he wrote,

> are poor in tradition and take as their first step a complete break with the past; both swim through endless valleys searching for their borders, and from different sides have traversed awesome expanses. They have everywhere marked their path with cities, villages and colonies, up to the shores of the Pacific Ocean, the Mediterranean of the future.[5]

From the Japanese perspective, on the other hand, the region bordering on the Okhotsk Sea was, during the seventeenth and eighteenth centuries, perceived as being part of a more restricted but no less vaguely defined area known as 'Ezo', which extended northward from the island now called Hokkaido into the dimly perceived mists beyond. Though furs and eagle feathers were among the booty brought back from Ezo to the markets of Japan, the most important resource here was not the 'soft gold' of Siberia but rather a more prosaic product – 'golden fertiliser' (*kinpi*), large quantities of herring and other fish that were caught and gutted by Ainu forced labourers and then sent south to enrich the rice fields of Honshu. By the 1750s, as the first Russian traders and missionaries were

---

4   Bassin, 'Inventing Siberia', pp. 771–75; Anton Chekhov, *The Island: A Journey to Sakhalin*, trans. Luba Terpak and Michael Terpak (New York: Washington Square Press, 1967).
5   Quoted in Bassin, 'Inventing Siberia', p. 789.

venturing into the northern Kurile Islands, the Japanese merchants were establishing their first fishing and trading posts at the southern end of the archipelago, in Kunashir.[6]

Just as Tartary or Siberia offered images of the exotic, which European Russians mobilised in creating images of self, so Ezo was a source of visions of otherness, which fed a slowly emerging consciousness of Japan as a nation. Perceived (following the Chinese model) as a 'barbarian periphery', Ezo was at first depicted in language full of magic and the monstrous. A fourteenth-century Japanese scroll described the 'thousand isles of Ezo' (*Ezo-ga-chishima*) as inhabited by cannibals, shape-shifters and female demons. With increasing contact, though, both geographical and social contours began to become more distinct. Travellers' tales from as far afield as Kamchatka (where a number of Japanese fishermen were cast ashore by storms in the seventeenth and eighteenth centuries) helped to resolve the vague image of 'northern barbarians' into a more complex awareness of a multiplicity of peoples: 'Ezo', 'Santan', 'Sumurenkur', 'Red Ezo' and others. Russian goods started to reach Japan through the trade route that extended from Kamchatka down the Kurile island chain to Hokkaido, and growing consciousness of a new colonising presence to the north encouraged the Japanese shogunate to dispatch the missions of Mamiya Rinzō, Mogami Tokunai and others to explore and map the further reaches of Ezo.[7]

One of the human groups that attracted the most interest from Japanese scholars of the region was (as we have seen) the tribe originally known as the 'Red Ezo' (because of the colour of their hair). By about the 1780s, it had been established that these warlike people, who were increasingly encroaching on Japanese fishing grounds in the north, were none other than the group described in foreign texts as 'Oroshiya' (Russians) and originating from the land of Muscovia, somewhere to the east of Holland (Holland being the European country most familiar to Japanese scholars).[8]

---

6   Kaiho Mineo, *Kinsei no Hokkaidō* (Tokyo: Kyōikusha, 1979), p. 89; Hokkaido was given its present name in 1869. Before that it, together with the rest of the region to the immediate north, was 'Ezo'. Here, however, I use the name 'Hokkaido' throughout for the sake of clarity.

7   Mamiya Rinzō, *Tōdatsu Kikō* (Dairen: Minami Manshū Tetsudō Kabushiki Kaisha, 1938), original written in 1810 and first published in 1911; Mamiya Rinzō, 'Kita Yezo Zustesu or a Description of the Island of Northern Yezo by Mamiya Rinsō', trans. John A Harrison, *Proceedings of the American Philosophical Society* 99, no. 2 (1955): pp. 93–111.

8   Kudo Heisuke, *Aka-Ezo Fūsetsukō* (1781), reprinted in *Hoppō Mikōkai Komonjo Shūsei*, ed. Terasawa Hajime et al., vol. 3 (Tokyo: Sobunsha, 1988), pp. 29–51; see also Donald Keene, *The Japanese Discovery of Europe, 1720–1830*, rev. ed. (Stanford: Stanford University Press, 1969).

When the Russian explorer Golovnin was captured by the Japanese in Iturup in 1811 and held as a prisoner for two and a half years, he found himself in the uncomfortable and unusual position of being the object of the insatiable curiosity of Japanese officialdom. Although he and his companions were generally well treated by their captors, he was later to complain of the endless stream of Japanese inquisitors who had insisted on asking him 'useless' questions, apparently arising from 'mere curiosity': 'what kind of dress does the Emperor of Russia wear – what does he wear on his head – what kind of birds are found in the neighbourhood of St Petersburg – what would be the price in Russia of the clothes which they were wearing'.[9] He was, in short, experiencing the trials and tribulations of being the object of early ethnographic research.

Figure 6.1. Golovnin being taken prisoner in Japan, c. 1811.
Source: Artist unknown, original held in Waseda University Library.

While images of 'Ezo' resembled images of 'Siberia' in their emphasis on the exotic qualities of the region, in other senses the early nineteenth-century Japanese vision of the frontier region differed from the Russian vision. The heterodox philosopher Andō Shōeki (1703–62) used travellers' accounts of Ainu society to depict his image of a utopian world without rulers or ruled, where all people lived in peace with one another. The 'Ezo' (Ainu), he wrote:

> catch fish, [and] gather fruit which they store up; they make clothes from the bark of trees and they never need suffer from cold, nor do they go hungry … People engage in direct cultivation and make their own clothes by their own labour. There is no circulation of bullion, and thus people are not avaricious. There is no instruction

---

9   VM Golownin, *Memoirs of a Captivity in Japan*, ed. J McMaster, vol. 1 (Oxford: Oxford University Press, 1973), pp. 200 and 211–12. I have used the standard modern transliteration of Golovnin's name.

on military strategy and no books of sages to disturb them about
the wars and turmoil in this world … There is no need to pass
judgment as between good and evil as the people live a peaceful
and quiet life.[10]

This wistful nostalgia has certain resonances with the writings of some
nineteenth-century Russian romantics, who wrote of Siberian villages
where ancient Russian traditions had been preserved in unadulterated
form, and praised the 'simplicity' and 'geniality' of the indigenous
peoples.[11] But although Japanese travellers' accounts, naturally enough,
emphasised the intensely cold climate of the northern regions, there was
little to suggest an image of 'Ezo' as a grim, dark or inhospitable realm.
By the eighteenth century a few Japanese scholars of Western learning
were beginning to propose schemes for the colonisation and 'opening
up' of Ezo, and this interest in the region was intensified by increasing
anxiety about events on the frontier, but there was also, as yet, nothing
to compare to the images of the Siberian frontier as a second America –
a land of boundless human progress. It was not until the second half of the
nineteenth century, and the advent of the modernising Meiji government,
that these schemes would be put into effect and the region (under a new
name) would become the focus of utopian dreams of progress.

Defining the Frontier

From the Russian perspective, then, until the middle of the nineteenth
century, the eastern fringes of the empire conjured up visions of a frontier
in Frederick Jackson Turner's sense: 'the hither edge of free land',
a phenomenon utterly different from the Western European frontier,
'a fortified boundary line running through dense populations'.[12] As one
political exile recalled:

> Not only did there exist no frontiers, but the two neighbouring
> empires [here the author is referring to Russia and China] did
> not know accurately what distance separated them, and what was

10   Quoted in E Herbert Norman, *Andō Shōeki and the Anatomy of Japanese Feudalism* (Tokyo: The
Asiatic Society of Japan, 1949), p. 233.
11   Sakakura Genjirō, *Ezo zuihitsu*, reprinted in *Hoppō Mikōkai Komonjo Shūsei*, ed. Terasawa
Hajime et al., vol. 1 (Tokyo: Sōbunsha, 1979). Original written in 1739.
12   Frederick Jackson Turner, *The Significance of the Frontier in American History* (Harmondsworth:
Penguin, 2008), p. 2. Original published in 1893.

in the interior. From the Siberian side, as well as from that of the Celestial Empire, stretched out uninhabited deserts, with their steppes, their gigantic cedar-forests, their endless prairies.[13]

From the Japanese point of view, on the other hand, an emerging awareness of Russian expansion into this frontier region produced (at first) a rather different image of the frontier, not as a zone of forward advance but as a buffer: an area necessary both for self-protection and for cautious interchange with the outside world. This notion was captured in the metaphor, popularised from the mid-eighteenth century onward, of Ezo as Japan's 'northern guard-house' or 'northern gate' (*hokumon*).

Increasing conflict with the 'Red Ezo' to the north of the gate, however, created a new imperative to define its geography more precisely, and this in turn gradually gave rise to a different vision of the frontier. In 1789, a revolt by Ainu broke out on the island of Kunashir and the neighbouring coastal area of northern 'Ezo' in protest against the treatment of local people by Japanese merchants, and in the autumn of 1806 and spring of 1807, two hot-headed Russian adventurers named Khvostov and Davydov, enraged by Japan's rebuff to a diplomatic mission from the Tsarina Catherine, attacked and burnt Japanese trading posts in southern Sakhalin and on the Kurile island of Iturup. Although the Russian government publicly disowned this exploit, it caused intense concern to the Japanese shogunate. One response was to dispatch Mamiya Rinzō and Matsuda Denjirō, to explore the northern regions of Ezo and to locate 'the limits of the territory of Great Japan' (*Dai-Nihonkoku no jizakai*).[14]

From a modern perspective, there is something slightly strange about this mission – this vision of the border as a tangible phenomenon, almost like a mountain range or a rift valley, which must exist out there somewhere, even though no one yet knows where. It suggests a notion of the frontier in some respects similar to the early nineteenth-century Thai concepts illuminated by the research of Thongchai Winichakul. Here the frontier is seen not as a sharp line, but rather as a zone, or perhaps more accurately a series of points, which mark the limit of the state's influence.[15] In this sense, it is not the outcome of negotiation between nation and nation, but is determined by discovering how far one can travel without arriving

13   Ludwik Niemojowski, *Siberian Pictures*, vol. 1 (London: Hurst and Blackett, 1883), p. 3940.
14   Hora Tomio, *Mamiya Rinzō* (Tokyo: Yoshikawa Kōbunkan, 1960), pp. 134–37.
15   Thongchai Winichakul, *Siam Mapped: A History of the Geo-Body of the Nation* (Honolulu: University of Hawai'i Press, 1994), pp. 74–80.

in something clearly 'hostile territory', and how far afield one can detect faint traces of trade or tributary connections to the state. Mamiya and Matsuda, journeying by foot and by small boat through Sakhalin, placed this limit somewhere around the region of Cape Rakka, up to which the indigenous people showed some familiarity with the existence of the *Sisa* (Japanese), but beyond which lay the sea to the west and impenetrable forest to the north.

Meanwhile, though, the Japanese shogunate, in response to the disturbing events to the north, was starting to engrave the frontier more firmly in the lives of the people of the region. In 1899 the eastern part of 'Ezo-chi' was placed under direct Shogunal rule, and in 1807 this was extended to the western part too. The shogunate used its new powers to attempt policies to 'Japanise' the Ainu by forcing them to learn Japanese language and wear clothes similar to those of Japanese peasants, but these measures proved to have limited success and were rather short-lived: in 1821, Matsumae Domain's authority over 'Ezo-chi' was restored and the 'Japanisation' measures lapsed until they were revived with new vigour by the modernising Meiji state from the 1870s onwards.[16]

A distinctly different concept of the border is evident in the major nineteenth-century Russian expeditions to the region: the Amur expeditions of the 1850s. Unlike the travels of Mamiya and Matsuda, these were large and well-equipped ventures involving military troops, geologists, botanists and ethnographers, and backed by the wealth of the Russian-American Trading Company and by the authority of the newly created Russian Geographical Society. The prime mover behind the missions, Count Nikolai Nikolaevich Murav'ev, governor of Eastern Siberia, saw the aim as being not to locate the limits of Russian rule, but rather to stake Russia's claim to the right to territorial expansion.

This right was interpreted in at least three ways. In moral terms, Russia was seen as occupying the unique position of a European power that also possessed an Asian dimension, and thus had a special mission to bring civilisation to Asia. Pragmatically, expansion on the Pacific coast was explained in terms of the power politics of the day: if Russia did not take control of the region around the mouth of the Amur, it was likely to fall

---

16   See Watanabe Kyōji, *Kurofune Zenya: Roshia, Ainu, Nihon no Sangokushi* (Tokyo: Yōsensha, 2010), ch. 6; also Tessa Morris-Suzuki, 'Creating the Frontier: Identity and History in Japan's Far North', *East Asian History* 7 (1994): pp. 1–24.

into the hands of France or Britain, with whom Russia was fighting the Crimean War. But at the same time, Russian redefinitions of its border were also justified in terms of a global system of international law, by reinterpreting the meaning of earlier interstate treaties or renegotiating the treaties themselves. So Murav'ev's emissary, Captain Gennadii Ivanovich Nevel'skoi, having explored the Straits of Tartary and coastline of Sakhalin, proposed that the island had never been part of the Chinese empire, but was rather a natural extension of the coastal regions granted to Russia by the highly ambiguous terms of the seventeenth-century Treaty of Nerchinsk.[17] To emphasise the point, he went on to establish a military camp adjacent to the main Japanese trading post in southern Sakhalin. Meanwhile, Murav'ev was also placing pressure on the northern borderlands of China, whose power was weakened by the ongoing Taiping rebellion (1850–64). This pressure was ultimately to result in the 1858 Treaty of Aigun, under which China ceded to Russia a large stretch of territory along the northern bank of Amur River and the northern borders of Manchuria.

It was this modern version of the national border as a line to be negotiated through complex power plays between state and state that was also to prevail in the negotiations between Japan and Russia. By the 1850s, Japan was being drawn into the global system of nation-states by pressures from the United States and the Western European powers, as well as from Russia. In 1853, Russian emissary Yevfimiy Putyatin arrived in Japan to negotiate the frontier with the shogunate. Building on Murav'ev's claims to territory extending the Siberian coast south to the Amur River, Putyatin argued that Sakhalin, as a mere offshore appendage of this coast, was equally Russian territory. In response, Japanese officials began to deploy a relatively new concept that would become central to their subsequent definitions of national sovereignty. They argued that the Ainu people who inhabited Hokkaido, the south Kurile Islands and the southern half of Sakhalin, had traditionally been under the 'protection' of the Japanese domain of

---

17   Mark Bassin, 'The Russian Geographical Society, the "Amur Epoch" and the Great Siberian Expedition 1855–1863', *Annals of the Association of American Geographers* 73, no. 2 (1983): pp. 24056, doi.org/10.1111/j.1467-8306.1983.tb01411.x; AI Alekseev, *Amurskaya Ekspeditsiya 1849–1855* (Moscow: Mysl', 1974), p. 77. Murav'ev himself expressed scepticism at this rather far-fetched interpretation of geography, although he was to claim that the 1858 Treaty of Aigun, which ceded the area south of the Lower Amur to Russia, also conferred sovereignty over Sakhalin; see Akizuki Toshiyuki, *Nichirō Kankei to Saharintō: Bakumatsu Meiji Shoki no Ryōdo Mondai* (Tokyo: Chikuma Shobō, 1994), p. 138.

Matsumae, and that Ainu territory was therefore Japanese territory.[18]
This was a crucial step in the gradual process of dispossession, by which
the indigenous people on both sides of the frontier were reassigned from
the role of exotic foreigners to that of national subjects, whose links to
the land no longer empowered themselves, but instead empowered the
territorial claims of the colonising nation-state. The Russians too were
intermittently to use the presence of Nivkh-speaking indigenous groups
on both sides of the Tartar Straits to reinforce their claims to Sakhalin.

Putyatin's negotiations resulted in the 1855 Treaty of Shimoda, which
divided the Kurile archipelago between Japan and Russia (with the
border running between the islands of Iturup and Urup) but left Sakhalin
under the joint sovereignty of both nations. In practice, however, joint
sovereignty proved a cumbersome arrangement, and in 1875 the frontier
was renegotiated, with Japan surrendering its rights to Sakhalin in return
for control of the entire Kurile archipelago. Predictably, this was done
without any reference to the wishes of the indigenous inhabitants,
whose lives were in many cases to be drastically affected by the new
arrangements. About one-third of the Ainu population of Sakhalin were
persuaded to move south to the island of Hokkaido where, concentrated
in large settlements for the first time in their lives, many died of infectious
diseases. In the northern Kuriles meanwhile, a large proportion of the
Ainu and Aleut inhabitants had been converted to Orthodox Christianity.
Of these, a few moved north to Kamchatka on the Russian side of the
border (where some of their descendants remain to the present day),
while the remainder were relocated by the Japanese government to the
southernmost island of Habomai, for fear that their presence near the
new boundary might create security problems.[19] They too were decimated
by poverty and epidemics resulting from their forced removal from their
homes. Japan's victory in the Russo–Japanese War in 1905 then enabled
Japan to regain control of the southern half of Karafuto, creating a new
borderline at the 50th parallel across the island (discussed further in the
following chapter).

18   See John J Stephan, *The Russian Far East: A History* (Stanford: Stanford University Press, 1994),
pp. 48–49; Akizuki, *Nichirō Kankei*, pp. 14–42.
19   Karafuto Ainu Shi Kenkyūkai, ed., *Tsuishikari no Ishibumi* (Sapporo: Hokkaidō Shuppan Kikaku
Sentā, 1992); VO Shubin, 'Zhizn "Kuril'tsev" na Kamchatke v 1877–1888 godax', *Kraevedechesk
Byulleten* (Yuzhno-Sakhalinsk) 3, no. 4 (1992): pp. 37–52.

Nation-Building and the Frontier Zone: Priamur and Hoppō

In the years that immediately followed the 1855 definition of the border, Russians and Japanese began to appropriate the frontier zone in new ways, both physically, though colonisation, and mentally, through a renaming of the region. From the Russian perspective, the area bordering the Okhotsk Sea ceased merely to be the remotest fringe of Siberia, and became a region geographically integrated by the labels 'Maritime Region' (*Primorye*) or 'Amur Region' (*Priamur*): labels that were to be deployed in various ways in the course of modern history. Initially, from 1856 onwards, Kamchatka, the Kuriles, Sakhalin and the Okhotsk coastline including the mouth of the Amur were incorporated into the Maritime Region (*Primorskaya Oblast*), and in 1884 this became part of the larger Priamur governor-generalship, subsequently renamed the Priamur Region (*Priamurskii Krai*).

At one level, increasing use of the region as a place of exile for the state's most feared criminals and political prisoners served only to intensify its grim reputation, and throughout the late nineteenth and early twentieth centuries, interwoven images of hostile nature and savage humanity often threatened to overwhelm more romantic depictions of the frontier. Russian convicts had first been brought to the island of Sakhalin in 1859 to dig for coal, and in 1881 the island was formally designated a penal colony; by 1897 its population was recorded as consisting of 23,251 convicts, 11,997 Russian free settlers, a small number of Chinese, Japanese and Koreans, and 4,151 indigenous people.[20] The terrible conditions of exile life, vividly depicted by Anton Chekhov and others, cast their shadow of images of the landscape itself. Sakhalin became 'the Banished Island' or 'the Isle of Misery', where even time, constrained by the bonds of the *katorga* (penal colony), seemed unable to flow freely as it did elsewhere. For the exile, wrote one observer:

> each year does not consist of twelve months … nor does it consist of 'four seasons', as it does for people in normal society. It is not made up of 365 days, as it is for everyone else. It is millions of minutes, of which many stretch as long as eternity.[21]

20   John J Stephan, *Sakhalin: A History* (Oxford: Clarendon Press, 1971), pp. 67–68; Tōa Dōbunkai, ed., *Karafuto oyobi Kita Enkaishū* (Tokyo: Tōa Dōbunkai, 1905), part 2, pp. 24–26.
21   VM Doroshevich, *Sakhalin: Katorga* (Moscow: I. D. Sytin, 1903), p. 324; see also Ferdinand Ossendowski, *Man and Mystery in Asia* (London: Edward Arnold, 1924), part 3; Stephan, *Sakhalin*, p. 187.

Figure 6.2. Prisoners in the Sakhalin penal colony.
Source: Charles H Hawes, *In the Uttermost East* (London and New York: Harper and Brothers, 1903).

Yet at another level, the redefined region provided a stage for a newly defined group of people, the 'Amurians' (*Amurtsy*), later 'Trans-Amurians' (*Zaamurtsy*), who promoted the study, exploration and colonisation of the Amur region, and, from the mid-1890s onwards, sought to use the area as a base for Russian expansion into Manchuria. Nationalist, scientifically minded and often possessing close links with scholars in China and Japan, they included such figures as the army-officer-turned-ethnographer Vladimir Klavdievich Arsen'ev (1872–1930), whose semifictional memoir *Dersu Uzala* (published in 1921) was to have an enormous impact on popular imaginings of the region. Arsen'ev's work can be seen as a classic example of 'imperial nostalgia'.[22] Told from the perspective of an army officer (Arsen'ev himself) sent to survey the coastal region south of the mouth of the Amur in the first decade of the twentieth century, it depicts the area as a wilderness of great and untapped natural wealth, an exotic realm where Nanai and other indigenous people coexist with Chinese brigands, Korean settlers and communities of Russian religious dissenters. Within this realm Arsen'ev plays the role of the bearer of modern

---

22   Renato Rosaldo, *Culture and Truth: The Remaking of Social Analysis* (Boston: Beacon Press, 1993), pp. 68–87.

civilisation, an irresistible force relentlessly sweeping across the face of the earth, and leaving in its wake towns, railways, steam baths and telegraph lines. Yet Arsen'ev himself, as the harbinger of modernity, grieves for the passing of the innocent power of the wilderness: characteristics embodied in the character of the book's central figure, the Nanai tribesman Dersu Uzala, whose final fate is not only death but the obliteration of his grave by the march of progress: 'The magnificent cedars disappeared, and in their place appeared roads, embankments, excavations, mounds, grooves and pits … Farewell Dersu!'[23]

Figure 6.3. Arsen'ev with Dersu Uzala, 1906.

Source: VK Arseniev, *Sobranie Sochinenii v 6 Tomakh*, vol. 1 (Vladivostok: Rubezh, 2007).

With the coming of Stalinism, Arsen'ev was to face disgrace and persecution, and his vision of the frontier was to be overshadowed by a far more simple triumphal image of the march of progress: '[T]wenty-five settlements on the once desolate shore of the Amur estuary', proclaimed one typical report from the 1930s, 'where there stood only one or two miserable Nivkh huts, have become large villages containing hundreds of houses with electricity'.[24] Yet Arsen'ev's image of the region, with its combined themes of national pride and exoticism, progress and nostalgia for lost wilderness, was to survive as an important undercurrent both in Russian and in Japanese imagery of the frontier zone, and to be given a belated revival many years later in the Japanese director Kurosawa Akira's acclaimed film version of *Dersu Uzala*, released in 1975.

On the Japanese side of the border, meanwhile, rapid political change was producing a new vision of the region, one which in some respects more closely paralleled earlier Russian imaginings of Siberia as a second America. In 1867, following more than 250 years of rule, the Tokugawa

23   VK Arsen'ev, *Dersu Uzala: Skvol' Taigu* (Moscow: Mysl', 1972), p. 228; on Arsen'ev, see also Stephan, *The Russian Far East*, pp. 170–72 and pp. 194–96; Slezkine, *Arctic Mirrors*, pp. 127–28.
24   Ni Kolesnikov, AM Boyarnik and VA Sharapov, eds, *Sotsialisticheskoe Stroitel'stvo na Sakhaline 1925–1945* (Yuzhno-Sakhalinsk: Arkhivy Otdel Sakhalinskogo Obispolkoma, 1967), p. 453.

Shogunate collapsed in the face of a military uprising by a miscellaneous group of opponents united under the banner of imperial restoration. After a relatively brief period of armed conflict, the supporters of the old regime were forced to flee north to Hokkaido, where one of their leaders, Enomoto Takeaki, sought to establish a base of opposition to the Restorationist forces by proclaiming the establishment of a 'Republic of Ezo', which drew inspiration in part from the model of the United States and in part from the ideas of Enomoto's French military adviser, Jules Brunet. Although the scheme was very short-lived, and it is uncertain how much Enomoto really knew of US political ideas, it seems likely that he (rather like Alexander Herzen) envisaged the frontier region as an unsettled space whose very emptiness made such radical political experiments possible.[25]

In the longer term, though, it was a new and subtly different vision of America that was to exert the greatest influence on Japanese imaginings of the north. The establishment of the Meiji government in 1868 opened the way to large-scale plans for the colonisation of Hokkaido, for which America served as a model, not simply in terms of geographical imagination, but also in much more practical ways. Of 65 Western advisers hired by the new regional administration to assist with the early development of Hokkaido, 48 were Americans, among them former US Commissioner of Agriculture Horace Capron, who in his earlier career had played a significant part in crushing Native American resistance to the colonisation of the American West.[26] Capron brought with him information on the ways in which indigenous lands had been appropriated and distributed to settlers in other colonial societies including India, Australia and the US, and argued against the creation of indigenous 'reservations' on US lines, instead favouring a wholesale policy of assimilation towards the Ainu.[27] This was, indeed, the policy adopted by the Meiji state, which gave the Ainu 'Japanese' names, prohibited their traditional hunting practices and instituted a vigorous program of assimilationist education for Ainu children.

25   Oyama Tsunao, 'Nichibei Bunka Sesshoku no Rekishi no naka no Hokkaido', in *Hokkaidō to Amerika*, ed. Sapporo Gakuin Daigaku Jinbun Gakubu (Sapporo: Sapporo Gakuin Daigaku Seikatsu Kyōdō Kumiai, 1993), p. 108.
26   Harada Kazufumi, 'Kaitakushi no Oyatoi Gaikokujin to Amerika', in Sapporo, *Hokkaidō to Amerika*, pp. 159 and 170; on Capron, see also Fumiko Fujita, *American Pioneers and the Japanese Frontier: American Experts in Nineteenth-Century Japan* (Westport, Conn.: Greenwood Press, 1994).
27   Ōsaka Shingo, *Ishida Kiyotaka to Hōresu Kepron: Hokkaido Kaitaku no Nidai Onjin – Sono Shōgai to sono Gyōseki* (Sapporo: Hokkaidō Taumusu Sha, 1962), pp. 166–81.

Under the influence of Capron and other American advisers, US farm tools and techniques were introduced to the region, and a system of allocating farm land to colonists (in part modelled on the principles used in the colonisation of the American west) was created. This, like equivalent schemes on the Russian side of the frontier, was of course based on the expropriation of villages and hunting grounds previously used by the indigenous people of the region. Although prison labour played an important part in the construction of roads and railways in Hokkaido, particularly in the north-eastern region surrounding the newly constructed Abashiri prison, the colonisation of the island was primarily based on the voluntary inflow of farmers and fishers from the south. In this context, 'America' was seen less as a model of political liberty than as an example of colonial development, centred upon the skill and hard work of migrant family farmers. The prominent agronomist Tsuda Sen, for example, saw Hokkaido as holding the potential for 'the creation of a United States of America within the Japanese Empire': and the America he had in mind was first and foremost the America of the Pilgrim Fathers – a place where development would be born of diligence, frugality and a pioneering spirit.[28]

This 'opening up' of the north was accompanied by a renaming of the region that symbolised changing official, and eventually also popular, perceptions of the frontier zone. The name 'Hokkaido' (North Sea District), based on proposals put forward by the Japanese explorer Matsuura Takeshirō, was officially bestowed on the largest and most southerly island of 'Ezo' in 1869. The name 'Ezo' itself fell into disuse, and the Okhotsk region in general came to be commonly referred to by the term 'Hoppō' (the Northern Regions). The shift was more than a semantic one. It both reflected and helped to shape changing images of the surrounding world. 'Ezo', as a word applied both to the region and its inhabitants, had been redolent with overtones of 'barbarism' in the Chinese sense of the word. 'Hoppō', on the other hand, was part of a new geography that redefined Japan in relation to the nineteenth-century global order. In this order, the two main coordinates were 'the Occident' (*Seiyō*) and 'the Orient' (*Tōyō*). These arrived, as it were, pre-packaged by Western geography, and were accepted into Japanese thought (by and large) as immutable spatial realities. Within this dichotomy, Japan was

28   Oyama, 'Nichibei Bunka Sesshoku', pp. 108–09.

inescapably assigned to the spatial realms of 'the Orient', even though various reformers might argue that, spiritually and socially, Japan should seek to escape from its Asian destiny and remake itself as part of 'the Occident'. But as far as the other two compass points – north and south – were concerned, Japanese writers had greater freedom to define their own sense of space. During the second half of the nineteenth century, the terms popularised to describe this space were, on the one hand, *Nanyō* or *Nanpō* (the South Seas or the Southern Region) and on the other *Hoppō* (the Northern Region). Significantly, unlike *Seiyō* and *Tōyō*, these terms located Japan at the centre, with the Northern Region extending outward from Hokkaido into the Okhotsk Sea and the Southern Region stretching southward from Okinawa into Taiwan, Micronesia and ultimately the islands of Southeast Asia. They offered an imaginary panorama of Japan as a long chain of islands stretching from the frozen north to the subtropical south, and embodying a potential for expansion in either direction, or in both at once.

Figure 6.4. A Japanese settlement in the Habomai Islands, c. 1920.

Source: Tetsudō Shō Hokkaidō Kensetsu Jimusho, *Nemuro, Nayoro, Mashike Zentsū Kinen Shashinchō* (Sapporo: 1922).

In the first half of the twentieth century it was the concept of 'southward advance' (*nanshin*) that would acquire the greater hold over popular imagination and practical policymaking, but during the Meiji period (1868–1912) 'northward advance' (*hokushin*) provided an essential testing ground for Japanese colonisation, as settlers moved first into Hokkaido and the Kurile Islands and then (after Japan's 1905 victory in the Russo–Japanese War) into the regained southern half of Sakhalin (known in Japanese as Karafuto). Just as the creation of Priamur created scope for Russian 'Trans-Amurians' to dream of an expanded Asian destiny, so this northern foothold encouraged some Japanese to nurture Siberian dreams. A brief Japanese incursion into Eastern Siberia and Northern Sakhalin during the post-revolutionary chaos of the early 1920s served to heighten Soviet suspicions of such dreams, but inspired certain Japanese politicians and intellectuals to press the cause of 'northward advance' with increasing vigour. It was in this context that some Japanese officials and intellectuals encouraged dreams of an independent Yakut Republic in Siberia under Japanese tutelage (see Chapter 7), and in 1939 the Central Scientific Research Laboratory of the colony of Karafuto staged an exhibition on the development of the area it labelled 'the Northern Region of East Asia' (*Tōa Hoppō*). This extended the earlier and more parochial version of the 'Northern Regions' to embrace not only Karafuto but also Manchuria, Mongolia, Eastern Siberia, and the Buryat and Yakut Autonomous Regions, an area that, the organisers proclaimed, contained a total population of over 43 million people.[29] In this region, just as in Southeast Asia, the exhibition's publicity argued that Japan's destiny was to reverse centuries of European colonisation and promote the vision of 'Asia for the Asians'.[30] All this remained, of course, no more than a dream; an illusion that was shattered by the defeat of the Japanese empire in the Asia-Pacific War.

---

29   Karafuto Chō Chūō Shikenjō, *Karafuto Chō Chūō Shikenjō Sōritsu Jūnen Kinenshū* (Toyohara: Karafuto Chō Chūō Shikenjō, 1942).

30   Anon., 'Toa Hoppo Kaihatsuten o Miru', *Karafuto Jihō* 29 (September 1939): p. 127.

Figure 6.5. 'The Northern Region of East Asia'.

Source: Map from the 1939 exhibition by the Karafuto Central Scientific Research Laboratory.

Reimagining the Frontier

During the very short Soviet–Japanese conflict of August to September 1945, Soviet forces swept into the southern half of Sakhalin and the Kurile island chain, creating a new national frontier that ran through the waters immediately to the north of Hokkaido. Throughout the postwar decades, Soviet ideology emphasised the image of the border zone as the vulnerable interface with the threatening forces of capitalism, and richly illustrated official publications with titles like *The Frontier Gives Birth to Heroes* [*Granitsa Rozhdaet Geroev*] glorified the courage of the soldiers and settlers who guarded the limits of the Motherland.[31] On the Japanese side, meanwhile, the frontier became in many ways a forgotten region. Though heavily fortified, and the subject of repeated attempts by an assortment of political groups to stir nationalist sentiment, its impact on the public imagination was small.

After its defeat in war, the Japanese government continued to argue that sovereignty over southern Sakhalin/Karafuto had not been determined under international law. Until the end of the twentieth century, official Japanese maps of the region still showed the island as bisected by a frontier line at the 50th parallel. But no serious efforts were made by Japan to reclaim its lost colony of Karafuto, and, in a quiet act of political pragmatism, in 2001 Japan opened a consulate in Yuzhno-Sakhalinsk (previously known as Toyohara), the former capital of its colony of Karafuto, thus de facto recognising the region as part of Russia and renouncing its claim to the territory.[32]

The Kurile Islands, though, were another matter. In 1956, as part of the process of restoring diplomatic relations, USSR and Japan came close to resolving the issue on the basis of a so-called 'two island solution', with the southernmost islands – Shikotan and the Habomai group – being returned to Japan, while the Soviet Union would retain control of Iturup and Kunashir. But this was the height of the Cold War, and the United States, which was concerned about this potential concession to its Soviet rival, privately warned the Japanese government that if it proceeded with the agreement, the United States might refuse to return Okinawa (which had

---

31   *Granitsa Rozhdaet Geroev* (Moscow: Izdatel'stvo Dosaaf SSSR, 1976); Stephan, *The Russian Far East*, pp. 274–84.
32   See Kudō Nobuhiko, *Waga Uchinaru Karafuto* (Fukuoka: Sekifūsha, 2008), pp. 60–67.

been under US occupation ever since Japan's wartime defeat in 1945).[33] The deal fell apart, though the two island solution remained a possible compromise that was to resurface whenever relations between Japan and the Soviet Union – or its successor state Russia – seemed to be thawing. One such brief moment of thaw occurred at the end of the twentieth century, when a rapprochement between Japan and Russia produced the 'Yeltsin-Hashimoto Plan', formulated at a meeting of the two countries' leaders at Krasnoyarsk in Siberia in November 1997 and reaffirmed by their meeting at Kawana in Japan in April 1998. This set a timetable for the resolution of the border issue between the two countries, committing both governments to work towards a settlement by the end of the year 2000, but the deadline was not met, and almost two decades later the two governments were still locked in efforts to define their border in the Okhotsk.

In the postwar period, use of the expressions *Nanyō* or *Nanpō* for the regions to Japan's south fell into disuse, but the expression *Hoppō* was revived specifically in the context of the *Hoppō Ryōdo* – the Northern Territories. The term 'Northern Territories' was first officially used by Japan's Foreign Ministry at the time of the 1956 negotiations, and became the official term used for the four southernmost islands from 1963.[34] By the late 1960s, the phrase had become the core of a nationalist appeal for the return of this 'lost territory' spearheaded by a government-sponsored Association for Countermeasures Related to the Northern Territories (*Hoppō Ryōdo Mondai Taisaku Kyōkai*),[35] and in 2018 the Ministry of Education announced that it would bring in guidelines to ensure that all high school students would be taught that the Northern Territories are 'an integral part of our territory'.[36] As researchers like Alexander Bukh and Iwashita Akihiro have shown, though, a complex politics lies behind this reconstruction of the region's identity. The 'Northern Territories' issue has repeatedly been used by various political groups across the ideological spectrum to boost their nationalist credentials, and has at times been

33   Nobuo Shimotomai, 'The Cold War in East Asia and the Northern Territories Problem', in *Northern Territories, Asia-Pacific Regional Conflicts and the Aland Experience: Untying the Kurillian Knot*, ed. Kimie Hara and Geoffrey Jukes (London and New York: Routledge, 2009), pp. 52–61, reference from pp. 56–57, doi.org/10.4324/9780203880166.

34   Alexander Bukh, 'Constructing Japan's "Northern Territories": Domestic Actors, Interests, and the Symbolism of the Disputed Islands', *International Relations of the Asia-Pacific* 12 (2012): pp. 483–509, particularly pp. 497–98, doi.org/10.1093/irap/lcs008.

35   Bukh 'Constructing Japan's "Northern Territories"', pp. 497–98.

36   '"Kōkyō Jugyō": Shinbun ya Tōkei Katsuyō – Kōkō Shidō Yōryo no Kaisetsusho Happyō', *Yomiuri Shimbun* (Tokyo Edition), 18 July 2018, p. 29.

strongly promoted by the Hokkaido Prefectural government to strengthen its hand in power struggles with the central government.[37] But the people most directly affected by the issue – the former residents of the islands and their descendants, many of whom now live in the town of Nemuro, nearest to the disputed territories – tend to have a distinctively different perspective on the matter. For many of them, the crucial issue is less the return of Japanese territory than the opportunity to visit family graves on the islands, and to have access to the vital fishing grounds that surround the area. Opinion surveys have shown that majority local opinion supports a compromise solution, rather than insistence on the return of all the disputed islands, if it can help to ensure that access.[38]

On the Russian side of the divide, as Paul Richardson has vividly shown, the Kurile Islands have become a similarly symbolic touchstone in domestic politics, deployed by diverse groups of political and intellectual elites in support of their own particular constructions of national identity. Richardson broadly defines three visions of the islands that have emerged in the post-Soviet Era. From the 1990s, a group of 'liberal institutionalists' argued for a compromise settlement with Japan as a means of demonstrating post-Soviet Russia's credentials as a 'good citizen' on the international stage. They were countered by a group of 'territorial imperativists' who evoked the history of the nation's past glories and sacrifices to support their insistence that the southern Kuriles should never be surrendered to Japan. Third, a group whom Richardson call's 'pragmatic patriots' (and who include President Vladimir Putin) argue for strategic negotiations and compromises with Japan, and are potentially willing to sacrifice some territory in search of their overriding goal of securing Russia's future as a global great power.[39]

Putin's strategic nationalism has been paralleled by that of Japanese Prime Minister Abe Shinzō. Abe takes a particularly hardline stance on Japan's two other territorial disputes – with China over control of the Senkaku or Diaoyu Islands and with Korea over the little islet of Dokdo or Takeshima – but in the Kurile Islands dispute, he evidently sees an opportunity for a diplomatic breakthrough in a region riven by international tensions. In November 2018, the governments of Japan and Russia announced

---

37   Bukh 'Constructing Japan's "Northern Territories"'; Akihiro Iwashita, *Japan's Border Issues: Pitfalls and Prospects* (London and New York: Routledge, 2015).
38   Iwashita, *Japan's Border Issues*, p. 51.
39   Paul B Richardson, *At the Edge of the Nation: The Southern Kurils and the Search for Russia's National Identity* (Honolulu: University of Hawai'i Press, 2018).

a renewed determination to reach an overall settlement on the basis of the compromise two island solution proposed in 1956, though this again has yet to produce results.[40] These moves were accompanied by the revival of even more concrete visions of a bridging of the divide between the two nations. During the first decade of the twenty-first century, Russian officials touted the idea of a cross-border tunnel linking Hokkaido and Sakhalin, and in June 2018 President Putin instructed his cabinet to develop a plan to build two bridges – one between Hokkaido and Sakhalin and the other between Sakhalin and mainland Siberia, thus linking Japan directly to the Asian continent.[41] What will come of this ambitious scheme remains to be seen. More surprisingly, perhaps, in December 2018 Putin also announced his government's intention officially to recognise the Ainu as one of the indigenous peoples of Russia[42] – a move that could be read either as a belated acknowledgement of a historical fact (that Ainu were in fact indigenous inhabitants of the Kuriles, the southern tip of Kamchatka and southern Sakhalin, and some of their descendants still live in Russia), or as a strategic move to undermine those Japanese claims to the territory that have been based on the status of 'our' Ainu as the original inhabitants of the Kurile Islands.

Meanwhile, other less official dreams for the region also began, more quietly, to make themselves heard. The Pacific War and the Cold War that followed completed the gradual process by which centuries of contact between indigenous groups in the Okhotsk region was severed. Most of the Ainu inhabitants of Sakhalin were 'repatriated' after the war to Hokkaido – a place many of them had never seen before – and they were later followed by a small number of other indigenous people who had lived in the Japanese half of the island before the war (see Chapter 7). For decades, the border left these people almost wholly isolated from friends and relatives on the Russian side of the frontier. But by the end of the twentieth century that was changing. Visiting Japan for the first time in September 1997, the Sakhalin Nivkh activist and poet Vladimir Sangi participated in a forum attended by a number of Hokkaido Ainu and descendants of Ainu and Uilta evacuated from Sakhalin to Japan after

---

40   Dmitri V Streltsov, 'Will Japan and Russia Really Settle their Territorial Dispute?' *The Diplomat*, 15 November 2018, thediplomat.com/2018/11/will-japan-and-russia-finally-settle-their-territorial-dispute/ (accessed 20 December 2018).

41   'Putin Poruchil Pravitel'stvu Prorabotat' Vopros Postroiki Mosta na Sakhalina', *RBC*, 24 June 2018, www.rbc.ru/society/24/07/2018/5b570abe9a79478fca3837da (accessed 2 January 2019).

42   'Ainu Minzoku wa "Roshia Senjū Minzoku": Pūchin Shi ga Nintei Hōshin', *Hokkaidō Shimbun*, 19 December 2018, p. 2.

the Pacific War.[43] There he and others spoke of the destruction wrought both on the environment and on the lives of the indigenous population by earlier policies of 'opening up' the frontier region and emphasised the need for the indigenous people of the region to have an active voice in any decisions about the future of the disputed islands.[44] Some Ainu activists, too, point out (with good reason) that it is the Ainu people who historically have the oldest claim to the disputed northern islands.[45]

These voices suggest other perspectives for looking at the past and present of the region. The frontier is a place where national governments negotiate or contest the geographical limits of their power, and where citizens of the nations on either side create their dreams of other worlds. But national borders are also lines that carve their way straight through the lives of those who inhabit the territories they bisect. In the following chapter we shall take one point on the border that bisected Sakhalin Island as a vantage point for exploring this experience of division and its implications for the indigenous people of the region.

This chapter is a revised version of an article that first appeared in the journal *Pacific Affairs* 72, no. 1 (1999): pp. 57–77.

43   Vladimir Sangi, address to seminar 'Saharin Shosu Minzoku no Kako to Genzai' ['The Ethnic Minorities of Sakhalin: Past and Present'], Hokkaido Museum of Northern Peoples, Abashiri, 20–21 September 1997.
44   Sangi, address to seminar 'Saharin Shōsū Minzoku no Kako to Genzai'.
45   See, for example, Alexander Bukh, 'Ainu Identity and Japan's Identity: The Struggle for Subjectivity', *The Copenhagen Journal of Asian Studies* 28, no. 2 (2010): pp. 35–53, reference from pp. 46–49, doi.org/10.22439/cjas.v28i2.3428.

7

INDIGENEITY AND MODERNITY IN COLONIAL KARAFUTO

For the natives of Otasu (Orok, Gilyak) there are no firewood for homes or logs to build houses, so we've got to ask for help. The Japanese living back of the Shimkuki River cut them down to their stumps, every year two miles long by a mile wide. That's why we've got to ask for help. We want to become Japanese quickly, so please help us.[1]

Some words echo across decades. Fragments of text speak into the imagination; sounds of life rise from the rubble of historical archives. The message translated here was written around 1930 by a villager from the little settlement of Otasu in the Japanese colony of Karafuto (southern Sakhalin).[2] As its angular sentences suggest, it was written with pain and difficulty in a foreign language (Japanese), for the author of this statement was member of the Nivkh-speaking community, whom the colonial bureaucracy called 'the Gilyak'. Not only were the complicated Japanese characters foreign, the very medium of written messages, addressed to unknown urban officials with unspecified powers over life and death, was alien.

---

1   Quoted in Tanaka Ryō and D Gendānu, *Gendānu: Aru Hoppō Shōsū Minzoku no Dorama* (Tokyo: Gendaishi Shuppankai, 1978), p. 61.
2   In this chapter I use the term 'Karafuto' to refer to Japanese-ruled southern Sakhalin, and 'Sakhalin' to refer to the island as a whole.

Written messages to officialdom were acts of desperation. By the time this letter was written, the forests of Karafuto were falling to make paper for that most literate of all societies, Japan, and the foundations of indigenous life had been uprooted. In 1926 the Uilta-speaking and Nivkh-speaking inhabitants of Karafuto began to be herded into the settlement of Otasu, and in 1930 a 'Native School' was opened, to teach the children of the village Japanese language, literacy, numeracy and loyalty to the emperor.[3] It was with the help of those schoolchildren that the Nivkh villager composed his halting plea to the colonial authorities.

This chapter explores the landscape of this small corner of the prewar and wartime Japanese colony of Karafuto. The village called Otasu, also sometimes known as 'the Forest of Otasu' (*Otasu no Mori*) was perched on a sandbank at the confluence of the Poronai and Shisuka Rivers about 70 miles from the Russo–Japanese frontier, and had just one road and a rickety ferry to link it to the outside world. Its houses varied from the substantial homes built by the reindeer-herding entrepreneur Dmitri Vinokurov (discussed further below) and the prominent Uilta shaman Uzlgush and her family[4] to very basic wooden structures built to a standardised design. Lives flowed out into the grassy spaces between the houses, where dappled dogs wandered among buckets, baskets and racks of drying fish. Beyond the village and the river, the tundra stretched flat to the edges of the sky: in places cleared by logging, but elsewhere still thickly wooded with larch and silver birch. The floor of the forests was cushioned in summer with moss-covered peat. Mosquitoes swarmed in the shadows, and only the reindeer and those who followed them could avoid the bog patches hidden under the tussocky surface.

In September the forests were briefly vivid with autumn colours and the ground covered with cranberries (*furep*), but in winter the temperature could drop to 30 degrees below zero. Engines seized up in the cold. The fastest travel was by dog or reindeer sled: icy journeys through tunnels of endless translucent whiteness.[5] Otasu was both short-lived and very small. It existed for just 20 years – roughly from 1926 to 1946, and the

3   Shisuka Dojin Jimusho, *Orokko sono ta Dojin no Seikatsu* (Shisuka: Yōsawa Chū Shōten, 1935), pp. 30–34.
4   See Nikolai Vishinevskii, *Otasu: Etno-Policheshie Ocherki* (Yuzhno-Sakhalinsk: Dal'nevostochnoe Knizhnoe Izdatel'stvo, 1994), pp. 133–34.
5   This description is based on Tanaka and Gendānu, *Gendānu*; Hishinuma Uichi, *Karafuto Annai Chimei no Tabi* (Tokyo: Chūō Jōhōsha, 1938); and Yamamoto Sukehiro, *Karafuto Genshi Minzoku no Seikatsu* (Tokyo: Arusu, 1943).

population at its peak was less than 200. Despite this, a surprisingly large number of records of life in Otasu remain, including official reports, anthropological essays, travel guides, memoirs and photographs.

Otasu was not a 'traditional' indigenous village, but a unique colonial artefact. That fact itself, together with the village's location and history, made it a particularly revealing embodiment of some important facets of colonial policy. Here I want to consider how the design of the village represented the structures and aims of imperial rule, but also the ways in which that design was experienced and reinterpreted both by people who visited Otasu and by the people who lived there. For a village or an urban district can never be seen as a whole, it is always viewed from specific standpoints, even though those standpoints change as the viewer moves on his or her trajectory through the landscape. It is the multiple visions that various individuals had of Otasu, as much as the village's physical design itself, that reveal the complexities of Japanese colonial rule over the indigenous people of Karafuto, and of the indigenous experience and reinterpretation of 'modernity'.

Figure 7.1. Traditional Uilta summer houses on the outskirts of Otasu.
Source: Karafuto Chō, ed., *Karafuto Kyōdo Shashinchō* (Toyohara: 1934).

Japan and the Indigenous People of Karafuto

The extension of Japanese influence over the southern part of Sakhalin had been a long and gradual process, going back to the late seventeenth century. As we saw in the previous chapters, by the middle of the nineteenth century, Japan had extensive fishing interests along the southern coasts of the island, while Russia had also established outposts further north. In the 1855 Treaty of Shimoda, Russia and Japan reached an agreement under which the island would be treated as the joint territory of both countries, but this proved impractical, and there were recurrent conflicts between Japanese and Russian settlers. Under the 1875 Treaty of St Petersburg, Japan agreed to transfer control of the island to Russia in return for Japanese sovereignty over the entire Kurile Island chain to the east. However, as part of the spoils of the Russo–Japanese War of 1904–05, Japan regained control of the southern half of Karafuto, as far north as the 50th parallel; and, during the period from 1921 to 1926, during its intervention in Siberia following the Russian Revolution, Japan also briefly occupied the northern half.[6]

All of these events had a massive impact on the lives of the indigenous people of Karafuto/Sakhalin. Figures for the last decade of the nineteenth century suggest that, at that time, the island had around 4,000 indigenous inhabitants, of whom the largest group were Nivkh (generally referred to by prewar officials and anthropologists as 'Gilyak'), who also inhabit parts of the eastern coastline of continental Siberia.[7] While most of the 2,000 or so Nivkh lived in the north of the island, most of the Ainu population of Karafuto was concentrated in the south. Before 1875, the number of Karafuto Ainu had also been estimated at around 2,000. But many Karafuto Ainu worked in Japanese fisheries and had close links to Hokkaido. At the time of the Treaty of St Petersburg, those who remained on Karafuto automatically became Russian citizens. Escaping this shift in nationalities, over 800 Karafuto Ainu chose or were persuaded move to Japan, where many had close links to Hokkaido Ainu communities or

6   Taisho Nakayama, 'Japanese Society on Karafuto', in *Voices from the Shifting Russo–Japanese Border: Karafuto/Sakhalin*, ed. Svetlana Paichadze and Philip A Seaton (London and New York: Routledge, 2015), pp. 19–41, reference from pp. 20–21, doi.org/10.4324/9781315752686.
7   See James Forsyth, *A History of the Peoples of Siberia* (Cambridge: Cambridge University Press, 1992), p. 219.

to Japanese fishing enterprises. Despite their wish to live in the north of Hokkaido, close to Karafuto, they were then forcibly transferred en masse to the village of Tsuishikari, near Sapporo, and where many succumbed to epidemic diseases.[8] The other main indigenous group on the island were the reindeer-herding Uilta (referred to by the colonial rulers as 'Orok'), who probably numbered around 700–800 at the end of the nineteenth century, and who lived in the centre of the island – the area that came to be bisected by the border between the Japanese colony of Karafuto and Soviet Sakhalin. Meanwhile, other reindeer-herding people from the Evenk and Saha (Yakut) language groups were also moving in small numbers into Sakhalin from the Siberian mainland, while small groups of Ul'chi people from the Siberian mainland also travelled to Sakhalin to trade, and sometimes settled there.[9]

Sakhalin thus became the focus of complex interactions between multiple cultural and linguistic groups. Intermarriage between indigenous groups was common,[10] and the Russian ethnographer Bronislaw Piłsudski, who conducted careful surveys of Sakhalin Ainu communities in the first decade of the twentieth century, noted that Ainu on the west coast of the island also sometimes married Chinese or Koreans who crossed from the continent to collect kelp.[11] Piłsudski estimated that about 10 per cent of the Ainu population of Sakhalin had non-indigenous (Japanese, Russian, Korean or Manchurian) ancestry, and also recorded numerous instances of intermarriage between Uilta women and Nivkh, Evenk and others.[12] Newly arriving groups like Evenk and Saha also had an important impact on the lives of older-established indigenous groups. Evenk influence seems to have been a major factor in the nominal conversion of many Uilta to Russian Orthodox Christianity,[13] and also helped to strengthen

---

8   Karafuto Ainu Shi Kenkyūkai, ed., *Tsuishikari no Ishibumi* (Sapporo: Hokkaidō Shuppan Kikaku Sentā, 1992); Kōichi Inoue, 'A Case Study on Identity Issues with Regard to Enchiws (Sakhalin Ainu): Reconsidering B. Pilsudski's "Draft Rules for the Establishment of Authority over the Sakhalin Ainu" (1905)', *Hoppō Jinbun Kenkyū* 9 (2016): pp. 75–87.

9   AV Smolyak, *Etnicheskie Protsessy u Narodov Nizhnevo Amura i Sakhalina* (Moscow: Nauka, 1975).

10   See, for example, Bronislaw Piłsudski, 'B. O. Pilsudski's Report on his Expedition to the Ainu and Oroks of the Island of Sakhalin in the Years 1903 to 1905', in *The Collected Works of Bronislaw Piłsudski*, vol. 1, *The Aborigines of Sakhalin*, ed. Alfred F Majewicz, Trends in Linguistics Documentation 15-1 (Berlin and New York: Mouton de Gruyter, 1998), pp. 192–221, doi.org/ 10.1515/9783110820768-013.

11   Piłsudski, 'B. O. Pilsudski's Report', p. 194

12   Piłsudski, 'B. O. Pilsudski's Report', p. 211; Bronislaw Piłsudski, 'From the Report on the Expedition to the Orok in 1904', in *The Collected Works of Bronislaw Piłsudski*, pp. 618–77, reference from p. 634, doi.org/10.1515/9783110820768-028.

13   Piłsudski, 'B. O. Pilsudski's Report', p. 207.

the Uilta reindeer-herding economy, though Evenk and Saha also seem to have used their greater wealth and connections to the continent to enter into exploitative trade relations with local Uilta and Nivkh. At least until the early twentieth century, Nivkh and Uilta from Sakhalin continued to travel regularly to the continent to trade goods at posts on the Amur River (as they had done in earlier times – see Chapter 5). A Uilta informant told British traveller Charles Henry Hawes in 1901 that wealthier members of his community in particular travelled to Nikolaevsk on the Amur to sell 'furs, reindeer etc. and bring back large quantities of rice, tea, tobacco'.[14]

For the people who lived in central Sakhalin, the division of their homeland between two increasingly hostile powers had a devastating effect. Unlike the borders of earlier empires, the frontier across the island did not meander along rivers or the crests of mountain ranges, but ran in a straight line along the 50th parallel: a course made possible by nineteenth-century improvements in the techniques of surveying. During the first years of its existence the frontier remained largely invisible at ground level, its presence signalled only by occasional wooden boundary-markers. The indigenous Nivkh and Uilta people, and the handful of Russian and Japanese settlers who lived near the border, continued to travel relatively freely to and fro though the swampy forest, which stretched unbroken across the limits of empire. When he visited the region in 1912, the Japanese ethnographer Torii Ryūzō was still able to cross the frontier unchallenged with the help of local guides, and was welcomed with gifts of tobacco and potatoes by a family living in an isolated outpost on the Russian side.[15]

But after the Russian Revolution, and even more as tensions between Russia and Japan intensified during the 1930s, the frontier acquired a physical presence that cut through the everyday lives of the region's inhabitants. Wooden boundary-posts were replaced by concrete blocks; a cleared space, like a wide straight road, was gouged out of the forest, and those who crossed it risked being shot or imprisoned for spying. So the trade route that had for centuries linked Hokkaido to the Amur region via Sakhalin was severed, just as the eastern trade route linking Hokkaido to Kamchatka via the Kurile Islands was also cut. Relatives, trading partners and former neighbours on either side of the border were involuntarily and irrevocably separated from one another. The practical consequences were

---

14   Charles Henry Hawes, *The Diaries of Charles Henry Hawes*, Book VII, transcript, MS. Eng. misc. b. 443, Bodleian Library, p. 109.
15   Torii Ryūzō, *Aru Rōgakuto no Shuki*, reprinted in *Torii Ryūzō Zenshū*, vol. 12 (Tokyo: Asahi Shinbunsha, 1976).

profound. There were, for example, more men than women in the small Uilta population of Japanese Karafuto, but the border made it increasingly difficult for the them to seek Uilta brides from Russian Sakhalin.[16] People who shared a common history, in some cases even members of the same family, found themselves incorporated into the modern state as subjects of two very different and generally hostile great powers: on the one side, the Japanese empire, on the other, the Tsarist Russian empire and its successor, the Soviet Union.

Most of surviving Ainu who had left the island in the 1870s went back to their homeland: some of them while it was still under Russian rule, and the remainder after Japan regained control of southern Karafuto/Sakhalin in 1905.[17] These Ainu had acquired Japanese family registrations, and were thus treated in legal terms as 'Japanese'; all other 'Karafuto Natives' had no family registers, but were enrolled in a 'Native List' (*dojin meibo*). This meant that they were not covered by the provisions of Japanese criminal and civil law, which made it virtually impossible for them to acquire property or run their own businesses. In 1932, after a prolonged campaign by Karafuto Ainu, the colonial government finally extended full Japanese citizenship to all of them, but not to the small group of other indigenous people, who in the 1930s numbered in total between 400 and 500, with the largest group being the community of around 300 Uilta.[18]

Resettlement, Farming and the Architecture of Modernity in Japanese Karafuto

A survey carried out in the first years of colonisation found Ainu living in 43 settlements, some of them with populations of less than 20 people.[19] From 1907 onwards, however, the Karafuto authorities amalgamated this scattered population into just nine villages: five on the east coast and four on the west coast.[20] Concentrated settlements were not only easier to

---

16   Nakanome Akira, *Karafuto no Hanashi* (Tokyo: Sanseidō, 1917), p. 37.
17   Inoue, 'Case Study on Identity Issues'.
18   Shisuka Dojin Jimusho, *Orokko sono ta*, p. 1.
19   Kasai Takechiyo, *Karafuto Dojin Kenkyū Shiryō* (Mimeographed report, 1927), pp. 97–98 and 120–21.
20   Karafuto Chō, ed., *Karafuto Chō shisei sanjūnen shi*, vol. 2 (Tokyo: Hara Shobō, 1973), p. 1984. Original published in 1936.

control and to fit into the norms of Japanese local government, they also provided the basis for other modernisation and assimilation measures: the building of schools, shops, roads and police stations.

One result of this resettlement was the creation of a sharper division between Ainu and other indigenous groups in the colony. Early colonial surveys had commented on the close contacts and frequency of intermarriage between different peoples, and nineteenth-century accounts suggest that a number of hamlets on the central parts of the Sakhalin coast had mixed populations of Ainu, Uilta and Nivkh; but the drawing of the frontier and the resettlement of populations made such interactions increasingly difficult. The forced movements of Karafuto Ainu population in some cases aroused bitter protests. One important cause of distress was the fact that relocation removed people from the places where their relatives and ancestors were buried.[21] The resettlement policy did, however, provide the colonial authorities with an opportunity to superimpose their vision of civilisation and order on indigenous life.

Figure 7.2. The Ainu 'model' village of Torandomari.
Source: Karafuto Chō, ed., *Karafuto Shashinchō* (Toyohara: 1929).

The new Ainu villages of Karafuto embodied a vision of modernity that, interestingly enough, closely resembled that of indigenous villages that were to be constructed at the same time across the border in Soviet Sakhalin, where the Nivkh population was gathered into villages of standardised two- or three-bedroom houses built according to a 'model plan'.[22] The new Ainu settlements in Japanese Karafuto were typically

21   Kasai, *Karafuto Dojin Kenkyū Shiryō*, p. 101.
22   See, for example, Chuner M Taksami, *Nivkhi: Sovremenoe Khozyastvo, Kul'tura i Byt* (Leningrad: Nauka, 1967), pp. 165–66.

constructed along a main road, with a row of identical houses on either side. The houses themselves were designed along the lines of Japanese urban housing, though little thought seems to have been given to anything other than providing basic shelter. It was left to the inhabitants themselves to give their standardised homes character and life. Shirakawa Shinsaku, who grew up in the Ainu village of Shirahama on the southeast coast of Karafuto in the 1930s, recalls that his home was one of a row of identical rectangular buildings with two six-mat rooms at the front and two six-mat rooms at the back. The houses had no cupboards for clothes or bedding, nor any inside toilets:

> Depending on the families, some people put in sliding doors and screens. It was the same with cupboards. Better-off families got their own proper furnishings, including cupboards, but poorer families had absolutely nothing in their houses. They were just totally empty. There was no money so they couldn't buy things, you see. But people who were good with their hands made things by themselves and so on. In our house, my elder sister bought and installed a thick paper sliding door herself.[23]

Otasu: Showplace of the Ethnicities

Yet, both south and north of the border that divided the island of Karafuto/Sakhalin, policies of assimilating and 'modernising' indigenous people, paradoxically, went hand in hand with an urge to preserve and display aspects of the 'exotic' culture of the empire's far-flung and ethnically diverse subjects. In Japanese Karafuto, the place that most symbolically embodied this paradox of empire was the settlement Otasu. During the first years of the colony's existence, the colonial government of Karafuto had paid little attention to the non-Ainu indigenous groups, who lived in relatively remote areas near the Russian border, though in 1912–13 it commissioned a survey of these groups by education expert Nakanome Akira, whose report, published in 1918, proposed an intense program of assimilation.[24] Little was done to follow up on these suggestions until

---

23   Shirakawa Shinsaku and Shirakawa Yaeko, with Fujimura Hisakazu, 'Shirahama Chihō no Kurashi', in *Henke to Ahachi*, ed. Fujimura Hisakazu and Wakatsuki Jun (Sapporo: Sapporo Terebi Kabushiki Kaisha, 1994), pp. 147–48.

24   Nakanome Akira, *Dojin Kyōka Ron* (Tokyo: Iwanami Shoten, 1918); see also Aoyanagi Fumiyoshi, 'Otasu no "Seiritsu" to Kyōikusho', *Aldo* 19 (2002): pp. 6–11, reference from p. 6.

the 1920s, but in 1923 a group of 18 Uilta and Nivkh were dispatched on a tour of the colonial capital Toyohara, which was intended to provide them with an introduction to the superior civilisation of the colonisers.[25]

From 1926 onward, assimilationism began in earnest, and the non-Ainu indigenous people of the colony began to be relocated into this single centralised settlement. Described colonial officials as 'the capital city of the natives' (*dojin no miyako*) and as a 'representative native village' (*dojin no daihyō buraku*), by 1938 Otasu had a population that was carefully enumerated and ethnically labelled as follows: 87 'Gilyak' (i.e. Nivkh) living in 16 houses; 78 'Orokko' (i.e. Uilta) living in 14 houses; two households of eight people who were a mixture of 'Gilyak' and 'Sandā' (i.e. Ul'chi); and one Yakut (i.e. Saha) household whose 10 members included two 'Yakuts', five 'Tungus' (i.e. Evenk), one 'Orokko' and two Japanese.[26] Although the official report fails to mention this, there were also other Japanese residents in the village: a couple named Kawashima Hideya and Nao, who jointly ran the local school, and their small children.

On the one hand, Otasu was a focus of modernisation policies that closely resembled those applied to the Ainu population of Karafuto. Nakanome Akira had proposed that assimilationary education was needed to turn the indigenous people of Karafuto into 'people of economic worth to the nation'.[27] The Otasu 'Native School' (*dojin kyōikusho*), opened in 1930, proclaimed its mission as being to 'foster sentiments of nationality (*kokuminteki jōsō*)', 'impart vocational training', 'nurture a spirit of cooperation', and 'develop a spirit of diligent labour'.[28] Lessons (all of which were conducted in Japanese) emphasised stories from Shinto mythology and the heroic moments of Japanese history, and the school received several visits from army officers who gave glowing accounts of Japanese military victories in Japan's expanding war with China.[29] The colonial authorities in the neighbouring town of Shisuka also approvingly noted the gradual shift of Uilta people from their traditional bark-roofed huts and tents to wooden houses, which seem to have been much like the houses built in the Ainu village of Shirahama and elsewhere.[30]

---

25   Aoyanagi, 'Otasu no "Seiritsu"', p. 6.
26   Shisuka Dojin Jimusho, *Orokko sono ta*, pp. 1 and 28.
27   Nakanome, *Dojin Kyōka Ron*, p. 108.
28   Shisuka Dojin Jimusho, *Orokko sono ta*, p. 31.
29   Vishinevskii, *Otasu*, pp. 126–27.
30   Shisuka Dojin Jimusho, *Orokko sono ta*, p. 28.

Figure 7.3. Colonial modern housing in Otasu.
Source: Karafuto Chō, ed., *Karafuto Shashinchō* (Toyohara: 1929).

At the same time, though, the village was presented to the outside world as a small model of the Japanese empire's rule over ever-expanding realms of exotic peoples. While the colonial government generally discouraged tourist visits to Ainu villages, Otasu was promoted as a highlight of the colonial Karafuto tourist experience, where guidebooks promised visitors the opportunity to see the indigenous people of the colony living 'a life which was close to its primitive state' (*genshi no chikai mama no seikatsu*).[31] The appeal of this promise was so great that by the late 1930s the village was said to be 'extremely busy with visitors (from Japan) in midsummer'.[32] Since, by this time, around 30 per cent of the colony's Uilta population and 75 per cent of its Nivkh population were living in Otasu (and the percentages were steadily rising), the village also became a focus for Japanese anthropological fieldwork on the indigenous peoples of Karafuto.

This presentation of the village as a symbol of Japan's rule over the exotic other was perfectly encapsulated in an exhibition of life in Karafuto, staged in Tokyo in 1940 as part of the national celebration of the '2,600th anniversary' of the mythical creation of the Japanese imperial line.

31   Hishinuma, *Karafuto Annai Chimei*, p. 77.
32   Shisuka Dojin Jimusho, *Orokko sono ta*, p. 28.

The exhibition included a life-sized panorama of the village of Otasu, where visitors could see waxwork models of the settlement's Nivkh and Uilta people engaged in traditional fishing and herding activities. The only tangible representation of the assimilation policies the authorities were so vigorously pursuing in the village was the background music, which featured a recording of the village children singing Japanese patriotic songs.[33] As a new 'native village' almost entirely designed by the colonising power, Otasu thus became a particularly vivid physical representation of the aims and contradictions of policies towards indigenous people, and of the indigenous people's response to the those policies.

The House of the 'Village Chief'

In the centre of the settlement, close to a landing point on the river, stood the key symbols of colonial rule – the school, a public bath house and a martial arts hall (*dōjō*) and behind them, on a slight rise in the sand dunes, the Shinto shrine. On either side of the central space occupied by these symbols of power were rows of houses, neatly divided by ethnicity – the Nivkh houses to east along a tributary of the Poronai River and the Uilta houses to the west along the Shisuka River. A ferry linked the settlement to the nearby town of Shisuka, and thus to the outside world, and from the pier where the ferry tied up, a tourist route took visitors in a loop around the village.

The first stop on this route was one of the village's largest buildings, the home of the 'village chief' Dmitri Vinokurov, which stood to the west of the village near the Nivkh side of the settlement. Here Vinokurov and his Evenk wife Anastasia offered visitors Russian coffee, and tourists were given a chance to photograph each other amongst the large herd reindeer that grazed peacefully in the woodland behind the chief's house. They were also treated to lectures on the ideology of Greater East Asia by Vinokurov, who told one group of visitors in the late 1930s that:

> originally the great land of northern Asia belonged to the gods of nature, and I believe it is therefore natural for them to seek salvation and protection from the power of Japan's rising sun flag. However, the great army of the Red Flag is seeking to spread over the great northern land, and all Asia is in crisis.[34]

---

33 'Hokumon no mamori Karafuto tenrankai', *Karafuto jihō* 33 (1940): pp. 69–77.
34 Hishinuma, *Karafuto Annai*, pp. 78–79.

'Behind the Red Flag', he added darkly, 'stands Roosevelt'.[35] Vinokurov employed his own interpreter, a Japanese man named Umemiya Tomisaburō, who was (like Vinokurov) married to a Evenk woman, Ulyana,[36] and it seems that much of the explanation of local customs tourists received came from Umemiya and his family.[37]

Vinokurov's physical location at the entrance to the village, and his title of 'village chief', are particularly interesting because none of the other Otasu villagers regarded him as a 'chief'. Indeed, he seems to have been regarded with considerable suspicion by his neighbours, and to have had a supercilious attitude to the other indigenous people of the village.[38] Vinokurov was in fact an immigrant from Siberia – a relatively prosperous member of the Saha (Yakut) indigenous people of Siberia. He had been born in 1884 in the settlement of Yarmonka on the banks of the Suola River in the Yakut region of Siberia, and worked as a guide for oil prospectors before moving to Sakhalin in 1910 in the hope of making money on the periphery of the newly emerging oil business there.[39] He was a shrewd merchant and entrepreneur and had amassed considerable wealth by the time the Japanese occupation of northern Sakhalin began. Vinokurov first came into contact with the Japanese authorities during the period from 1921 to 1926 when Japan, as part of its so-called Siberian Expedition following the Russian Revolution, occupied the northern half of Sakhalin. In 1921, the Japanese ethnographer Torii Ryūzō travelled to the Tym River, which had long been a meeting place for the indigenous communities from various parts of Sakhalin and Lower Amur. There he encountered Vinokurov with a group of other Saha from the mainland engaged in building a road along the banks of the river.[40]

During the occupation, the Japanese military attempted to organise and distribute propaganda to the indigenous people of northern Sakhalin, in the hope of turning them into an advance guard for resistance to a return of Soviet forces to the region. In this, they appear to have had

---

35   Hishinuma, *Karafuto Annai*, p. 79.
36   See Vishinevskii, *Otasu*, p. 39.
37   See Hishinuma, *Karafuto Annai*, p. 80.
38   *Minzoku Saigo no Hitobito: Otasu no Dojin* (Shisuka: Karafuto Insatsusha, 1937), p. 9; see also Hokkaidō Dōritsu Hoppō Minzoku Hakubutsukan, 'Tenji Kaisetsu: Karafuto 1905–45 – Nihonryō jidai no shōsū minzoku', in *Karafuto 1905–45 – Nihonryō jidai no shōsū minzoku*, ed. Hokkaidō Dōritsu Hoppō Minzoku Hakubutsukan (Abashiri: Hokkaidō Dōritsu Hoppō Minzoku Hakubutsukan, 1997), pp. 5–14, reference from p. 11.
39   Vishinevskii, *Otasu*, p. 7.
40   Torii, *Aru Rōgakuto*, pp. 294–300.

ON THE FRONTIERS OF HISTORY

little success. Vinokurov, however, did enthusiastically embrace the
Japanese cause, apparently hoping that Japanese support would help
him establish an independent Yakut Republic in his homeland. He was
appointed a community leader, and began to cultivate powerful friends
within Japanese military and political circles.[41] When Japan withdrew
from the northern half of the island in 1925, Vinokurov moved to an area
close to the dividing line between the Soviet and Japanese sectors, where
he herded reindeer and continued his trading activities, but in 1926,
while on a hunting trip on the northern side of the still porous border, he
was arrested by the Soviet security forces on a charge of collaborating with
the Japanese, and released only when he promised to gather intelligence
on Japanese Karafuto for the Soviet Union. He then fled south to the
town of Shisuka, and soon after was installed as 'chief' of the native village
of Otasu.

Throughout the late 1920s and much of the 1930s, Vinokurov was
encouraged in his dream of creating a Yakut Republic by Japanese politicians
and activists, among them the well-known nationalist thinker Tōyama
Mitsuru (1855–1944). He visited Tokyo three times for negotiations on
the subject, as well as writing a lengthy article for a Japanese colonial
newspaper setting out his vision for the liberation of Eastern Siberia
by the Japanese empire.[42] With support from the Japanese colonial
authorities, he also helped to create an experimental station to develop
more scientific methods of reindeer breeding and raising. Meanwhile,
the Japanese colonial authorities seem deliberately to have created the
'native capital' around him, using him as a focus for an imperial vision
of Japan's relationship with the indigenous peoples of the North. Because
the reindeer herders who worked for Vinokurov could easily cross the
border undetected, and because Vinokurov maintained communication
with people in Northern Sakhalin and Siberia, the Japanese government
(like the Soviet administration to the north) clearly saw him as a valuable
source of intelligence.

41 Vishinevskii, *Otasu*, pp. 7–10 and 21–25.
42 *Minzoku Saigo no Hitobito*, p. 10; see also Vishinevskii *Otasu*.

178

Figure 7.4. A reindeer herd near Otasu.
Source: Karafuto Chō, ed., *Karafuto Kyōdo Shashinchō* (Toyohara: 1934).

The Reindeer Herders' Tents

After visiting Vinokurov, tourists continued on their path around the village, generally focusing their eyes and their camera lenses not on the modern 'barrack-style housing' in which most of the Nivkh and Uilta population of Otasu lived nor on the agricultural projects in which they were required to participate, but rather on the visual signs of 'tradition', such as the distinctive Nivkh and Uilta graves that lay scattered in the forest near the village. Their photographs often picked out the bark-roofed houses where some Uilta families still lived in summer, and the conical tents they inhabited when they followed the reindeer in winter. Tourists also visited the school to buy examples of the beautiful neo-traditional embroidery made by the village girls in the handicraft lessons.[43]

Anthropologists and linguists spent longer in the village and interacted more intensively with its inhabitants. Yet, viewing Otasu through the prism of the anthropological quest for pristine culture, their descriptions of local society too have a remarkable capacity to foreground some details

---

43 Hishinuma, *Karafuto Annai*, p. 79; see also Kitagawa Aiko, '"Otasu" no kurashi to watashi', in Hokkaidō Dōritsu Hoppō Minzoku Hakubutsukan, *Karafuto 1905–45*, p. 15.

while blotting out others altogether. A striking example is ethnographer Yamamoto Sukehiro's account of the *Life of the Primitive People of Karafuto* [*Karafuto Genshi Minzoku no Seikatsu*], published in 1943. Yamamoto was the director of the museum built by the colonial authorities in the Karafuto capital of Toyohara, and his fieldwork was conducted in and around Otasu, yet his study almost entirely erases the signs of colonial modernity. The photographs that fill his small but richly illustrated book show dog sleds racing across the frozen tundra, reindeer herders in their birch-bark houses or winter tents, and indigenous men and women engaged in traditional handicrafts.[44]

Yamamoto's ethnographic vision of Otasu is encapsulated in his discussion of the 'Yakut' (Saha) people of Karafuto. The sample he had to work with here was small, since there were only two Saha families in Japanese Karafuto: the Vinokurovs and the family of a man named Ivan Petrovich, who was employed by Vinokurov to look after his reindeer herds. Yamamoto only briefly mentions Vinokurov, whom he describes as a 'ruling class Yakut'.[45] The Otasu 'village chief', who read Russian newspapers and drank Russian coffee, and whose daughter collected French dolls, did not readily fit into Yamamoto's ethnographic framework. His description of the life of Karafuto's Yakuts is therefore a rhapsodic account of Ivan Petrovich's timeless existence in the Karafuto tundra as he follows the reindeer, sleeping in a tent and living life in tune with the rhythms of nature. There is no hint in any of this that the Petrovich family was in fact part of Vinokurov's extended household, and presumably spent a fair amount of their existence in Vinokurov's Russian-style house, being regularly treated to their employer's extended monologues on Pan-Asianism, Marxism and FD Roosevelt.

The same extraction of the 'indigenous' from the 'modern' recurs throughout Yamamoto's accounts of Otasu's indigenous people. It continues, too, in the numerous ethnographic works he published in the postwar period on the basis of his 1930s and 1940s fieldwork, as it does in the work of other prominent ethnographers like Ishida Eiichirō, who also performed fieldwork in prewar Otasu.[46] A common theme of

---

44   Yamamoto, *Karafuto Genshi Minzoku*.
45   Yamamoto, *Karafuto Genshi Minzoku*, p. 12.
46   See, for example, Ishida Eiichrō, 'Hōryō Minami Karafuto Orokko no Shizoku ni tsuite - 1', in *Ishida Eiichirō Zenshū*, vol. 5 (Tokyo: Chikuma Shobō, 1970), pp. 333–75.

these ethnographic works is a lament that the pristine traditional lifestyle is on the brink of disappearing, and yet it is constantly re-created in the minds of the ethnographers as a kind of essence extracted from the more messy realities they encountered on their visits to the field.

Farm Fields and School Classrooms

In these ethnographic accounts, therefore, we receive no glimpse of the other Otasu that emerges forcefully from the writings of visitors like Kasai Kōmuru. Kasai, visiting the village in 1941, saw only the transformations wrought by the modernising hand of Japanese colonialism. He depicts the past of the indigenous inhabitants as one of degradation and 'defeat', in which they had become spectacles for the entertainment of others. Now, thanks to the impact of assimilation and development policies, he writes, the Uilta and Nivkh have shifted from their hunting and herding existence and begun to cultivate fields and eat vegetables; the young speak Japanese, and the doors of houses are adorned with name plates showing both indigenous names and the new Japanese names villagers had been encouraged to adopt. 'The wind of a new century', proclaims Kasai, 'is sweeping through the lives' of the indigenous people of Otasu. The men of the village, he observed, were almost all absent during his visit, having gone off to undertake paid work at construction sites, farms or fisheries, etc.; and (as Kasai noted with amazement) even the young man working in the engine room of the steam ferry that plied the route across the Poronai River between Otasu and Shisuka could be identified by his 'dull and expressionless face' as a member of the indigenous community: 'When I noticed this I was astonished – they're even working in places like this!'[47] The subject of the condescending comment was a young Uilta man named Daaxinneeni Geeldanu (discussed further below), who would later recall how the tourists on the boat would often ask him weird questions about 'natives' and recount wildly inaccurate stories about strange 'Orok' customs, as though they regarded the indigenous people as 'some kind of monsters'.[48]

---

47   Kasai Kōmuru, 'Otasu no Dojintachi', *Karafuto* 13, no. 10 (1941): pp. 104–07, reference from p. 104.
48   Tanaka and Gendānu, *Gendānu*, p. 65.

In these various 'readings' of the landscape of Otasu, then, we can see how different observers adopted contrasting viewpoints that made one aspect of the village's ambivalent symbolism visible, and another invisible. Observers like Kasai saw little but the modern housing, the newly created farm fields (which were largely unsuited to the Otasu environment, and were repeatedly washed away by floods) and the school with its Japanese-speaking pupils who would soon be 'taking their place in the workplaces of life just like Japanese people'.[49] Tourists and many anthropologists, meanwhile, chose paths through this landscape that concealed the school, the farm fields and the modern housing, and revealed vistas of fur-clad hunters, grazing reindeer herds and tent-dwelling indigenous people.

The underlying assumption that framed both these fields of vision was that it was possible to be indigenous and traditional, or to be modernising and 'on the way to becoming' Japanese, but it was not possible to be both at once. From this perspective, the category of 'Japaneseness' could contain both a 'traditional' and a 'modern' aspect – the indigenous people of Otasu, for example, could in some circumstances be 'patriotic Japanese' while also herding reindeer – but the category 'indigenous' could only equate to 'traditional': they could not simultaneously be 'Uilta' or 'Nivkh' and 'modern'. There was no space within this vision for a recognition that indigenous culture was itself dynamic, rapidly adapting to circumstances by the absorption and creative use of outside influences: no space, for example, for discussing how the tents used by the reindeer herder Ivan Petrovich were in fact Russian military tents adapted to Saha needs.

A few Japanese observers of Otasu, however, did manage to view the village from a somewhat more complex perspective. One of these observers was the schoolteacher, Kawamura Hideya, who spent some 15 years in Otasu, living in quarters attached to the schoolhouse in the middle of the village. Kawamura seems to have been genuinely liked and respected by many of his pupils, and he left some careful and sympathetic accounts of the indigenous society of Otasu. In these, Kawamura acknowledged, not only that indigenous society was rapidly changing in response to Japanese colonialism, but also that this was just part of a long history of cultural interaction and change that had produced the forms of 'tradition' so eagerly sought out by tourists to Otasu. He described, for example, the variety of clothing worn by the people of Otasu, which for men varied

49   Kasai, 'Otasu no Dojintachi', p. 104.

from embroidered outfits worn with fur boots to suits and neckties, and for women were often plain blouses with skirts and jackets. 'Tourists to Otasu', Kawamura noted,

> sometimes see the women's clothes and say 'Hey, the natives are wearing western clothes!' However, this sort of hasty conclusion is problematic. Their undershirts are called *uribaf* or *uribaashika* [in the Uilta language], and this is derived from the Russian *rybashka* [shirt], because they are like the undershirts worn by Russian peasant women.[50]

Figure 7.5. Kawamura Hideya teaching a class at the 'native school', Otasu.
Source: Karafuto Chō, ed., *Karafuto Kyōdo Shashinchō* (Toyohara: 1934).

He himself was indeed actively promoting this type of creative hybridisation by (for example) encouraging his female pupils to apply traditions of Uilta and Nivkh embroidery to the production of artefacts like purses and table mats for sale to visiting tourists.[51]

---

50 Kawamura Hideya, 'Orokko, Giriyāku no Seikatsu to Fuyū', *Karafuto Chōhō* 6 (October 1937): pp. 155–65, quotation from p. 157.
51 Kitagawa, '"Otasu" no kurashi', pp. 15–18, reference from p. 15.

Kawamura's own position, however, was also a profoundly problematic one. His official role was to 'modernise' and 'Japanise' his students by inculcating in them 'sentiments of nationality' and 'a spirit of diligent labour', and yet (like others in similar colonial roles) he clearly valued the indigenous languages and ways of life his school was seeking to eradicate, and tried to record them even as his school undermined their survival. The ambivalence of his position in the paradoxical landscape of Otasu were (as we shall see) to end both in disaster for many of his pupils and in a personal sense of defeat for Kawamura himself.

Pathways Through Colonial Modernity

The accounts left by former indigenous inhabitants of Otasu themselves tell yet another story. For them, the relatively loose and flexible links that had long connected them to other societies were now replaced by a much more intense and forcible process of exposure to the 'Japanese modern', creating a perilous landscape though which they had to pick their way as best they could. Often, this involved processes of hybridisation, through which new colonial experiences were married with older traditions in ways that made them comprehensible and usable.

A particularly vivid illustration of the way in which unfamiliar knowledge and experience could be reinterpreted in the framework of more familiar ways of knowing comes from some of the indigenous legends ethnographer Yamamoto Sukehiro collected in Otasu in the colonial era. The following legend, for example, told to him by a local Nivkh storyteller, is full of haunting suggestions of local responses to the arrival of the imported diseases that had ravaged the indigenous communities of Sakhalin/ Karafuto in the late nineteenth and early twentieth centuries:

> Rōhen of the Kīrin (Evenk) people was watching over his reindeer on the banks of the Mui River, and then he went to set traps for rabbits beyond the Poronai River. But, sitting on the bank of the river, there was a Russian woman smoking a cigarette. When Rōhen approached her, she stood up and asked 'I am trying to go south towards the coast; which way should I go?' Rōhen replied, 'from here, the river is winding, and the journey is long. You had better cut straight across the tundra.' Rōhen had understood that this woman was the spirit of influenza, and so he told her to go across the tundra where no-one lived. The woman walked a little

way ahead, passed two or three trees, and disappeared into the shadows of the forest. After he had seen this, a tornado arose, and whirled all the way to Taraika on the coast.[52]

From internal evidence, this story would seem to have originated in the early years of the twentieth century, and may perhaps refer to the particularly severe 1905 influenza epidemic that caused many deaths in Sakhalin indigenous communities.[53] By the 1930, the pressures of colonial assimilation had become much more intense, and the challenges faced by a younger generation are well illustrated by the stories of two members of the Daaxinneeni clan,[54] one of six Uilta clans living in Japanese-ruled Karafuto. The Daaxinneeni clan had migrated in earlier times from the north-eastern coastal area of Sakhalin Island to the shores of Lake Taraika (now known as Lake Nevskoye) in the south, and then a number of the clan members had moved to Nokoro (now known as Vladmirovo).[55] Among them were Gergulu, who had been born sometime in the 1890s, and was known for his shamanic powers. When the 'native village' of Otasu was created, Gergulu, his wife Anna and their children were moved into the village.[56] The residents of Otasu continued to consult shamans (both male and female) about health problems and other problems, and Gergulu's position in the village, both as a shaman and a skilled hunter, was an important one. He was a major source of information for visiting ethnographers like Ishida Eiichirō.[57]

During the 1930s, Gergulu and Anna, who had two daughters but no son, adopted a boy named Geeldanu,[58] who was then aged about five or six, and was also a member of the Daaxinneeni clan.[59] Adoption was quite common amongst the indigenous people of the Okhotsk region, and Geeldanu maintained close contact with his birth mother, who lived just across the road from his adoptive parents: since she was blind, she summoned him to help with daily tasks around the house. Geeldanu grew up in Otasu, attending the village school along with other members of his

---

52   Yamamoto Sukehiro. 'Giriyaku, Yakūto no Minwa', *Minzokugaku Kenkyū* 27, no. 3 (1963): p. 573.
53   See, for example, Piłsudski, 'B. O. Pilsudski's Report', p. 215; Bronislaw Piłsudski, 'Selected Information on Individual Ainu Settlements on the Island of Sakhalin', in *The Collected Works of Bronislaw Piłsudski*, pp. 311–30, particularly p. 311, doi.org/10.1515/9783110820768-018.
54   The transliteration of the Uilta language is complex, because the sounds do not correspond precisely with those of European languages or of Japanese. Here I use the romanisation followed by the linguist and scholar of the Uilta language Ikegami Jirō.
55   Ishida, 'Hōryō Minami Karafuto', p. 355.
56   Tanaka and Gendānu, *Gendānu*, p. 26.
57   Ishida, 'Hōryō Minami Karafuto', p. 335.
58   Sometimes transcribed via Japanese as 'Gendānu'.
59   Tanaka and Gendānu, *Gendānu*, pp. 26–31.

double family. There they received an intensive program of 'Japanisation', which included being given Japanese names – Daaxinneeni Geeldanu became 'Kitagawa Gentarō' – learning the Japanese language and Japanese patriotic songs, and being taught the art of growing vegetables and buckwheat (relatively unfamiliar foods as the Uilta diet had consisted mostly of meat and fish supplemented with wild plant food such as *furep*).[60]

Like many of his schoolmates, Geeldanu generally began his day by going fishing in the river for trout that was sold to customers who crossed over to the village from the nearby town of Shisuka. The pocket money he earned from these and other tasks was spent on trips to Shisuka to see samurai movies at the local cinema, followed by a meal of fried udon on the way home, or on visits to the town's summer festival, where you could buy ice cream. The visits to Shisuka were a source of both delight and pain. The town, with its shops and restaurants, trucks and motorcars, and the smokestacks of the Ōji paper mill sending their plumes billowing over its outskirts, was exotic and exciting, but also a place of painful encounters with the sharp end of colonialism. Within the Otasu school (as Geeldanu's adoptive sister recalled) 'we didn't even know that discrimination existed', but when the children and their parents went to town, they would sometimes face mockery and insults from the local Japanese residents.[61]

The desire to escape from the pain of discrimination was, perhaps, one of the powerful forces that made Geeldanu and other children internalise the messages conveyed by their school education, longing to 'become Japanese'.[62] For Geeldanu, serious education in Uilta hunting techniques came only after he had completed six years of school, when his adoptive father Gergulu took him to the coast to learn the techniques of shooting seals on the floating ice shoals, and of shaping the handmade bullets used in the Murata rifles that most Uilta then used for hunting. Bullets were often made by cutting up strips of lead and placing the pieces in a bottle, which was given to children to use as a rattle; after a few months of use, the constant shaking and friction would turn the lead into beautifully smooth and rounded bullets.[63] Geeldanu's main employment after graduation, though, was not in hunting and reindeer herding, but in

---

60   Tanaka and Gendānu, *Gendānu*, pp. 32–34; Kitagawa, '"Otasu" no kurashi', p. 16.
61   Kitagawa Aiko, *Watashi no Oitachi* (Abashiri: Jakka Dukhuni, 2001), pp. 7–8.
62   Tanaka and Gendānu, *Gendānu*, pp. 33–35.
63   Kitagawa Aiko (address to seminar 'Saharin Shōsū Minzoku no Kako to Genzai' ['The Ethnic Minorities of Sakhalin: Past and Present'], Hokkaido Museum of Northern Peoples, Abashiri, 20–21 September 1997).

a job with Shisuka city administration, who employed him as a ferry-boat ticket collector and as a clerk before promoting him to captain the ferry between Shisuka and Otasu.[64]

Figure 7.6. Indigenous people hunting marine mammals near Otasu.
Source: Karafuto Chō, ed., *Karafuto Shashinchō* (Toyohara: 1929).

Geeldanu's adoptive sister, who was given the Japanese name Kitagawa Aiko, also attended the village school, and took part enthusiastically in the headmaster's schemes to encourage the production of embroidered items for sale to Japanese tourists. She learnt the skills of Uilta embroidery, not from her own mother but from the mother of a schoolfriend – a woman who was known for her particularly fine sewing.[65] Uilta embroidery is both distinctive and symbolic of the long history of trade and interaction amongst the many communities of the Okhotsk and Lower Amur. Its designs bear a strong resemblance to those found in Nivkh, Ul'chi, Nanai and other neighbouring societies, though Uilta designs have a particularly strong tendency to symmetry, and demanded very delicate stitching of reindeer hides to ensure that the design was visible only on one side.[66] The development of these embroidery skills had long relied on commercial relationships with neighbouring societies that could provide access to

---

64 Tanaka and Gendānu, *Gendānu*, pp. 63–70.
65 Kitagawa, '"Otasu" no kurashi', pp. 15–16.
66 Hokkaidō Kyōiku Iinkai, *Uiruta Minyō Bunkazai Kinkyū Chōsa Hōkokusho*, no. 10 (Sapporo: Hokkaidō Kyōiku Iinkai, 1989), pp. 84–101.

steel sewing needles. The traveller Charles Hawes, who visited a Uilta community at Chaivo on the east coast of Sakhalin at the beginning of the twentieth century, described how metal needles were treasured, carefully stored in special needle cases made of ornamentally carved bone, and passed down from one generation to the next as heirlooms.[67]

Figure 7.7. Uilta needle case, early twentieth century.
Source: Charles H Hawes, *In the Uttermost East* (London and New York: Harper and Brothers, 1903).

The stories told by Otasu residents like Daaxinneeni Geeldanu and Kitagawa Aiko give some sense of the complex world through which young indigenous residents of Karafuto sought a path in the 1920s and 1930s – rapidly absorbing newly imported elements of Japanese culture while also learning older Uilta skills and knowledge from their elders, and often finding creative ways to combine the two. Thus the Murata rifle could fit conveniently into, and enhance, Uilta hunting skills, and Uilta embroidery could be applied to the creation of tourist souvenirs.

The Martial Arts Hall

But on the border, culture was never really separable from politics. In August 1942, museum director Yamamoto Sukehiro composed an introduction to his account of the traditional lifestyles of the 'primitive peoples of Karafuto' in which he wrote:

> These are people whose ancestors or fathers migrated to Karafuto at some point in the past; sometimes they fought with blizzards and sometimes they struggled with ice-floes, and they spent many generations in wild areas which are not blessed with natural wealth; today they live by the waters of the Poronai River, having created their home in the icy tundra of our Karafuto and made the snowfields their garden. Now they have been blessed by the

---

67 Charles H Hawes, *In the Uttermost East* (London and New York: Harper and Brothers, 1903), p. 221.

beneficence of the Emperor, and their original primitive life is disappearing. However, their life with the reindeers in the depth of the tundra still continues to survive, and their everyday existence hunting sea mammals on the ice floes still appears unchanged.[68]

In the very month when Yamamoto wrote these words, every indigenous young man in Otasu received an official conscription notice from the Japanese military secret service requiring him to report to the village's martial arts hall on a certain morning. On the appointed day, about 30 Uilta, Nivkh and other young men gathered in front of the hall, where they were told that they would now become imperial Japanese soldiers. Many of the young men apparently welcomed conscription as a sign that they had finally been fully accepted as subjects of the Japanese emperor, and as an opportunity to disprove the demeaning stereotypes of inferiority and backwardness that had so often been applied to them by the colonisers. They were given medical inspections, and those who were passed as fit were provided with uniforms and ordered to move to the martial arts hall for intensive training. The recruitment of colonial subjects, who were not covered by Japan's wartime conscription laws, was in part apparently a response to reports that the Soviet Union was using indigenous people for spying missions on the island.[69]

The young Uilta woman Kitagawa Aiko, who was by then in her late teens, recalled:

> In Otasu there was a thing called the youth martial arts hall. It was a residential camp, and its purpose was to gather together the young men of Otasu and train them as spies. After I graduated from school, I and a Nivkh girl called Matsuko went to work there, serving food. As I'd just finished school, I didn't really know how to do catering properly, but any way, there was this kind of atmosphere where we felt we should cooperate to do our bit for Japan. Not only we two but a lot of others applied for the job, but in the end they just took us … Senior people from military intelligence [*Tokumu Kikan*] kept coming to stay the in hall. It wasn't just a place where the young men stayed, you see, so we had to make separate meals for those people and the young men. I used to get up at three in the morning and boil rice. Then, at the same time as serving breakfast, we had to fill the mess tins with

68 Yamamoto, *Karafuto Genshi Minzoku*, p. 1.
69 Tanaka and Gendānu, *Gendānu*, pp. 92–94; Hokkaidō Dōritsu Hoppō Minzoku Hakubutsukan, *Karafuto 1905–45*, pp. 12–13.

packed lunches. In the evening when the young men came back there would be a mountain of empty mess tins to clear up, as well as dinner to be sorted out. I used to get back home after 11 pm.[70]

Kitagawa's adoptive brother, Daaxinneeni Geeldanu was one of those who had passed the medical and was being trained for the spy missions. After their initial training, these young men were sworn to secrecy and allowed to return to 'civilian' life for a while, but then intermittently summonsed to be sent on missions to the border area, where their intimate knowledge of the forest landscape was put to use in tasks such as observing the movements of border guards and conducting surveillance in case of possible infiltration from the Russian side.[71] After Japan's defeat in August 1945, the Soviet army swept into Sakhalin and the Japanese population of Shishuka and surrounding areas crowded the railway station and roads, fleeing southwards in the direction of Japan. Many of the indigenous people of Otasu attempted to join them, but before they could find transport to take them southwards, the Soviet forces arrived and promptly arrested the young men who had been trained for spying missions by the Japanese. Daaxinneeni Geeldanu and his comrades-in-arms were sent to a military court in the city of Toyohara (now Yuzhno-Sakhalinsk) for trial as 'war criminals', found guilty and transported to labour camps near Krasnoyarsk in Siberia. Other indigenous people from Karafuto were also sent to labour camps for 'espionage', and many of them died in the harsh conditions of the Siberian camps – among them Kitagawa Aiko's Evenk husband, whom she had married just six months before his arrest.[72] Kitagawa herself was also held for questioning by the Soviet authorities for about three months; she was released and went to work in a factory on Shisuka (by then renamed Poronaisk).

Meanwhile, the Saha 'village head' Dmitri Vinokurov, who had probably been engaged in intelligence gathering for both sides many years, had finally come under suspicion from the Japanese authorities in 1938 and been arrested and imprisoned in Toyohara for two years. He was released in 1940, but died in Otasu two years later of health problems contracted while in prison, having in his final year of life abandoned his dream of

---

70   Kitagawa, '"Otasu" no kurashi', p. 17.
71   Tanaka and Gendānu, *Gendānu*, pp. 95–128.
72   Kitagawa, *Watashi no Oitachi*, p. 11.

an independent Yakut Republic.[73] After Japan's defeat, the few remaining inhabitants of Otasu moved out of the village, and the 'capital city of the natives' disappeared from the map.

While almost all the Japanese inhabitants of Karafuto were repatriated to Japan after the war, the fate of the island's indigenous groups was more complex. Karafuto Ainu, who were regarded as Japanese nationals, were 'repatriated' to Hokkaido – a place where most had never lived. Many of them were resettled in coastal areas of northern Hokkaido, in villages like Wakasakanai in the north-west and Tokoro near Abashiri, whose harsh environment made them relatively unattractive to majority Japanese.[74] Meanwhile Uilta, Nivkh and other small indigenous groups had never been given full Japanese nationality and (together with the thousands of Koreans who had been brought to the colony to work in coal mines and construction projects) were left in a postwar limbo. It was not until the 1950s that some survivors of the disaster that had befallen the community of Otasu were allowed to migrate to Japan, where most settled around the city of Abashiri on the north coast of Hokkaido. Among them were Daaxinneeni Geeldanu, who arrived in Japan in April 1955 after being released from a Siberian labour camp,[75] as well as his adoptive parents Gergulu and Anna, and his sister Kitagawa Aiko, who had remarried, her second husband being a Korean man who been brought to Karafuto as forced labourer in the coal mines.[76]

As for the school teacher Kawamura Hideya, who had spent the past 15 years teaching the children of Otasu how to become good imperial subjects, in his final encounters with his students before his own repatriation in 1947, he wept and asked their forgiveness for his part in the colonial system. During his time in Otasu he had amassed a mountain of notebooks filled with his 18 years of careful observations of life in Otasu, but most of these were abandoned during his return to Japan. Kitagawa Aiko recalled how she met Kawamura shortly before he was repatriated from Karafuto to Japan.

---

73   Vishinevskii, *Otasu*.
74   See Inoue, 'Case Study on Identity Issues'; also Emiko Ohnuki-Tierney, *Illness and Healing Amongst the Sakhalin Ainu: A Symbolic Interpretation* (Cambridge and London: Cambridge University Press, 1981).
75   See Ikegami Jirō, *Giryaku, Orokko Kibutsu Kaisetsusho: Kitagawa Gentarō Hitsuroku 'Uilta no Kotoba' 1* (Abashiri: Abashiri Hoppō Minzoku Bunka Hozon Kyōkai, 1986).
76   Kitagawa, *Watashi no Oitachi*, pp. 16–18.

He apologised to me and said 'what I taught you was wrong'. Then he said, 'from now on, you can do things the way you think right.' I thought, 'OK, I can do that. But in that case I am not going back to being Uilta, nor am I going to become Japanese'. That was what I decided at that time.[77]

Off the Map

The architecture of Otasu was filled with colonial paradoxes. The functional modernity of new 'barrack' housing, the school and the martial arts hall shared space with the 'exotic' forms of reindeer herders' tents and the sacred symbols of the indigenous graveyard. Visitors to the village could choose their perspective, avoiding its unsettling ambivalence by focusing on one aspect or the other. But the indigenous people who lived in Otasu did not have that luxury. They were required to live lives that constantly moved between the uneasy juxtapositions of the 'representative native village'. The theories of modernity and development prescribed a one-way journey: from 'indigenous' to 'national', and from 'traditional' to 'modern'. But in practice, life for the villagers of Otasu did not flow in this simple one-way direction. Instead, each day they found it necessary to negotiate a path that crossed back and forth across these boundaries. Neither Japanese nor indigenous society offered much in the way of mental maps to help them on this journey, and there can be no doubt that many found it a painful and disorienting journey.

One remarkable expression of that journey is a tiny book – a miniature autobiography – written by Kitagawa Aiko in the early 1980s.[78] The book is handwritten, and illustrated with beautiful drawings of the traditional Uilta designs that Kitagawa and her brother Geeldanu were to spend much of the later part of their lives seeking to preserve (see Chapter 8). But the text that accompanies these drawings is not an account of 'Uilta tradition', but rather a vivid account of Kitagawa's determination to be 'neither Uilta nor Japanese'. It is a stark personal story of a life lived first in Otasu, and then the town of Poronaisk, where social isolation and grim economic conditions left her struggling with thoughts of suicide. Although she and other family members chose to migrate to Japan in the late 1950s, seeing this as the best option open to them, they found themselves confronting

77 Kitagawa, '"Otasu" no kurashi', p. 18.
78 Kitagawa, *Watashi no Oitachi*.

ongoing struggles with prejudice and dislocation: struggles that also profoundly affected the lives of the next generation.[79] The story has no simple end. The harsh story of Kitagawa's life and the charming drawings with which she illustrated it are in irreconcilable tension with one another. The design and structure of Otasu had the power to tear societies apart, and more than half a century after the village and colony Karafuto itself disappeared, the rifts it engendered have yet to be fully healed.

---

79   Kitagawa, *Watashi no Oitachi*; see also Ikegami, *Giryaku, Orokko*.

8

JAPAN AND ITS REGION: FROM TARTARY TO THE EMERGENCE OF THE NEW AREA STUDIES

In May 2018, indigenous people from Australia, New Zealand, North America, Hawai'i and Japan gathered in Canberra to share knowledge and ideas about an issue of profound concern to all of them: the task of reclaiming and repatriating the remains of the dead, dug up by colonial scholars or trophy collectors and removed to museums and universities around the world. The European imperial knowledge system, in its nineteenth- and twentieth-century search for the raw materials to build theories of race and progress, profoundly affected not only ways of life of colonised societies, but also their ways of death. Skeleton-gathering became a scientific tool practised by scholars and trophy hunters alike in all corners of the globe, and evolved into a global network of trade in human remains. As a result, for example, the National Museum of Australia and at least one other Australian institution hold skulls of Ainu people, which appear to have been excavated in Hokkaido and traded to Australia by the Japanese anthropologist Koganei Yoshikiyo in the first half of the twentieth century, while the University of Tokyo and other Japanese institutions hold Australian Aboriginal remains that Japanese scholars received in return. The repatriation of such remains to their places of origin is now an important issue, not only for the communities where the dead once lived and for the institutions that hold their mortal remains, but also for governments and international organisations around the world.[1]

In Japan, intense debate about the return of indigenous remains was sparked in 1995, when a group of academics and students, while clearing out a storeroom at Hokkaido University, came upon cardboard boxes containing six human skulls. Three of these were labelled 'Orok aerial burial, Otasu village' and had evidently been removed by an unknown visitor to Otasu (the indigenous village in Sakhalin discussed in the previous chapter). Another box held the skull of a Korean participant in the Donghak uprising of 1894, which was suppressed with the participation of Japanese troops. Reports of this discovery sparked protests by indigenous activists and an investigation by the university, and after a prolonged struggle by indigenous rights groups, in 2003 the skulls from Otasu were returned to Sakhalin for reburial. A memorial was also erected on the site, and the university authorities apologised for the actions of the researchers who had removed the remains.[2] But Hokkaido University remained in possession of over 900 other Ainu remains, while many hundreds more were still held in museums and universities around Japan, and indeed around the globe. After prolonged campaigns and court cases by Ainu community leaders, a small number of these began to be returned to the communities from which they were taken in 2017.[3] But, although similar repatriation processes in Australia, Canada and the United States began in the late 1980s to 1990s, the process in Japan has barely begun, and remains the subject of intense controversy.

The Ainu participants in the 2018 meeting, all of whom had been actively involved in the repatriation of the Ainu remains from Hokkaido University, discovered that their stories shared many common threads with those of the indigenous speakers from places such as the Kimberley region of Western Australia, the Torres Strait Islands, the Waikato region of New Zealand and the island of Molokai in Hawai'i. One particular

1   See Brigit Katz, 'Australia to Return Remains of Japan's Indigenous Ainu People', *Smithsonian. com*, 15 June 2017, www.smithsonianmag.com/smart-news/australia-return-remains-indigenous-japanese-group-180963697/ (accessed 3 January 2019).

2   See Tanaka Ryō, 'Hokudai "Jinkotsu Mondai" Chōsa Iinkai: "Ninkichū ni Hōkokusho o Otodoke suru" to Mochizuki Bungakubuchō', *Aldo* 41 (December 2009): pp. 4–5.

3   For further information, see Tessa Morris-Suzuki, 'Performing Ethnic Harmony: The Japanese Government's Plans for a New Ainu Law', *The Asia-Pacific Journal: Japan Focus* 16, no. 2 (1 November 2018).

shared concern was to find ways of returning the dead to their homelands with dignity and proper ceremony, despite the fact that there are, of course, no 'traditional' ways to welcome home the remains of the dead that have been stolen from their resting places and removed to alien and distant locations.

Discussions of Japan and its region, or of Japan's regional role, often focus exclusively on the grand narratives of interstate relations or of regional institution-building. The agendas of debate encompass items such as the power relationship between Japan and China, the contribution of Japan to regional economic integration, or the successes and failures of Japan's negotiations on border disputes with its neighbours. These are all important issues. But the grand narratives of regionalism often neglect a complex underlying social fabric that political scientist TJ Pempel calls 'regionalization', the mass of fine intertwined threads that bind particular localities and groups within Japan across national frontiers to places and people throughout Asia and beyond.[4] The stories told at the meeting in Canberra rediscovered the threads created by the journeys of the indigenous dead, while creating new threads of knowledge between those seeking their repatriation.

One important feature of this example is the way that it connects unexpected points on the map. There is nothing in physical or political geography that would have enabled us to predict the existence of a link between places such as Hokkaido, the Torres Strait Islands and Molokai. The thread has been spun by a gradually accumulating history of human movement and action, and the relationships of power and suffering these have forged. It is, in its small way, (I think) an example of the 'architecture' that Arjun Appadurai had in mind when he wrote that 'we need an architecture for area studies that is based on process geographies'; based, in other words, not on visions of great blocks of shared territory or 'civilisations', but on the social and cultural 'precipitates of various kinds of action, interaction and motion – trade, travel, pilgrimage, warfare, proselytization, colonization, exile, and the like'.[5] In this chapter,

---

4   TJ Pempel, 'Remapping Asia: Competing Patterns of Regionalization and Regionalism', in *A Changing Korea in Regional and Global Contexts*, ed. Lee-Jay Cho, Ching-Si Ahn and Choong Nam Kim (Honolulu: East-West Center, 2004), pp. 363–400.
5   Arjun Appadurai, 'Grassroots Globalization and the Research Imagination', in *Globalization*, ed. Arjun Appadurai (Durham and London: Duke University Press, 2001), pp. 7–8.

I should like to explore the possibilities of such alternative architectures for understanding the many societies of Japan and its multiple regions in a time of far-reaching and sometimes disorienting change.

Transforming Area Studies: Geopolitics and Chronopolitics

In the second decade of the twenty-first century, East Asia has been in the midst of profound transformation. The rise of China, the economic and social problems that beset Japan, tensions on the Korean Peninsula, and the United States' changing relationship to the region are all elements in this moment of change. One way of describing the current moment is to say that, whereas the Cold War on the Atlantic side of the globe ended in the period from the late 1980s to early 1990s, in Northeast Asia the Cold War has never truly ended. The region is therefore still in the process of a transition to a post–Cold War era, and the outcome of this process will help determine the nature of the global post–Cold War order. Despite all the changes of the past two decades, China and North Korea remain one-party states; Cold War treaties still underpin the security policies of Japan and South Korea; and Korea remains divided. Efforts to move forward towards new forms of regional cooperation and integration have produced some results over the past two decades, but progress has been slow and Northeast Asia is still repeatedly described by observers as 'one of the most dangerous places in the world'.[6]

My purpose in this chapter is not to analyse this moment of transformation itself, but rather to ask: what does it mean for the study of Japan, and more broadly for East Asian studies? How has the study of Japan and its region been shaped by the changing nature of the regional order? How should area studies be responding to the challenges posed by the profound changes underway in the region? How might Japan's relationship with its region be reimagined? Since my main focus of research is Japanese history, I am particularly interested in the changing ways in which historians of Japan and of East Asia have conceptualised their area of study, and how they have been influenced by, and responded to, contemporary shifts in

6   See for example, Kent Calder, 'Northeast Asia: The "Organizational Gap" and Beyond', in Cho et al., *A Changing Korea*, pp. 27–74, quotation from p. 27; Li Xing and Zhang Shengjun, 'One Mountain with Two Tigers: China and the United States in East Asian Regionalism', *Perspectives on Federalism* 2, no. 3 (2010): pp. 111–29, quotation from p. 125.

the regional order. In tracing this story, I draw some inspiration from the postwar Japanese scholar of world history, Uehara Senroku, whose vision of history always revolved around a search for the meaning of 'the present era' (*gendai*).[7] How does the ever-moving, ever-changing 'present era' influence the frameworks of time and space that are applied to the study of Japan's past? Of course, the literature on Japanese and East Asian history is vast and multilingual, and here all I attempt to do is to look at a few examples of writings (mostly in English, some in Japanese) that suggest some answers to that question. But I hope that even a limited attempt to address the question may be a useful starting point for reflection about our own role as students of Japan and its region in an age of transformation.

As we saw in Chapter 1, the rise of area studies was largely a mid-twentieth-century phenomenon. Indeed, some scholars have argued that area studies were both a product of the Cold War era and deeply permeated by the politics of the Cold War world. As the Cold War in Europe came to an end, area studies too came to be subject to growing criticism, not only for its ideological connections but also for its vision of geographical and social space. So, for example, Willem van Schendel, drawing on the work of Lewis and Wigen, Appadurai and others, reimagines areas as the product of human interaction, so that a 'region', rather than being fixed in the unchanging bedrock of physical geography, may start to assume 'unfamiliar spatial forms – lattices, archipelagos, hollow rings, patchworks'.[8]

But the foundations that sustained the architecture of postwar Japanese studies and East Asian studies are deeply embedded in our patterns of thought, and rethinking them is a challenging task that involves the excavation of subterranean assumptions that underpin the very language that we use in our discussion of areas and regions. Those foundations, moreover, were laid well before the Asia-Pacific War, and I would suggest that any rethinking of East Asian and Japanese studies needs to go back at least a hundred years, to an age of an earlier transformation that convulsed the East Asia from the last decade of the nineteenth century to the first decade of the twentieth. So here I will start with some thoughts on the emergence of Japan and East Asia as fields of historical research in the

---

7   Uehara Senroku, 'Gendai wa donna Jidai ka', *Sekai*, August 1950; Uehara Senroku, *Sekaishi ni okeru Gendai no Ajia* (Tokyo: Miraisha, 1961).
8   Willem van Schendel, 'Geographies of Knowing, Geographies of Ignorance: Jumping Scale in Southeast Asia', *Environment and Planning D: Society and Space* 20, no. 6 (2002): pp. 647–68, quotation from p. 664, doi.org/10.1068/d16s.

English-speaking world, before going on to consider more recent and alternative ways of approaching Japanese history. I shall reflect on the way in which the distinctive vision of space embodied in twentieth-century area studies is interwoven with a distinctive vision of time: borrowing Johannes Fabian's term, to consider not only the implicit geopolitics but also its implicit chronopolitics of studies of Japan and its region.[9]

From Tartary to the Far East

When he published the fifth edition of his bestseller *Things Japanese* in 1905, the famous British Japanologist Basil Hall Chamberlain (1850–1935) ended his entry on 'History and Mythology' with the tart comment 'it is not possible to conclude this sketch of Japanese history with the usual formula "books recommended" – for the reason that there are no general histories of Japan to recommend'.[10] In Chamberlain's view, as late as the end of the Russo–Japanese War 'a trustworthy history of Japan remains to be written – a work which should do for every century what Mr. Aston has done for the earliest centuries only, and Mr. Murdoch for the single century from 1542 to 1651'.[11] Chamberlain was of course referring to works in English, and he was well aware of the historical information contained in classic Western accounts of Japan by Siebold and other travellers, and of the English-language compilations put together from these accounts by more recent authors (such as Charles MacFarlane and Richard Hildreth).[12]

---

9   Johannes Fabian, *Time and the Other, How Anthropology Makes its Object* (New York: Columbia University Press, 2014), p. 144. Original published in 1983.
10   Basil Hall Chamberlain, *Things Japanese: Being Notes on Various Subjects Connected with Japan for the Use of Travelers and Others*, facsimile of the 1905 5th ed. (Teddington: Wildhern Press, 2009), p. 242.
11   Chamberlain, *Things Japanese*, p. 243.
12   Charles MacFarlane, *Japan: An Account Geographical and Historical* (London: George Routledge and Co., 1852); Richard Hildreth, *Japan as it Was and Is* (Boston: Phillips, Sampson and Co., 1856). Chamberlain describes Hildreth's work as 'an excellent book' but 'now difficult to obtain'; Chamberlain, *Things Japanese*, p. 73.

Figure 8.1. Illustration from Charles MacFarlane's *Japan*.

Source: Charles MacFarlane, *Japan: An Account Geographical and Historical* (London: George Routledge and Co., 1852).

But his comment is a reminder of the fact that academic work on Japanese history in the English-speaking world was still in its early formative stage during the crucial years from the late nineteenth century to the first decade of the twentieth, when Japan's political and economic dominance of 'the Far East' (as it was then called) became internationally recognised. In fact, these years were also the period when the very idea of 'the Far East' was in formation, shifting from being a vaguely defined world on the horizons of European vision to being a much more clearly bounded 'area', and Japan's growing dominance in the region was a key factor in that formation. This context, I shall argue, had a deep structural impact on the way in which Japanese studies, Far Eastern studies and later East Asian studies came to be envisaged and practised.

The term 'Far East' was widely popularised in nineteenth-century English-language travel writings, but was at first very hazily delineated. For most Europeans of the early to mid-nineteenth century, 'the East began where the Ottoman Empire began' – that is, in Belgrade, and almost anything east of Turkey might therefore be labelled the 'Far East'.[13] Daniel H Mackinnon's account of his *Military Service and Adventures in the Far East*, published in London in 1849, for example, dealt largely with Afghanistan and India, while GF Davidson's 1846 *Trade and Travel in the Far East* focused on Java, Singapore, China and Australia.[14] Area terms indeed remained fluid and malleable well into the twentieth century – one of my favourite examples being Arnold Wright and TH Reid's study of British colonialism in Malaya, published in 1912, which is entitled *The Malay Peninsula* and subtitled *A Record of British Progress in the Middle East*.[15] The elasticity of the terms 'Far East' and 'Middle East' resembles that of the term 'Orient', which, as Edward Said and others have pointed out, was most often applied by Europeans to the region immediately to the east of Europe, and was laden with images of exoticism and ancient origins, while the North American 'Orient' more often referred to China and Japan and surrounding regions, and was 'less dense' in the richness of its imagery.[16]

Between the 1890s and the first decade of the twentieth century, though, a subtle but significant shift in European and American visions of the world was beginning to become evident. The terms 'the Near East' and 'the

---

13   Roderic H Davison, 'Where is the Middle East?' *Foreign Affairs* 38, no. 4 (1960): pp 665–75, citation from p. 666.

14   Daniel H Mackinnon, *Military Service and Adventures in the Far East, including Sketches of the Campaigns against the Afghans in 1839 and against the Sikhs in 1845–46* (London: John Ollivier, 1849), doi.org/10.1017/cbo9781139178730; GF Davidson, *Trade and Travel in the Far East* (London: Madden and Malcolm, 1846).

15   Arnold Wright and TH Reid, *The Malay Peninsula: A Record of British Achievement in the Middle East* (London: Unwin, 1912); on changing geographical depictions of the 'Middle East', see also Daniel Follard, *Dislocating the Orient: British Maps and the Making of the Middle East, 1854–1921* (Chicago and London: University of Chicago Press, 2017), doi.org/10.7208/chicago/9780226451473.001.0001.

16   Edward Said, *Orientalism* (London: Routledge and Kegan Paul, 1978), pp. 9–10.

Middle East' appeared for the first time in geopolitical debates, and 'the Far East' began to acquire more precisely delineated frontiers, embracing Japan, China and Korea, and sometimes also extending to Indo-China, the Philippines and other parts of what would later be labelled 'Southeast Asia'.[17] Behind this redefined vision of the Far East lay seismic shifts in regional politics. Japan's victory in the Sino–Japanese War (1894–95) was seen as 'proclaiming to an astonished world the birth of the New Far East', centred no longer on China but on Japan.[18] The Russo–Japanese War of 1904–05 was even more intensively covered by the Western press, and resulted in an outpouring of publications on 'the New Far East', most of them focusing on Japan's growing dominance over a region encompassing eastern China and Korea.[19] A pair of maps of the 'Far East' published by the famous Scottish map publishing company Bartholomew's at the time of the Russo–Japanese war illustrates the processes of focusing in from the broader to the narrower definition of the 'Far East'.

The emerging infrastructure of empire, developed by the expanding Japanese state from the 1890s onward, helped to weave together this integrated Far East centred on Japan. The Korean and South Manchurian railways, over which Japan had assumed control by 1905, carried local and foreign journalists, scholars and tourists on routes linking the southern Korean port of Pusan via Northeast China to the Trans-Siberian Railway. Japanese shipping lines extended these links to the ports of Japan, and southwards to the British colony of Hong Kong and to Manila, which from 1898 became the administrative centre of the first US colony in Asia: the Philippines. Although the outer limits of 'the Far East' continued to vary according to the perspectives of the author, one commonly used framework was defined by Alexis Krausse's *The Far East: Its History and its Question*, published in 1900. This envisaged the region as divided into two spheres – the 'indigenous kingdoms of the Far East' – China, Korea and Japan – and, surrounding these, the 'outlying bulwarks of Western empires' – Far Eastern Russia, French Indo-China and the Philippines.[20]

---

17   Davison, 'Where is the Middle East?' pp. 666–67.
18   Arthur Diósy, *The New Far East* (London: Cassell and Co., 1898), quotation from p. 1.
19   For example, Thomas F Millard, *The New Far East* (London: Hodder and Stoughton, 1906); BL Putnam Weale, *The Re-Shaping of the Far East*, 2 vols (London: Macmillan and Co. 1905); Ernest FG Hatch, *Far Eastern Impressions* (London: A. C. McClurg and Co., 1905).
20   Alexis Krausse, *The Far East: Its History and its Question* (London: Grant Richards, 1900).

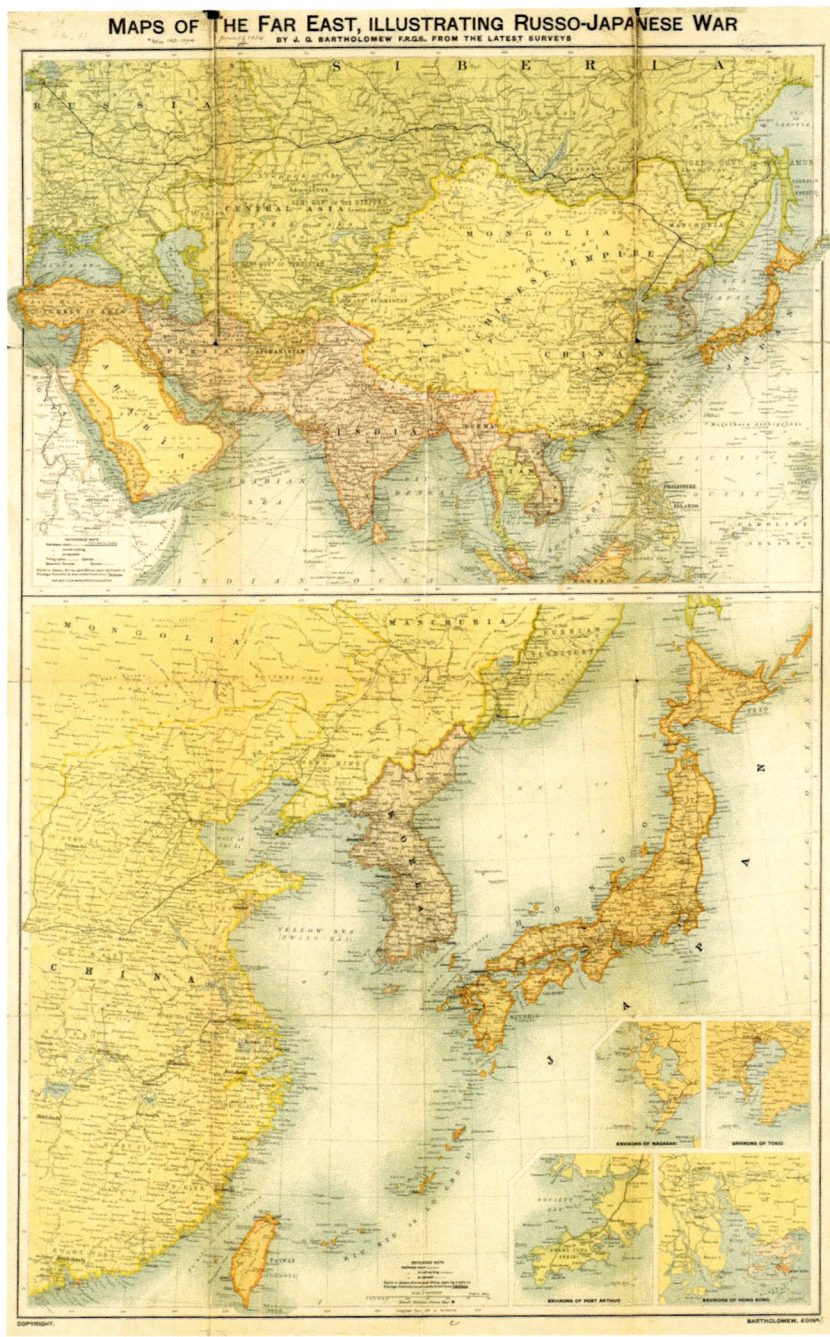

Figure 8.2. John George Bartholomew, 'Maps of the Far East, Illustrating Russo–Japanese War', 1905.

Source: Boston Public Library, Digital Commonwealth, Massachusetts Collections Online.

As the 'Far East' emerged – like a photograph in developing fluid, taking on clear outlines and colours – so it displaced other older European regional concepts, most notably the idea of 'Tartary'. In seventeenth-, eighteenth- and even early nineteenth-century English-language writings, as we have seen, Tartary was a vast realm that extended from the Caspian Sea to the frontiers of Japan itself. For example, eighteenth-century Scottish writer Thomas Salmon's fascinating and encyclopedic *Modern History, or the Present State of All Nations* (1739) – written at a time when the very notion of 'modern history' was assuming its 'modern' form[21] – concludes its section on the 'Present State of Japan' with a discussion of 'the Land of Jesso, Said to be a Tributary to Japan, and of the Various Opinions Concerning its Joining to America'. This notes of Jesso (Ezo, present-day Hokkaido and the northern islands beyond): 'whether it doth not join to the north part of Japan, which is but little known to the Japanese themselves, is not yet determined … Neither does it as yet clearly appear, whether this land of Jesso is a part of Tartary, or whether by an arm of the sea divided from it'.[22]

Salmon, of course, only had access to a potpourri of second-hand knowledge about Japan and the surrounding countries (which contains surprisingly accurate details on some issues, side by side with fascinating confusions and misapprehensions on others[23]). But the difference between his work and those of early twentieth-century writers on the Far East is not just a gap in access to accurate information, nor is the difference between Tartary and the Far East simply a matter of the redrawing of geographical boundaries between regions. There is also (I think) an important qualitative difference between these two regional concepts. 'Tartary' was not a realm occupied by nation-states; indeed, the 'nations' of Thomas Salmon's modern history are not necessarily *nation-states* at all. Rather, they are a miscellany of 'peoples' who are variously described as tribes, kingdoms, principalities, etc.

---

21   Reinhard Koselleck notes that 'modern' or *'neue Zeit'* shifts during the course of the eighteenth and early nineteenth centuries from being a purely chronological marker of recent times to having a particular content associated (as it is in the writings of Salmon) with the Western voyages of exploration, the spread of the printed word and the new intellectual currents of the Reformation. See Reinhard Koselleck, *Futures Past: On the Semantics of Historical Time*, trans. Keith Tribe (New York: Columbia University Press, 2004), pp. 224–36.

22   Thomas Salmon, *Modern History; or, The Present State of All Nations*, vol. 1 (Dublin: George Grierson, 1727), p. 65.

23   On the practice of *seppuku* in Japan, for example, 'when a great man makes an entertainment, 'tis usual at the end of the feast to call his servants together, 'tis said, and demand which of them will kill themselves before the guests; and that thereupon they contend who shall first rip up their bowels'. Salmon, *Modern History*, p. 57.

Tartary, in other words, was a fluid world where a whole range of societies – which might or might not have identifiable political structures – intermingled, exchanged goods and ideas, did battle and migrated across the face of the land. This of course reflects the fact that in the eighteenth century the authority of centralised states such as China, Korea, Japan and Russia only extended across limited parts of the area we call 'East Asia'. Between were wide realms occupied by very small kingdoms (such as the Ryukyu Kingdom) or by non-state societies such as those of the Ainu, Nivkh, Uilta, Nanai and other indigenous groups of the north-eastern parts of the Asian continent.

By the time we come to early twentieth-century writings on 'the New Far East', though, these regions had almost entirely been incorporated into states, and the Far East was therefore envisaged as a space entirely occupied by state-controlled territories, even if some of these were colonised states and others are colonising states. The bounds of Tartary could only be described by reference to physical features – mountains, rivers and seas – and its peoples were described largely through ethnographic accounts of their customs. The twentieth-century Far East, on the other hand (as in Krausse's work), was defined by a catalogue of clearly bounded states, and the narratives that described the Far East were overwhelmingly state-centred narratives. Importantly, this state-centred vision of the region then came to be projected backward onto history: the history of the Far East became the history of its major states, and many of the peoples of 'Tartary' and beyond lost their place in history except to the extent that they impinged (because of wars, invasions, etc.) on the historical narratives of those states.

While states provided the spatial architecture for the early twentieth-century 'Far East', its temporal architecture was provided by narratives of progress. Of course, ideas of civilisation, barbarism and progress were present to some extent in pre-nineteenth-century works like Salmon's *Modern History*, but they played a different and more limited role. In this eighteenth-century 'modern history', true civilisation is the prerogative of Protestant Western Europe, while, at the other end of the scale, some extremely unfamiliar social forms are identified as survivals from the archaic past. When he deals with nations outside Europe, however, Salmon is much more likely to judge them in ethical or aesthetic terms than to rank them in terms of progress.

The twentieth-century narratives of the New Far East, on the other hand, focused on the struggle of nation-states to obtain temporal, as well as spatial, superiority over others by becoming if possible larger and stronger, but above all more *advanced*. The rank ordering of nations on the ladder of progress, and the task of explaining their position on the ladder, had become the core task of Far Eastern history, and this was of course reflected not only in studies of the region as a whole, but also in the first major European and American scholarly histories of Japan.

Japan in the Far East: Time and Space in the Prewar Region

In 1917 Scottish migrant to Australia James Murdoch (1856–1921) completed the third volume of his *History of Japan* (a history whose narrative covers the span from the ancient origins of the Japanese to the fall of the Tokugawa Bakufu). The work, which runs to over 2,000 pages and was completed with the help of Japanese collaborators including Murdoch's wife Takeko, is in many ways as remarkable as its author, a radical teacher and journalist who, among other things, taught English to the renowned Japanese novelist Natsume Sōseki, wrote novels set in Japan, and participated in the unsuccessful utopian 'New Australia' commune in Paraguay.[24] His book is very much a product of its time. By the time it was written, Japan was a recognised world power that controlled Hokkaido in the north, Okinawa in the south and colonial territories beyond. China was fragmented and struggling, but it was nonetheless a modern state with clearly defined national boundaries, and a participant in the global interstate system. Korea, on the other hand, was a Japanese colony. Murdoch's fourth volume, which would have covered the years from the Meiji Restoration onward, remained unfinished on his death in 1921. But, even though his work does not address 'contemporary history', its narrative is framed by contemporary concerns.

---

24   David Sissons, 'James Murdoch (1856–1921): Historian, Teacher and Much Else Besides', in *Bridging Australia and Japan: The Writings of David Sissons, Historian and Political Scientist*, ed. Arthur Stockwin and Keiko Tamura, vol. 1 (Canberra: ANU Press, 2016), pp. 319–77. Original published in 1987.

For Murdoch, and for most of his contemporaries, the big historical issue was to explain:

> the sudden, the almost meteor-like rise of an Empire with such a strange and peculiar culture to the proud position of by no means the least among the Great Powers of the modern world.[25]

This rise was made particularly intriguing, in Murdoch's eyes, because it had been accomplished by a 'Non-Aryan' people to whom 'most of what is considered to be most distinctive in the common heritage of Western Culture was utterly alien'.[26] In the search for answers to the enigma, Murdoch drew up a balance sheet of the pre-existing strengths and weaknesses that underpinned Japan's rise as a modern state: on the credit side, a large population, a stable social system, a 'keen sense of honour and of conduct',[27] the 'alertness and receptivity of the Japanese intellect',[28] and 'a seemingly inherent capacity for organization';[29] on the debit side, resource poverty and the 'mosaic patchwork' of the Tokugawa political system of a mass of domains linked by the overarching power of the Shogunate.[30] The overall message, though, is not simply that credits outweighed the debits, but also that the credits were very deeply embedded in many centuries of Japanese history and culture. So, for example, discussing the Meiji Restoration, Murdoch is at pains to emphasise how little it relied on borrowing from the West and how much it drew on organisational ideas that could be traced back to the Taika Reforms of the seventh century CE.[31] A similar view was expressed even more strongly by the aristocratic French historian Antoine Rous de la Mazelière, whose monumental eight-volume *Japon: Histoire et Civilisation* was published between 1907 and 1923.[32]

---

25 James Murdoch, *A History of Japan*, vol. 1, 2nd ed. (London: Kegan Paul, Trench, Trubner and Co., 1925), p. 2. The work is in many ways as remarkable as its author: a radical journalist and teacher who (among other things) wrote fierce critiques of the working conditions of Japanese miners and of Australia's race-based immigration policies, lived for 27 years in Japan, married a Japanese wife, participated briefly in an unsuccessful utopian community in Paraguay, and taught English to Natsume Sōseki.

26 Murdoch, *History of Japan*, p. 1.

27 Murdoch, *History of Japan*, p. 5.

28 Murdoch, *History of Japan*, p. 6.

29 Murdoch, *History of Japan*, p. 14.

30 Murdoch, *History of Japan*, pp. 17–20.

31 Murdoch, *History of Japan*, pp. 20–21.

32 De la Mazelière aimed to show his French readers that 'in broad outline, the history of Japan is no different from that of the West. Like them, the Japanese cultivated themselves, while accepting the morals and arts of already cultivated nations; like them, they were able to transform and render original an assumed civilisation'. He also stressed that 'before appreciating the originality of the Japanese, it is necessary for us to distinguish their distinctive spirit from that of the Chinese … To those who study it, the political, economic and social history of Japan shows no relationship to the history of China, whereas the various peoples of Europe seem to have experienced a shared evolution'. See AR de la Mazelière, *Essai sur l'Histoire du Japon* (Paris: Libraire Plom, 1899), pp. vii and 452.

James Murdoch's Japanese friends, it should be said, did not universally share his positive assessment of their country's recent history. Natsume Sōseki expressed affection and admiration for his former English teacher, but wrote a response to Volume One of Murdoch's history in which he stressed the social and psychological burdens imposed on the Japanese people by the nation's rapid industrial modernisation.[33] Murdoch's history has also had bad press from subsequent generations of historians. George Sansom, who wrote one of the most enduring of prewar English-language histories of Japan – *Japan: A Short Cultural History* (1937) – respected Murdoch's prodigious researches, but felt repelled by his sweeping generalisations and cumbersome prose, and accused of him of depicting Japan 'as seen through spectacles made in Aberdeen about 1880'.[34] Sansom wrote in clear and elegant prose, and was very wary of generalisation and theorising: he described himself as a 'convinced empiricist'.[35] Yet Sansom's own careful scholarly narratives of Japan's history in fact contain implicit (and occasionally explicit) judgements on the factors that had contributed to Japan's economic strength and political power. For example, Sansom suggests that the 'absence of a universalist tradition' allowed pragmatic responses to new challenges and was therefore 'one of the factors that made for a rapid change in the nature of the Japanese state in the nineteenth century'.[36]

The general histories of the Far East that appeared from the 1920s to the 1940s often (like Murdoch's history of Japan) incorporated balance sheets of the factors that promoted or held back progress. They used contemporary political units to provide their spatial frameworks, and their narrative arcs frequently highlighted contrasts in progress, particularly between the region's two largest nation-states – China and Japan. I shall look more closely at one example of this narrative structure in a moment, but first it is important to remind ourselves that the 'the Far East' was of course not the *only* spatial framework for early twentieth-century understandings of the region's history.

---

33 See Sukehiro Hirakawa, *Japan's Love–Hate Relationship with the West* (Folkstone: Global Oriental, 2005), pp. 268–69.

34 Quoted in Marius Jansen, *The Making of Modern Japan*, reprint (Harvard: Harvard University Press, 2002), p. 769.

35 George B Sansom, *Japan in World History* (Tokyo: Charles E. Tuttle and Co. 1977), p. 83. Original published in 1951.

36 Sansom, *Japan in World History*, p. 36.

Within Japan itself, from the 1890s onward history had come to be institutionalised around the tripartite divide between *Tōyōshi* (Oriental – in practice, overwhelmingly Chinese – history) *Seiyōshi* (Western history), and *Kokushi* (national – i.e. Japanese – history). In this partitioning of space and time, 'Japan' was treated separately from 'the Orient' (which in fact lay to the geographical west of Japan), and tended to be temporally suspended between a *Tōyō*, identified with the past, and a *Seiyō*, which represented the modernity to which Japan aspired, and by whose standards it would be judged.[37] Some English-language writings also drew on different visions of regional space. Owen Lattimore's work viewed the region from the perspective of the borderlands of China, in a way that contained echoes of earlier narratives of the ebb and flow of the peoples of Tartary.[38] Robert Kerner, approaching the region from his perspective as a scholar of Russia, promoted a vision of 'Northeast (or Northeastern) Asia' (a previously unfamiliar term) in which Russia was a key player.[39] Kerner also produced a remarkable multilingual bibliography of works in and on the region – a valuable reminder of the ways in which Chinese and Russian historians were participating in debates on the changing nature of the region.[40] Neither Lattimore's nor Kerner's regional vision, however, seriously challenged the place of 'the Far East' as the most widely accepted English-language framework for understanding the region in the first half of the twentieth century.

37   See, for example, Jie-Hyun Lim, 'The Configuration of Orient and Occident in the Global Chain of National Histories: Writing National Histories in Northeast Asia', in *Narrating the Nation: Representations in History, Media and the Arts*, ed. Stefan Berger, Linas Eriksonas and Andrew Mycock (Oxford and New York: Berghahn Books, 2008), pp. 290–308, particularly pp. 295–97; the distinction between *Tōyōshi* and *Seiyōshi* seems to have been introduced into Japanese history teaching in 1894 at the suggestion of historian Naka Michiyo (1851–1908), who hoped the correct the Eurocentric bias introduced by too great a reliance on translated European histories. See Stephan Tanaka, *Japan's Orient: Rendering Pasts into History* (Berkeley: University of California Press, 1993), pp. 48–49.
38   For example, Owen Lattimore, *Manchuria: Cradle of Conflict* (New York: Macmillan, 1932).
39   Stephen Kotkin, 'Robert Kerner and the Northeast Asia Seminar', *Acta Slavica Iaponica* 15 (1997): src-h.slav.hokudai.ac.jp/publictn/acta/15/kotokin/kotokin.html (accessed 25 November 2018).
40   Robert Kerner, *Northeastern Asia: A Selected Bibliography*, 2 vols (Berkeley: University of California Press, 1939).

Japan in East Asia: The Development of Postwar Area Studies

The impact of these prewar legacies on postwar area studies can be glimpsed by considering one of the first histories of the Far East to appear after Japan's defeat in the Asia-Pacific War. Kenneth Scott Latourette's *A Short History of the Far East* was first published in 1946, and was in its fourth edition and still being widely used as a college text in the mid-1960s.[41] It was, in other words, an influential force in the burgeoning world of postwar area studies. But at the same time, it was the summation of the author's career as a prewar scholar, particularly of China and Japan. Like many of the first generation of European and American academic scholars of East Asia, Latourette (1884–1968) had a Christian missionary background: he had worked in the missions in China before becoming an academic, taking up the position of Professor of Missions and Oriental History at Yale University from 1949 to 1953. He had been among the first authors of general English-language histories of modern China and Japan, publishing *The Development of China* in 1917 and *The Development of Japan* in 1918. Latourette's *Short History* is in this sense a bridge between prewar Far Eastern studies and postwar area studies of East Asia.

In *A Short History of the Far East*, the great watershed in Asian history is the coming of the Western powers. The book is therefore divided into two parts: the Far East before and after the West. Each part begins with a chapter on India, which is treated not as part of the Far East, but as a crucial influence upon it. In part one, India provides the seeds of the culture and philosophy of lands to the east; in part two, it is the gateway through which the West enters the Far East. The discussions of India are followed by relatively detailed accounts of Chinese and Japanese political, cultural and social history, placed side by side and divided into several chronological chapters, and one chapter in each section on 'The Lesser Lands', stretching from Mongolia and Korea to the Philippines, Burma and Ceylon, all of which receive fairly short shrift: 'All played minor roles in Far Eastern history. None developed a strikingly original advanced culture'.[42] Pre-Western Korea is covered in two and half pages, and

---

41   Kenneth Scott Latourette, *A Short History of the Far East* (New York: Macmillan, 1947).
42   Latourette, *Short History of the Far East*, p. 290.

Mongolia in half a page. In the post-Western Far East, the binary presence of China and Japan again dominate, and Korea is subsumed into the colonial history of Japan.

This story is framed, from the very beginning, by 'the present predominance of Japan', and much of the narrative of Chinese and Japanese history is implicitly a search for explanations for that predominance. This in itself is interesting, when we consider that the book was first published at a moment when Japan lay in ruins, and future predominance can hardly have seemed assured. Like James Murdoch 30 years earlier, Latourette begins with a list of Japanese assets: in this case, 'the ability, the initiative, the perseverance, the industry, and the self-confidence of the Japanese'; Japan's strategic island position, which protected it from invasion; Japan's commercial experience and skills; its temperate climate; its natural beauty (which promotes aesthetic sensibility); and the role of Japan's compact and insular landscape in promoting national consciousness and patriotism.[43]

By the time that Latourette published his *Short History*, the region was in the midst of its second great modern convulsion: the collapse of the Japanese empire, revolutions in China and elsewhere, the Korean War and the emergence of the Cold War order. But in important respects, I would argue, this new regional order, rather than prompting a radical rethinking of scholarly visions of the region, instead served to reinforce some of the tendencies that had already become apparent in prewar Far Eastern studies. It is true that the term 'the Far East' gradually fell out of fashion, to be replaced by the ambiguous term 'East Asia' (which sometimes includes and sometimes excludes 'Southeast Asia'). But the underlying spatial and temporal architecture of postwar East Asian studies was not radically different from that of its prewar precursors. Cold War divisions, superimposed on mid-twentieth-century nationalisms, intensified the tendency to see the region as sharply divided along nation-state lines. Interaction between scholars and others in the various countries of East Asia became restricted, limiting scope for exploring common themes and ideas. For European, American and other foreign scholars of the region too, movement between the various countries of Northeast Asia became difficult.

---

43 Latourette, *Short History of the Far East*, pp. 25–27.

In this respect, East Asia's experience of the Cold War was very different from Europe's. While both were divided, Europe west of the so-called 'iron curtain' quickly became relatively integrated, allowing a new wave of postwar interactions between the countries of the region, and promoting the flourishing of European history as a field that sought out commonalities between the pasts of nation-states of Europe (particularly Western Europe). Northeast Asia, on the other hand, was divided by multiple Cold War fissures. Not only did the Sino–Soviet split draw a new dividing line across the region, the legacy of war and colonialism, combined with Cold War security concerns, imposed restrictions on human contact even between Japan, South Korea and Taiwan – countries on the same side of the ideological divide.

Meanwhile, Japan's postwar recovery and the 'economic miracle' of the 1960s once again focused academic attention on the developmental gap between Japan and China, and between Japan and other countries of the region. Postwar area studies grew and flourished alongside modernisation theory, which provided the temporal vector for the work of many leading scholars of the region, including Edwin Reischauer, Robert Bellah, Ronald Dore, Marius Jansen and others. All of this intensified the tendency towards comparative studies, which sought to divine the 'secrets of Japan's success', and (often) to derive lessons of that success for other Asian countries. Some sense of the continuities and shifts in postwar area studies can be gained by placing Latourette's *Short History* alongside those two area studies classics, Fairbank and Reischauer's *East Asia: The Great Tradition* (1958)[44] and Fairbank, Reischauer and Craig's *East Asia: The Modern Transformation* (1965).[45] For Fairbank, Reischauer and Craig, as for Latourette, the great historical watershed is the coming of the West, which marks the end of 'the Great Tradition' and the beginning of 'The Modern Transformation'. In *East Asia*, Korea has made a comeback – redeemed from its position as a 'Lesser Land' or 'an Outerlying Dependency of the Japanese Empire', the independent (if divided) Korea now has a 'Great Tradition' of its own, even though this tradition is covered in one chapter as against the three devoted to Japan and the eight devoted to China.

---

44   Edwin O Reischauer and John K Fairbank, *East Asia: The Great Tradition* (London: George Allen and Unwin, 1958).
45   John K Fairbank, Edwin O Reischauer and Albert M Craig, *East Asia: The Modern Transformation* (London: George Allen and Unwin, 1965).

Fairbank and Reischauer's *East Asia* changes shape and expands over time. The first volume – *The Great Tradition* – is confined to 'China, Japan, Korea and, to a lesser extent, Vietnam',[46] while the second – *The Modern Transformation* – embraces Southeast Asia:

> that area has become more and more closely involved with China and Japan. We have therefore included in this volume a survey of the recent history of the various countries of Southeast Asia, together with some background on their traditional cultures.[47]

The changing scope is justified by the historical role of Western imperialism in linking this wider region (though more recent scholars like Hamashita Takeshi would emphasise that it was already linked well before the coming of the Western powers).[48] But it also fits comfortably with the contemporary context in which the authors were writing. By the mid-1960s close economic ties were being re-established between Japan and Southeast Asia, and area studies – focused strongly on the Southeast Asian region – were beginning to flourish in Japan itself. The two *East Asia* volumes are relatively cautious in making explicit comparisons between Japan's 'advance' and China's 'stagnation'. There is no balance sheet of assets and liabilities here. Yet the whole framework is a national comparative one. The histories of the nation-states of the region are set side by side, allowing the reader to observe their commonalities and trace the points where their trajectories diverge.[49] In this framework, the premodern interstate world largely disappears from view. I shall also argue that this 'nation-state comparative' structure for understanding the region, which is carried forward into the final chapter on the postwar decades, tends to obscure some important inter-society interactions and cross-border historical processes.

---

46   Reischauer and Fairbank, *East Asia: The Great Tradition*, p. 3. Mongolia, which is defined as 'Central Asia', and Russia are both excluded.

47   Fairbank, Reischauer and Craig, *East Asia: The Modern Transformation*, p. 4.

48   See, for example, Takeshi Hamashita, *China, East Asia and the Global Economy: Regional and Historical Perspectives*, ed. Linda Grove and Mark Selden (London and New York: Routledge, 2008).

49   This nation-state focus in postwar Asian studies was later highlighted by Harry Harootunian, who wrote of the US Association for Asian Studies that 'although the association's committees are divided along area lines, its membership and officers serve as metonyms – stand-ins – because they are, at bottom, not specialists of Northeast Asia, South Asia, or Inner Asia but of nation-states'. See Harry Harootunian, *History's Disquiet: Modernity, Cultural Practice and the Question of Everyday Life* (New York: Columbia University Press, 2002), p. 26.

History Across Frontiers

The most visible fruit of the flourishing of area studies in postwar Europe and North America was, of course, an enormous expansion and deepening of research on the region. A whole generation of scholars of Japan, many of them trained during the war, took up teaching posts in universities, and they and their students – figures like Edwin Reischauer, Donald Keene, Edward Seidensticker, Ronald Dore, Marius Jansen, Carmen Blacker and many others – generated a wealth of scholarship on Japanese history and society that would have been unimaginable two or three decades earlier. But the deep structures of postwar area studies continued to have some limiting effects. Partly because of linguistic barriers, but also very much because of historical legacies and contemporary political circumstances, area studies in East Asia became highly compartmentalised on national lines. Japanese studies flourished, as did studies that placed Japan's experience side by side with that of China or other Asian countries for comparative purposes. But throughout the 1950s, 1960s and 1970s there were relatively few scholars of East Asia who were able to do what scholars such as Benedict Anderson and Anthony Reid have done for Southeast Asian studies[50] – move comfortably across national borders to draw out common region-wide themes for debate and theorisation.

In this respect, one exception was Marius Jansen. Deeply immersed both in Japanese and Chinese history, Jansen was able to write not only on the state-to-state relationship between the two neighbours, but also on their profound cultural and social interrelationships. His work on *The Japanese and Sun Yat-Sen* in particular suggests a way of looking at regional history very different from the comparative ranking of nation-states on the scale of modernisation.[51] Here, Jansen explored the twisting and interweaving of ideas that came about as Japanese and Chinese intellectuals and activists came together in the search for national power and regional collaboration. Rather than comparing and contrasting the modern development processes of Japan and China, this work exposes

---

50   See, for example, Anthony Reid, *Southeast Asia in the Age of Commerce, 1450–1680*, vol. 1, *The Lands below the Winds* (New Haven: Yale University Press, 1988); Anthony Reid, *Southeast Asia in the Age of Commerce, 1450–1680*, vol. 2, *Expansion and Crisis* (New Haven: Yale University Press, 1993); Benedict Anderson, *The Spectre of Comparisons: Nationalism, Southeast Asia, and the World* (London: Verso, 1998).

51   Marius B Jansen, *The Japanese and Sun Yat-Sen* (Cambridge, Mass.: Harvard University Press, 1954).

the complex ways in which, at the level of society and ideas, the processes were intertwined across national boundaries, at the same time illustrating the paradoxes of Pan-Asianism and the difficulty, in the turbulent context of prewar East Asia, of distinguishing nationalism from regionalism and internationalism. Published in the first half of the 1950s, *The Japanese and Sun Yat-Sen* seems in retrospect a pioneering work that prefigures the more recent upsurge of research on the cross-regional sharing of ideas and culture – for example, on the regional spread of 1920s socialism and feminism, and the simultaneous emergence in Japan, China and colonial Korea of the New Woman and the Modern Girl, and the social response to the spread of consumerism in various parts of East Asia from the 1920s onward.[52]

Also in retrospect, though, it seems a little surprising that there was so *little* research of this type between the publication of *The Japanese and Sun Yat-Sen* in 1954 and the revived interest in research on the social history of the Japanese empire and of East Asian cross-border interactions that began around the mid-1990s. Jansen himself of course returned to the topic of connections between the modern history of Japan and China several times, particularly in his larger study of *China and Japan: From War to Peace, 1894–1972,* written at the time of the establishment of diplomatic relations between Japan and the People's Republic in the early 1970s. Other than this, however, only a handful of books spring to mind: among them Gavan McCormack's pioneering study of Zhang Zuolin and Japan, published in the 1970s[53] and Ramon Myers' research on Japan's economic role in Manchuria, which was carried out as part of his doctoral program in the 1950s but not published in book form until the 1980s.[54] Whole swathes of fascinating and important history concerning intellectual and cultural connections between Japan and East Asia since the nineteenth century, the social and cultural history of the Japanese

52 For example, Tani E Barlow, ed., *Formations of Colonial Modernity in Modern East Asia* (Durham and London: Duke University Press, 1997); Barbara Molony, Janet Theiss and Hyaeweol Choi, *Gender in Modern East Asia* (London and New York: Routledge, 2018).
53 Gavan McCormack, *Chang Tso-Lin in Northeast China: China, Japan and the Manchurian Idea* (Stanford: Stanford University Press, 1977).
54 Myers' *The Japanese Economic Development of Manchuria, 1932–1945* was completed as a PhD thesis at the University of Washington in 1959, and published by Garland Publishing (New York) in 1982; research examining cross-border linkages between Japanese and Korean history is even rarer. Works like James W Morley's *Japan and Korea: America's Allies in the Pacific* (New York: Walker, 1965) is not only brief but focuses centrally on a comparative study of political developments set in the context of US strategic interests at the time of the normalisation of diplomatic relations between Japan and the Republic of Korea.

empire, and histories of the multiple migrations within and across the borders of that empire remained largely unexplored, leaving open wide fields of research that have only begun to be actively cultivated by English-speaking researchers of Japan in the past 25 years.

The relative neglect of these regional connections is all the more surprising when we consider that some aspects at least – particularly the intellectual and social connections between Japan and China – were the subject of intense research and debate by Japanese scholars (most famously by the Japanese Sinologist Takeuchi Yoshimi [1910–77]) in the postwar decades.[55] The underlying spatial architecture of postwar East Asian studies is also, I would argue, reflected in the relative neglect of the long pre-modern history of the region's non-state areas. Area specialists, for example, directed almost no attention to the history of the Ainu and other indigenous peoples of the north (research on whom was largely confined to the fields of anthropology and folklore). The one exception here was the history of the Ryukyu Kingdom/Okinawa – generally marginalised by European and American scholars of Japan and of East Asia in the prewar decades, but suddenly given new prominence on the context of the identity debates that accompanied the US occupation of Okinawa from 1945–72.[56]

Japan–China Reversal and the New Area Studies

Go into any bookshop in Japan today and you will find yourself confronted by shelves of works – ranging from the scholarly to the sensational – on Japan's relationship with its surrounding region, and particularly on the China–Japan relationship. The more lurid titles, such as *This Troublesome Country – China* [*Kono Yakkai na Kuni, Chūgoku*] or *Japan Will Become an 'Autonomous Region' of China* [*Nihon wa Chūgoku no 'Jichiku' ni Naru*][57] convey the flavour of anxiety, alarm, confusion and sometimes paranoia evoked the apparent inversion of the fates of Japan and China. Some more sober works, meanwhile, express the issue directly and succinctly – most succinct of all, perhaps, a work published by the Nihon Keizai Shinbun in

---

55   See, for example, Takeuchi Yoshimi, *Nihon to Chūgoku no aida* (Tokyo: Bungei Shunjūsha, 1977).
56   See, for example, George Kerr, *Okinawa: The History of an Island People* (Tokyo: C. E. Tuttle, 1958).
57   Okuda Hidehiro, *Kono Yakkai na Kuni, Chūgoku* (Tokyo: Wakku Bunkō, 2001); Bandō Tadanobu, *Nihon wa Chūgoku no 'Jichiku' to naru* (Tokyo: Sankei Shinbun Shuppan, 2010).

2010 and entitled *Japan–China Reversal* [*Nitchū Gyakuten*].[58] For at least
the past decade, it has been China's remarkable economic growth that has
attracted the headlines, while Japan's ongoing economic stagnation – the
'lost decade' that extended into a 'lost twenty years' – has sent theorists
both within Japan and abroad back to the analyses of the 'Japanese
economic miracle' in search of the hidden flaws that might explain the
subsequent loss of momentum.[59]

The message of the books that have resulted is not, of course, a simple story
of China's rise and Japan's decline. Many writers point to potential risks
and weaknesses in the economic and political order of the new Chinese
superpower, and many also emphasise residual sources of strength in
the Japanese system. But the underlying premise is certainly the notion
of a reversal of power relations in Asia. The big issue is no longer the
'secret of Japan's success', but rather the secret sources of relative failure,
or sometimes simply the stark question 'what went wrong?' Of course,
the reasons for China's expanding power and Japan's relative decline are
important issues that warrant serious research, but for many researchers
of Japan's modern history, the 'what went wrong?' question is not only
a rather depressing and unappealing one, but one that obscures a host
of fascinating aspects of the recent history of Japan's relationship with
its region. The problem, in other words, is that the fascination with the
'Japan–China Reversal' employs precisely the same conceptual architecture
for examining the region that was used by most prewar studies of the Far
East and much postwar area studies, but simply inverts the positions of
China and Japan. The region is still seen as a geographical block occupied
by nation-states, in which the main task of the historian is to rank the
position of the nations on a scale of progress, development or power, and
explain the reasons for their ranking.

While the Japan–China reversal has been taking place, however, new
approaches (referred to in Chapter 1 and earlier in this chapter) were
challenging the conceptual frameworks through which we study regions,
whether East Asia or elsewhere. Intense debate about globalisation and
about area studies versus disciplines has given rise to what may be called

58 Nihon Keizai Shimbunsha, ed., *Nicchū Gyakuten: Bōchō suru Chūgoku no Shinjutsu* (Tokyo: Nihon Keizai Shimbunsha, 2010).
59 For example, WR Garside, *Japan's Great Stagnation: Forging Ahead, Falling Behind* (London: Edward Elgar, 2012); Yoichi Funabashi and Barak Kushner, eds, *Examining Japan's Lost Decades* (London and New York: Routledge, 2015).

'the new area studies'.[60] The new area studies approach continues to emphasise the value of in-depth research on particular places, grounded in knowledge of local languages and ways of life, and developed through work in the 'field', but takes a fresh approach to spatial boundaries. Vincent Houben suggests that the new forms of area studies emerging in the twenty-first century focus on the relationship between theme and area, in which 'the determination of area depends on its relevance for the research theme chosen, and can have any size, location or temporality'.[61]

This new approach, in other words, can be seen differing from traditional postwar Asian studies in three main respects. First, traditional area studies generally accepts the 'area' as a geographical or cultural given. Studies of the Far East or of East Asia normally begin by providing their own definition of the boundaries of the regions, but whatever the definition, they accept the premise that the region has some form of inherent cultural coherence that makes it a meaningful framework for study. By contrast, as reflected in Arjun Appandurai's notion of 'process geographies', new area studies sees 'regions' not as fixed in physical or cultural geography, but as constantly created and re-created through human interaction and experience. Consequently, regions are multiple, overlapping and can take the range of unusual shapes – a vivid example being the concept of 'Zomia', put forward by geographer Willem van Schendel as a region of mainland Southeast Asia, which makes sense in terms of social history but was never viewed as a region by political scientists and political historians because it lacked strong state centres.[62] A second and related point is that new area studies tends to treat the 'area' not as an independent variable – a fixed frame within which history is studied – but rather as a dependent variable. A core object of research is to examine how historical events and forces have created and shaped the spatial system.

Third, new area studies raise questions not only about the geographical framing of the 'area', but also about the politics of knowledge creation. In other words, they pose the questions: 'Who is an area scholar?'

---

60   Also sometimes referred to as 'Third Wave' Area Studies – the first two waves being nineteenth- to early twentieth-century colonial area studies and the Cold War area studies of the second half of the twentieth century – see James D Siddaway, 'Foreword: A Third Wave of Area Studies', in *Area Studies at the Crossroads: Knowledge Production after the Mobility Turn*, ed. Katja Mielke and Anna-Katharina Hornidge (London: Palgrave-Macmillan, 2017), pp. v–vii.
61   Vincent Houben, 'New Area Studies, Translation and Mid-Range Concepts' in Mielke and Hornidge, *Area Studies at the Crossroads*, pp. 195–211, quotation from p. 202.
62   Van Schendel, 'Geographies of Knowing, Geographies of Ignorance', pp. 647–68.

'Who creates knowledge, and for whom?' One facet of the problem is the question very directly posed by Ariel Heryanto in the title of his 2002 article 'Can There be Southeast Asians in Southeast Asian Studies?'[63] In other words, area studies was developed largely in Europe and North America to research other areas of the world. What does this mean for Asians, Latin Americans or Africans who research the societies in which they themselves live? How are local voices heard in global (often English-language dominated) area studies? This question has perhaps not been as vexed in the case of Japan as in the case of some other parts of the world. Japan, as one of the richest Asian nations with its own strong postwar tradition of area studies, and Japanese are (and have long been) very active participants in international debates on East Asia's past and future. However, important debates still surround the distinctive position of those who study areas from within; and the problem of 'who creates knowledge for whom' has further dimension that are becoming increasingly visible with the rapid transformation of communications media and of education systems as a whole.

Thinking While Walking: *Bananas and the Japanese* and *The Eye of the Sea Cucumber*

'New area studies' largely took shape in the 1990s, with the spread of debates on postcolonialism and the emergence of a 'post–Cold War' order in Europe, and has continued to be discussed, developed, criticised and reworked into the twenty-first century. The alternative approaches to space and society that new area studies embody are not entirely new, though. In fact, by the 1970s and 1980s, various strands in Japanese social thought were already exploring new approaches to 'regionalisation' very different from those of mainstream postwar area studies. I would therefore like to conclude by looking at a couple of examples of these earlier rethinkings of the space of 'the region', because I believe that they contain valuable suggestions of future directions for new area studies in a rapidly changing East Asia.

---

63   Ariel Heryanto, 'Can there be Southeast Asians in Southeast Asian Studies?', *Moussons* 5 (2002): pp. 1–30, doi.org/10.4000/moussons.2658.

My first example comes from the work of a Japanese scholar who was not a historian but is generally regarded as an anthropologist, sociologist or Asian studies (*Ajiagaku*) scholar, though his work and career defy simple categorisation. The life trajectory of Tsurumi Yoshiyuki (1926–94) was profoundly shaped by his family background as the son of a prewar diplomat. Tsurumi was born and spent a significant part of his childhood in the United States, but was also haunted throughout adulthood by a sense of personal connection to Japan's invasion of Asia, because during the war his father had headed the military administration of Japanese-occupied Malacca. After graduation, Tsurumi worked for a long time for International House of Japan, and became well-known as a writer, peace activist and co-founder of the Pacific Asia Resources Center (PARC – *Ajia Taiheiyō Shiryō Sentâ*, established in 1973), a social movement that works mainly on issues of human rights and social justice in Asia and on problems emerging from Japan's relationship to other Asian countries. He did not obtain his first formal academic post, at Ryūkoku University, until he was in his 60s.

Tsurumi's writings on Japan's relationship to its region have sometimes been criticised for presenting a dichotomy between a poor and exploited 'Asia' and a rich and exploitative 'Japan' that implicitly stands outside of 'Asia'.[64] The 'Japan/Asia' dichotomy seems particularly evident from the titles of two of his works: *Ajiajin to Nihonjin* (*The Asians and the Japanese*, first published in 1980) and *Ajia wa naze Mazushii no ka* (*Why is Asia Poor?* published in 1982, at a time when Japan clearly was not).[65] But I think that it is too simple to assume from these uses of the term 'Asia' that Tsurumi was just echoing Japanese orientalist stereotypes of advanced Japan versus backward Asia. Tsurumi's use of the word 'Asia' (like that of Uehara Senroku whom I quoted earlier) was deeply influenced by the background of the Bandung Asian-African Conference of 1955 and the non-aligned movement that grew out of that conference, in which 'Asia' was frequently used a virtual synonym for the experience of colonisation and exploitation.

---

64   See, for example, John Lie, *Multiethnic Japan* (Cambridge, Mass.: Harvard University Press, 2004). Lie writes: 'When I lived in Tokyo in the mid-1980s, several of my politically progressive friends recommended that I read *Ajia wa naze Mazushiika* (*Why is Asia Poor?*) by Tsurumi Yoshiyuki (1982). Asia for my progressive friends did not include Japan. In fact, postwar Japanese intellectual and political life has largely ignored Asia (Sonoda 1993:22–25). Only recently has scholarly interest in Asia begun to revive (Ishida 1995:78–82)', p. 41.
65   Tsurumi Yoshiyuki, *Ajiajin to Nihonjin* (Tokyo: Shobunsha, 1980); Tsurumi Yoshiyuki, *Ajia wa naze Mazushii no ka* (Tokyo: Asahi Shimbunsha, 1982).

Far from emphasising the separation of Japan from 'Asia', Tsurumi developed an imaginative and innovative approach for understanding the interconnection of Japan to its region; an approach that in some senses interestingly prefigures later discourses on globalisation and its social effects. His approach to the topic, which he theorised as 'thinking while walking' (*arukinagara kangaeru*), is best illustrated in his two widely sold short studies, *Banana to Nihonjin* (*Bananas and the Japanese*, 1982) and *The Eye of the Sea Cucumber* (*Namako no Me*, 1990).[66] *Bananas and the Japanese* uses the simple but, at the time, quite radical device of examining Japan's relationship to its region by exploring how the humble banana finds its way onto Japanese dining tables. Starting from the arrival of the first bananas in Japan in 1903, Tsurumi takes his readers on a journey through the development of plantation agriculture in colonial Taiwan to the 1960s and 1970s, when the rise of mass consumption in Japan was linked to the massive expansion of plantation agriculture on the Philippines Island of Mindanao. Tsurumi's work, in other words, makes visible the invisible social relationship between Japan and Mindanao forged by consumer culture. In tracing the journey of the banana from tree to table, through a long line of intermediaries, Tsurumi shows how minor changes in consumption patterns in Japan can have huge effects on the lives and social structures of people many thousands of miles away in the producing villages. *The Eye of the Sea Cucumber* undertakes a similar exploration of the historical development of the trade in the delicacy *namako*, this time revealing a deep thread of connection between Japan and the Indonesian Island of Sulawesi.

Tsurumi's work precisely explores the 'precipitates of various kinds of action, interaction and motion' that form the core of Appadurai's 'process geographies'. At the same time, it poses challenges to some conventional notions about the production of area studies knowledge: Tsurumi not only conducted most of his research outside the bounds of academic institutions, but also emphasised the importance of engaging in social action together with the people who were the subjects of his research. His work is very clearly a call for 'engaged scholarship', which demands that the researcher not only talks the talk but also walks the walk. For Tsurumi, 'thinking while walking' implied that research is a physical activity carried out by the body as well as the mind: it engages all the senses of sight,

---

66 Tsurumi Yoshiyuki, *Banana to Nihonjin: Firipin Nōen to Shokutaku no aida* (Tokyo: Iwanami Shoten, 1982); Tsurumi Yoshiyuki, *Namako no Me* (Tokyo: Chikuma Shobō, 1990).

hearing, touch, taste and smell, as well as faculties of reasoning and reflection. His approach had a continuing influence on the work of a range of scholars (most notably Japanese scholars such as Murai Yoshinori and Utsumi Aiko), and I would argue that it deserves more attention than it has received so far from Asian studies scholars; for Tsurumi's readable and seemingly simple accounts of Japan's material relationships with its region contain rather profound suggestions of alternative ways to envisage social space and to practise the art of research.

Excavating the Past: The Case of the Okhotsk People's History Workshop

My second example of an alternative approach to Japan and its region comes from the work of a study group that is relatively little known even in Japan, let alone internationally: the Okhotsk People's History Workshop (*Ohōtsuku Minshūshi Kōza*, hereafter abbreviated to Okhotsk Workshop), which was established in the early 1970s and provided the seed bed for a range of study groups and social movements that are still active today.[67] Based in the northern Hokkaido town of Kitami, the Okhotsk Workshop was both small and local, but it is important to emphasise that it was not an isolated phenomenon. Broadly similar study groups exist in many parts of Japan. Their activities are a fascinating part of the process of 'doing history' in Japan,[68] though these activities have only recently begun to attract much serious study from university-based historians.[69]

---

67   The group was initially created as the 'Society for Telling the History of Kitami' in 1972, and changed its name to the Okhotsk People's History Study Group in 1973. See Koike Kikō, 'Ohōtsuku Minshūshi Kōza', in *Iwanami Kōza: Nihon Tsūshi*, appendix vol. 2, *Chiiki Kenkyū no Genjō to Kadai* (Tokyo: Iwanami Shoten, 1994), pp. 229–43, reference from pp. 231–32; Hiroshi Oda, 'Unearthing the History of Minshū in Hokkaido: The Case Study of the Okhotsk People's History Workshop', in *Local History and War Memories in Hokkaido*, ed. Philip A Seaton (London: Routledge, 2015), pp. 129–58, doi.org/10.4324/9781315733685-7; Oda Hiroshi, 'Koike Kikō: "Itami" kara Hajimaru Minshūshi Undō', in *Hitobito no Seishinshi*, vol. 2, *Chōsen no Sensō – 50-nendai*, ed. Tessa Morris-Suzuki (Tokyo: Iwanami Shoten, 2015), pp. 313–39.

68   I borrow the term 'doing history' from Minoru Hokari. See Minoru Hokari, *Gurindji Journey: A Japanese Historian in the Outback* (Sydney: UNSW Press, 2011); see also Hokari Minoru, *Radikaru Ōraru Hisutorī: Ōsutoraria Senjūmin Aborijini no Rekshi Jissen* (Tokyo: Ochanomizu Shobō, 2004); see also Sachiko Shōji, ed., *Rekishi Suru! Doing History!* (Fukuoka: Fukuoka City Art Museum, 2017).

69   The best study of the subject in English, focusing mainly on women's study groups in the 1950s, is Curtis Gayle's *Women's History and Local Community in Postwar Japan* (London: Routledge, 2010).

The emergence of these local groups needs to be understood in the context of the rise in 1960s and 1970s Japan of the phenomenon that US historian Takashi Fujitani calls 'Minshūshi as a critique of Orientalist knowledge'.[70] Inspired by the work of historians like Irokawa Daikichi (1925–) and Yasumaru Yoshio (1934–2016), 'people's history' sought to explore the lives of non-elite 'ordinary people' as the motive force of Japanese history, while questioning the relatively rigid theoretical apparatus of Marxist dialectics that had dominated much history research in postwar Japan.[71] This search for the lost voices of the people had obvious appeal to historians operating outside the realms of the elite universities, in relatively poor and outlying parts of Japan.

The central figure in the Okhotsk Workshop was an energetic and charismatic local history teacher named Koike Kikō (1916–2003), who originally came from Tokyo but had been purged from his position as a high school teacher in 1948 because of his involvement in trade unionism and his opposition to the content of the officially approved history textbooks. In 1953, he obtained a position as a teacher at a school in Kitami, where he spent the rest of his career.[72] Few of the participants in the Okhotsk Workshop, indeed, were university historians. Most were schoolteachers, local public servants, housewives, Buddhist priests and Christian ministers, retirees and other local people with an interest in history – people often condescendingly referred to as 'amateur historians'. They were, however, part of an amazingly rich tradition of local history research that exists all over Japan, and whose work has not only yielded a wealth of empirical historical knowledge, but also poses interesting conceptual challenges to mainstream academic concepts of the role of the historians and the process of 'doing history'. Other significant local groups include the Ehime Women's History Circle in Shikoku,[73] which dates back to the 1950s, and the vibrant people's history movement which developed in the Kyushu city of Minamata in response to that region's problems of industrial pollution.[74] In the mid-1970s, the Okhotsk

---

70 Takashi Fujitani, 'Minshūshi as Critique of Orientalist Knowledge', *Positions: East Asia Cultures Critique* 6, no. 2 (1998): pp. 303–22, doi.org/10.1215/10679847-6-2-303.
71 See Carol Gluck, 'The People in History: Recent Trends in Japanese Historiography', *Journal of Asian Studies* 38, no. 1 (1978): pp. 25–50.
72 Oda, 'Unearthing the History of Minshū'; Oda, 'Koike Kikō'.
73 Gayle, *Women's History*, ch. 6.
74 For example, Okamoto Tatsuaki, ed., *Minamata no Minshūshi*, 5 volumes (Tokyo: Nihon Hyōronsha, 2015).

Workshop was attracting audiences of several hundred to its regular lecture series, and its 10th anniversary conference in 1982 was attended by around 900 people.[75]

If 'walking' is the key term in Tsurumi Yoshiyuki's approach to history, 'digging' – or, more precisely, 'excavating the past' (*kako o horiokosu*) – is the key term in the work of the Okhotsk Workshop. The term 'excavation' appears repeatedly in Koike's writings: so often, indeed, that it is sometimes difficult to be sure whether he is using the term metaphorically or literally, since the group both conducted actual archaeological digs and also 'unearthed' the past through oral history interviews. The purpose of this excavation was to uncover, record and preserve the forgotten voices of those local residents whose experiences had been lost in mainstream grand narratives of the settlement of Hokkaido, which tended to present relatively triumphalist stories of the achievements of pioneer settlers. Among the early subjects for 'excavation' by the Okhotsk Workshop were dissident members of the Meiji Era Freedom and People's Rights movement who had been exiled to the far north of Japan as a punishment for their activism, and convict labourers who had been brought to northern Hokkaido to work on construction projects. (Kitami's neighbouring city of Abashiri is still home to one of Japan's largest prisons, with a history dating back to the nineteenth century.) Even after the abolition of convict labour in the 1890s, poor and unemployed men continued to be shipped to Hokkaido from other parts of Japan to work as *takobeya* (literally 'octopus pot') labourers (contract workers who were kept confined in barracks on mining or construction sites, often working in very harsh conditions for minimal wages). The Okhotsk Workshop formed teams to research the experiences of workers on these sites, and published detailed volumes containing archival records, oral history transcriptions and other historical material. They also erected monuments and performed memorial ceremonies for the repose of souls of those who had died on these sites.[76]

---

75   'Ohōtsuku Minshūshi Kōza Hyakukaime ni', *Mainichi Shimbun* (evening edition), 10 May 1982, p. 4.

76   See, for example, Jōmon Tonneru Kōji Junnansha Tsuitōhi Kensetsu Kiseikai, ed., *Tonneru no Kabe no naka kara: Jōmon Tonneru Kōji Junnansha Tsuitōhi Kansei Kinenshi* (Rubeshibe: Jōmon Tonneru Kōji Junnansha Tsuitōhi Kensetsu Kiseikai, 1983); Chūō Dōro Kaishō Giseisha Tsuitōhi Kensetsu Kiseikai, ed., *Ru-beshi-be no Bohyō: 'Chūō Dōro' ni Taoreta Torawarebito e no Chinkonfu*, 4th ed. (Rubeshibe: Chūō Dōrō Kaishō Giseisha Tsuitōhi Kensetsu Kiseikai, 2006). Original published in 1990; also round-table interview with Tsurumaki Hiroshi, Satō Takumi, Mori Ryōichi, Nakagawa Isao and Tonohira Yoshihiko, Abashiri, 4 November 2011.

Figure 8.3. Memorial for convict labourers near Abashiri.
Source: Photograph by author.

As oral history collection and the physical excavation and restoration of
historical sites progressed, however, the spatial contours of the Okhotsk
Workshop's work began to change. As they dug down into the past they
struck (as it were) underground veins or rivers connecting their local area
not just to other parts of Japan but also across borders to other parts
of Asia. Research on the *takobeya* labourers, for example, proved to flow
into the story of the importation of forced labour from Korea and China,
which began as a trickle in the early to mid-1930s and became a flood
after the passing of the first of a series of labour recruitment laws in 1939.
Particularly large numbers of forced labourers from the colonies were
brought to Hokkaido to work on projects that included mining and the
construction of dams and airfields. Members of the Okhotsk Workshop
discovered that some of these labourers had remained in their region
after the end of the war, and began to collect their oral testimony, as well
as documentary and archaeological evidence about the sites where they
had laboured. One result was the construction of a memorial in Abashiri
to the colonial forced labourers who had worked and died there.[77] This
research theme was particularly energetically pursued by the Sorachi
People's History Workshop (*Sorachi Minshūshi Kōza*), one of a number
of new groups established in neighbouring regions by local people who
had been inspired by the work of the Okhotsk Workshop. In 1997 the
Sorachi Group in turn established the East Asia Collaborative Workshop

---

77 'Chū Chō Jinmin no Tamashii, Yasukara ni Nemure', *Ohōtsuku Minshūshi Kōza Nyūsu* special
issue 1 (November 1976): p. 1.

(*Higashi Ajia Kyōdō Wākushoppu*), which regularly brings together groups of young people from Japan, Korea and elsewhere to excavate sites associated with wartime forced labour, discuss issues of cross-border history and (in some cases) return the remains of Japanese and Korean workers who died on labour sites in northern Hokkaido to their families.[78]

Meanwhile, members of the Okhotsk Workshop in Abashiri were excavating another historical channel that linked their locality across Japan's borders: in this case to communities in the central areas of the island of Sakhalin/Karafuto. During the colonial period, the population of Japanese-ruled Karafuto (as we have seen) included relatively small communities of indigenous people from three language groups: the Ainu, the Nivkh and the Uilta. Under colonial rule, the indigenous inhabitants of the island were moved into villages created by the colonial authorities and subjected to intense assimilationist education, while also (particularly in the case of the non-Ainu groups) being exposed to the intrusive exoticising gaze of tourists and anthropologists. Members of the Nivkh and Uilta communities were also trained to conduct spying missions across the border into Soviet northern Sakhalin (just as members of the same communities in the north were trained by their Soviet rulers to conduct missions across the border into Japanese Karafuto).

On Japan's defeat at the end of the Pacific War, almost all the Ainu people of Karafuto were evacuated to Japan, where many settled in the northern part of Hokkaido. The Nivkh and Uilta, who were not regarded as 'Japanese citizens', were left behind in Sakhalin, and a number were subsequently sent to Soviet labour camps as punishment for their work as 'Japanese spies'. From the mid-1950s, however, some Uilta and Nivkh survivors from former Japanese Karafuto migrated to Japan, where many settled in or around Abashiri. As a very tiny minority who had experienced both ethnic discrimination and the intrusive scrutiny of Japanese and other foreign ethnographers in colonial Karafuto, members of these indigenous communities were often reluctant to speak about their backgrounds. In Japan itself, they struggled to make a living, often in low-paid jobs,

---

78 Sorachi Minshūshi Kōza, ed., *Shumarinai no Kyōsei Renkō, Kyōsei Rōdō* (Fukagawa: Sorachi Minshūshi Kōza, 1994); Tonohira Yoshihiko, *Wakamonotachi no Higashi Ajia Sengen: Shumarinai ni Tsudou Nichi-Kan-Zainichi-Ainu* (Kyoto: Kamogawa Shuppan, 2004); see also Tessa Morris-Suzuki, 'Letters to the Dead: Grassroots historical dialogue in East Asia's borderlands', in *East Asia Beyond the History Wars: Confronting the Ghosts of Violence*, ed. Tessa Morris-Suzuki, Morris Low, Leonid Petrov and Timothy Y Tsu (London and New York: Routledge, 2013), pp. 87–104.

but the exoticisation of their presence continued, particularly in the form of a so-called 'Orochon Fire Festival', which was initiated in Abashiri in the late 1950s – soon after the postwar arrival of the Uilta and Nivkh migrants from Sakhalin. The festival itself was essentially invented as a tourist event by the local authorities, and bore very little resemblance to any known Uilta or Nivkh tradition, but a number of postwar indigenous migrants from Sakhalin, including Sakhalin Ainu, were persuaded to take part, to some degree at least out of a sense of obligation to the community in which they had settled.[79]

By the 1970s, though, things were beginning to change. The Ainu rights movement was gathering momentum across Hokkaido, and this encouraged some of the other indigenous migrants from Sakhalin to begin publicly to reclaim their own identities, and to try to educate the wider community about their own history and culture. Key figures in this process were members of the Daaxinneeni clan, whom we encountered in the previous chapter – shaman and elder Daaxinneeni Gergulu (who was by now in his 80s) and his adopted son Geeldanu (Kitagawa Gentarō) and daughter Aiko. Their resolve to tell their own histories to a wider audience was strengthened by the support of the Okhotsk Workshop, which in February 1975 invited artist and schoolteacher Tanaka Ryō – a long-time friend of Gergulu and his family – and Daaxinneeni Geeldanu to address a special lecture session they had organised on Uilta human rights and culture.[80] The talk evoked a strong response from members of the Okhotsk Group, and helped to inspire a local movement that persuaded the Abashiri City government to support the creation of a resource centre (*shiryōkan*) to preserve and promote the cultures of the indigenous peoples of Sakhalin.

---

79   See Tanaka Ryō and D Gendānu, *Gendānu: Aru Hoppō Shōsū Minzoku no Dorama* (Tokyo: Gendaishi Shuppankai, 1978), pp. 220–27.
80   Tanaka and Gendānu, *Gendānu*, pp. 175–77.

Figure 8.4. The Jakka Duxuni, Abashiri, 2011.
Source: Photograph by author.

The centre was eventually opened in August 1978, just a few weeks after the death of Daaxinneeni Gergulu, and was given the name *Jakka Duxuni* ('storehouse for precious objects' in Uilta).[81] Under the directorship of Daaxinneeni Geeldanu, the Jakka Duxuni brought together a rich collection of Uilta clothing, religious artefacts, musical instruments and other items, some of which had been brought from Sakhalin, while others had been made locally by members of the migrant Uilta community. It also displayed items made by other indigenous groups from Sakhalin, Hokkaido and Kamchatka, and provided a focal point for the activities of the Uilta Association (*Uilta Kyōkai*). The association, established in 1976, worked not only to record and preserve Uilta history, but also to campaign for the former military recruits from Otasu (see Chapter 7) to be given the pensions awarded to other Japanese members of the wartime army. With the thawing of Cold War tensions, it became possible to reopen the connections between Hokkaido and Sakhalin, which had been severed during the war, and members of the Uilta Association made several visits to the island, and in 1982 constructed a memorial in Otasu to the villagers who had died in Soviet labour camps.[82]

---

81   Tanaka Ryō, 'Hoppō Shōsū Minzoku Shiryōkan Jakka Dofuni no Ayumi', in *Hoppō Shōsū Minzoku Shiryōkan Jakka Dofuni Tenji Sakuinshū*, ed. Uilta Kyōkai Shiryōkan Uneikai (Abashiri: Uilta Kyōkai, 2002), pp. 11–16.
82   Tanaka, 'Hoppō Shōsū Minzoku Shiryōkan', p. 13.

By collecting and preserving records and traces of forced labour and of the colonial history of the indigenous people of Sakhalin/Katafuto, members of the Okhotsk Workshop, the Sorachi Workshop and the Uilta Association shed light on a very neglected corner of Japan's past and present relationship with its region. Their work subverts nation-state-centred narratives of Japan's place in its region, while also (I would argue) posing far-reaching challenges to traditional narratives of modernisation and progress, as well as to traditional Marxist models of stages of development. The colonial linkages forged between specific places within and outside the nation of Japan (between Hokkaido and parts of Korea or Hokkaido and Sakhalin, for example), force us to think of regional history in more complex spatial terms, and to re-examine the intricate imbrication of the historical trajectories of large state systems and smaller non-state communities.

These grassroots historical initiatives are themselves always vulnerable, as illustrated by the story of the Jakka Duxuni. Daaxinneeni Geeldanu died in 1984, and his adoptive sister Aiko, who had taken on the role of director of the resource centre, died in 2007. The 1970s and 1980s 'people's history' wave that had helped to support their initiatives was by now waning, and the next generation of indigenous migrants from Sakhalin to Hokkaido often found that the sheer demands of everyday existence left them without the time or enthusiasm to maintain the work begun by their elders. The Jakka Duxuni closed its doors in 2010,[83] and its collection was moved to Abashiri's Museum of Northern Peoples (*Hoppō Minzoku Hakubutsukan*). Thereafter, the most visible perpetuation of distinctively Uilta tradition were the embroideries that continued to be produced by local Japanese residents who had been taught Uilta embroidery techniques by Kiatagawa Aiko. Yet the small examples of the work of the Okhotsk Workshop, the Jakka Duxuni and other groups like them suggests possibilities for the rethinking of Japan's frontiers and of the human history that overflows those frontiers. I believe that, for those studying the region from outside as well as people within Japan itself, closer interaction with the work and legacy of such groups can offer one avenue for reimagining possible frameworks of area studies and revitalising the study of Japan and East Asia.

---

83 'Uilta Shiryōkan: 32-nen no Rekishi ni Maku – Rōkyūka "Iji ga Konnan" – Shōsū Minzoku no Bunka', *Asahi Shimbun*, 10 November 2010, p. 31.

Figure 8.5. Uilta embroidery: (above) by Kitagawa Aiko's Japanese students; (below) by Kitagawa Aiko.

Source: Author's collection.

Making Space

The stories told in the latter part of this chapter are reminders of the fact that the study of history and society is an active process of constituting and reshaping space. Research may reinforce existing senses of spatial belonging – to a locality or a nation, for example – or create awareness of links to places that previously seemed remote and unimportant. By rediscovering concealed or lost connections, researchers and 'history activists' participate in the building of conscious relationships based on those connections. Tsurumi's writings, by making visible the growing economic ties between Japan and Southeast Asia, provided a basis for new social connections, though which Japanese and Southeast Asian activists would share knowledge about and protest against labour exploitation and environmental damage. The work of the Okhotsk People's History Workshop and its offshoots opened up new perspectives on social links between northern Hokkaido, Korea and Sakhalin, and created a framework for the growth of social and cultural networks within this Northeast Asian region.

Compared to the big regional histories presented by Latourette, Fairbank, Reishauer and others, the projects pursued by Tsurumi, Koike and the Okhotsk Workshop may seem rather small and marginal. But, as I shall argue in the concluding reflections that follow, there is a very important place for such bottom-up 'small histories' in the rethinking of traditional categories of space and time.

This chapter is a revised version of an article that first appeared in the journal *Sungkyun Journal of East Asian Studies* 11, no. 2 (2011): pp. 123–42.

CONCLUDING THOUGHTS: ON THE VALUE OF SMALL HISTORIES

The chapters of this book have been written and reworked over a period of more than two decades. I started writing them at a time when area studies were facing new challenges, and when civilisational theories and Marxian stage theories were subject to critiques from post-structural and postcolonial perspectives: critiques that questioned the possibility of historical grand narratives, and indeed sometimes of empirical historical 'truth' as a whole. Since then, though, we have seen a resurgence of grand narratives of history – on a more sweeping scale than ever – with the growing interest in the teaching of world or global history, and with the rise of the very large-scale approach known as 'big history' (discussed briefly in Chapter 4).

'Big history' places the human past in the – spatially and temporally – much vaster context of the history of the universe, thus encouraging awareness of the inseparable interconnection between human history and the long-term dynamics of geological, climatic and environmental change. It induces a sense of modesty and of wonder by making us realise how small the histories of human communities, nations or civilisations seem when we view them within the vast spatial and temporal unfolding of the universe. In the process, big history takes us beyond the limits of narrowly national or ethnocentric stories of the past and makes us think about the past of humanity as a whole. It is also driven by a passion to use understanding of past patterns of change as a tool for elucidating possible future changes, particularly those driven by current environmental crises. Its contributions to historical knowledge have therefore been very great.

This book, though, is by contrast a plea for *small* histories: a call to appreciate the value of looking at the world from the standpoint of small societies and language groups, particularly those that live in the borderlands between nations and empires. Viewing the past in this way does not mean abandoning the big questions of history; but it does involve looking at them from a different point of view, and may make us aware of questions that are sometimes obscured by grand totalising narratives.

What comes into focus when we look at the past and present from this viewpoint – from the ground-up perspective of places (for example) like Tomarioro or Otasu or Abashiri? First, I would argue, we are able to appreciate the astonishing variety of social and cultural forms that human beings have created in different environments over time; and second, we start to see the complex 'imbricated' ways in which multiple social forms have interacted. Third, it enables us to question some of the relatively rigid spatial and temporal frameworks that have conventionally been imposed upon the past by area studies. It helps us to see unexpected connections created by migration routes, trading networks and the transmission and adaptation of cultural traditions. Fourthly, these small stories also make us look more closely at the fundamental questions that are posed by grand historical narratives, and that are being posed today by big history: for a defining characteristic of big history is not only its vast temporal and spatial timescale, but also the specific set of historical questions that it seeks to answer.

The quest at the heart of big history is to find a continuous narrative thread that takes us from the beginning of time to our present-day high-population, energy-dense global society. This narrative therefore comes to be structured around populations and energy flows, and around a series of thresholds or transformations that bring about fundamental changes in the flows of energy through matter. These thresholds are (to simplify) the Big Bang; the emergence of stars; the appearance of new chemical elements; the appearance of the solar system (including the earth); the emergence of life on earth; the development of human life; the discovery of agriculture; and the 'modern revolution', which saw the formation of a globalised system, industrialisation and the transition to the Anthropocene.[1] As a result, although this perspective extends the origins of history much further back than any previous model, it also draws quite

---

1   For a synoptic view, see the Big History Project website – www.bighistoryproject.com/home.

extensively on older civilisational models (in the works of Arnold Toynbee, Vere Gordon Childe and others), which saw the 'agricultural revolution' and the 'industrial revolution' as the key defining events of human history.

A history that centres around 'the agricultural revolution' and 'the modern/ industrial revolution' as the defining events of the human past tends to direct the gaze to the imperial heartlands: the places that had so-called 'Goldilocks circumstances' – ecological and geographical conditions that were 'just right' for the early emergence of agricultural or industrial civilisation.[2] When we focus on these areas, we tend to see the past as an ineluctable march towards societies of greater size and energy intensity. The regions and societies with very different environmental conditions, which were not central to that march, may easily come to be regarded either as frozen remnants of the ancient past or at least as irrelevant to the core narrative of history. This in turn makes us less aware of the immense diversity of the human past, and of the multiple ways in which societies have developed and shared knowledge over time. This book, therefore, chooses to consider the past from a place where circumstances for agriculture, dense human populations and large-scale industry were almost as far removed as could be from a 'Goldilocks' state.

In Chapter 4, I argued that the many decentralised knowledge systems of the past – the many ways in which small language or cultural groups have created an intimate understanding of very specific environments, while networking with other neighbouring societies – may contain important lessons for humanity as a whole as we confront the environmental and social challenges of the future. Large centralised knowledge systems have tended to be the ones that created great cities, enduring physical monuments and military might. In the past 200 years, these centralised systems have extended their power across the globe, destroying or subsuming small societies like those of Okhotsk region. These large systems, therefore, have also come to occupy a dominant and sometimes domineering place in grand narratives of the past.

But the small societies continue to have a profound and enduring value. Their decentralised knowledge systems are founded on the intimate ecological 'niche' knowledge that enabled people to survive in harsh and changing environments. Far from being frozen in timeless tradition, their

2   See, for example, Fred Spier, *Big History and the Future of Humanity* (Oxford: Wiley-Blackwell, 2010), pp. 36–40.

history demonstrates innovation, adaptation and the capacity to learn from others and to adjust to changing social and ecological conditions. They are, thus, part of the extraordinarily rich diversity of human history, and therefore also reminders of the richness of human potential. By deepening our knowledge of small societies – not only those of Northeast Asia but those of all parts of the world – we can come to appreciate that history is not a single road from past to future, but a multitude of diverging and intertwining paths. Ways of life that seem triumphant and successful sometimes reach an impasse. Empires grow and collapse, and minor ways of life acquire new significance as new systems take shape among the ruins of the old.

Small histories teach us to question reifying generalisations about national and civilisational pasts. They help us appreciate the capacity of human beings to flourish in seemingly inhospitable conditions and to adapt to changing environmental and political circumstances. Just as the preservation of biological diversity is crucial to the survival of humans and other species, so preserving and deepening knowledge of the cultural diversity and dynamism embodied by the small societies of the frontier is, surely, essential to the future of our world. I hope, then, that the ideas offered here can provide some pointers for further learning, both from the remarkable histories of the Okhotsk Sea and surrounding regions, and from the stories of small frontier societies worldwide.

Made in the USA
Monee, IL
24 April 2022

95350725R10148